Praise for *Connect!*

"Anne Zelenka has written a terrific book with a mountain of useful information for the connected age of web-working. If you're still mostly using knowledge-work tools and practices, then read this book immediately and tell your friends. It will transform your work habits, productivity, and attitude. I especially liked what she had to say about the advantages of 'bursty' over busy work styles, open source thinking, and the relevance of network science to creativity. This is a book about the future that is arriving now."

> —Richard Ogle
> Author of *Smart World*

"The dawn of the Industrial Revolution brought with it great changes to the workplace; lots of things we don't totally appreciate today, such as child labor laws. The same can be said for the Information Age and the dawn of the Web Worker Revolution. In her book, Anne Zelenka gives every web worker—be they corporate or indie—an array of invaluable tips and insights to survive what surely is the beginning of a golden era of work."

> —Steve Rubel
> SVP/Edelman and author of the Micro Persuasion weblog

"Contrary to popular misconception, time spent online is not time wasted. Zelenka demonstrates how putting the web to its best use can actually boost your productivity, if not entirely transform your career. Now when people ask me how they too can become web workers, I can direct them to this book."

> —Gina Trapani
> Editor of Lifehacker

"With all the hype and froth around the Web, it's a pleasure to read a no-nonsense, straightforward guide to how you actually work and thrive in the Internet business. Full of great tips and terrific suggestions, it's a must-read how-to guide for the digitally minded."

> —Kara Swisher
> Co-Executive Editor, All Things Digital website

"This is an awesome resource for independent web workers! Anne's written a creatively practical guide to maximizing the resources available to be as successful as possible in this bursty, fast paced world. It's going to sit on my desk permanently!"

> —Tara Hunt
> Founder, Citizen Agency

Connect!

A Guide to a New Way of Working from GigaOM's Web Worker Daily™

Anne Truitt Zelenka

with Judi Sohn

BICENTENNIAL
1807
WILEY
2007
BICENTENNIAL

Wiley Publishing, Inc.

Executive Editor: Chris Webb
Development Editor: Julie M. Smith
Technical Editor: Judi Sohn
Production Editor: Angela Smith
Copy Editor: C.M. Jones
Editorial Manager: Mary Beth Wakefield
Production Manager: Tim Tate
Vice President and Executive Group Publisher: Richard Swadley
Vice President and Executive Publisher: Joseph B. Wikert
Project Coordinator, Cover: Lynsey Osborn
Compositor: Kate Kaminski, Happenstance Type-O-Rama
Proofreader: Sossity Smith
Indexer: Melanie Belkin

Connect! A Guide to a New Way of Working from GigaOM's Web Worker Daily™

Published by
Wiley Publishing, Inc.
10475 Crosspoint Boulevard
Indianapolis, IN 46256
www.wiley.com

ISBN: 978-0-470-22398-7

Manufactured in the United States of America

10 9 8 7 6 5 4 3 2 1

About the Authors

Anne Truitt Zelenka is a writer and web technologist. As editor at large of Web Worker Daily, Anne brings a mix of career and technical advice to readers looking to find success and satisfaction in the new ways of working enabled by the web.

Anne has been in software and web development since the nineties, and worked through the dot-com boom as a database and web application developer. She lives in Denver with her husband Rick and three children. You can reach her via her website at annezelenka.com.

Judi Sohn, editor of Web Worker Daily, has over 10 years experience as a home-based graphic designer, technology consultant, and blogger. Now remotely managing a patient advocacy nonprofit organization, she truly lives the web worker life and brings her practical experience to Web Worker Daily readers.

Judi lives in Central New Jersey with her husband Eric and two daughters. She maintains a personal blog at momathome.com.

Acknowledgments

Today's web allows us to come online as authentic individuals, to join with others for profit and support, and to do more than we could before we were so connected. That's not just a nice story; it's the truth I've lived that led to this book.

Thanks to those who made *Connect!* possible: Om Malik for launching Web Worker Daily and inviting me to be its lead writer in November of 2006, Wiley executive editor Chris Webb for spotting a potential book in the site, and publisher Joe Wikert for getting behind it, even as I revised Chris' vision for the book into the book I wanted to write and thought needed writing.

Development editor Julie Smith shepherded me through the manuscript writing process with wit and kindness, encouraging me while keeping me on schedule. I hope to work with her again some day.

Technical editor and peer reviewer Judi Sohn balanced my theorizing and philosophizing with practical examples and realistic caveats. Working with her on Web Worker Daily has to be one of the greatest partnerships of my career. Both the site and I are lucky to benefit from her pragmatic wisdom, facility with technology, and energy for web work.

In my three plus years of blogging, I've been inspired by so many people that I hesitate to even start listing them. I want to mention a few specifically, though. Leisa Reichelt has provided friendship and insight in equal measure. James Governor, Steve O'Grady, and Michael Coté allowed me to try out industry analysthood with them—an experience that will inform my thoughts on virtual teams for a long time into the future—and they each continue to make me think more and better about what today's web means for software, work, and life in general. Stowe Boyd's ideas on flow, on individuals as the new group, and on more practical matters such as working as an independent consultant have informed and enlightened me. Mike Gunderloy's advice on writing a book, his thoughtful articles for Web Worker Daily, and his funny homeschooling-dad tweets make him one of my favorite friends and thinkers online.

There are a few writers I've mainly admired from afar, though this book gives me an excuse to connect personally to at least a couple of them. Richard

Ogle's book *Smart World* made sense of network science for me, and his ongoing insight and support makes it tangible. Gina Trapani has set the standard for life hacks websites with Lifehacker. I envy her easy, conversational writing style and her effortless grasp of all things tech. Daniel Pink's books *Free Agent Nation* and *A Whole New Mind* should be required reading for anyone who wants to understand the web work shift. Piers Anthony was my favorite author when I was a teenager and he suggested by example one of the few career dreams I had growing up: book author.

I credit my mom, Christie Cave, for my appreciation for words and writing as well as for my pragmatic streak, skinny though it may be. I thank her also for having me over to paint at her house when I wanted to play with pictures instead of with words while writing this book.

My dad Leigh Truitt bought the family an Apple IIe when I was in junior high, leading me to a lifelong fascination with software and with the ways that it brings people together. He's the most dedicated reader of my blogs and supports me in more practical ways also, helping with kids' carpooling, meeting for coffee, and sharing books and articles that he knows I'll enjoy.

My sisters Allison and Sarah listen with patience and even interest when I offer career or financial or real estate or relationship advice. I appreciate their kindness and indulgence. I just wish Allison were living in Colorado with the rest of us.

Of all the decisions I've made in my life, the second best was to move back to Denver after 20 years away. We lucked onto the most ideal of streets just a mile away from my childhood home. My neighbors on Deep South Clayton may not understand what I do in my home office, but maybe one or another of them will read this book. Thanks to Lisa, Harris, John, Sherry, Ingerid, Steve, Jennifer, David, Frances, Bill, Jenny, Vern and everyone else for good conversation, good food, good drinks, and good friendship. But Harris: no more appletinis, please. I can't web work like that.

Special thanks to neighbor Steve Lubowicki for showing genuine and ongoing interest in the book, for sharing his experiences as a business owner, and for being an example of choosing authenticity in your work.

Behind every successful working mother is a good childcare arrangement. I am lucky to have had two responsible and dedicated au pairs in the past few years: Rose Usadee Eckert and Susana Garcete. I am grateful to both these women for the time and attention they have given to my children and for the freedom they've given me.

The first best decision I've made in my life was marrying Rick Z. more than 13 years ago. We've taken a wild ride together from California to D.C. to Maui and finally to what we plan is our permanent home in Denver. Our marriage, along with the family and friends that surround us here in our great Rocky Mountain state, reminds me that it's not money that makes you happy; it's your relationships with people. With Rick and all the other people I'm connected to online and off, I feel wealthy indeed.

And finally I want to thank you, reader, for picking up this book from the bookstore or at the library or from a friend. I hope you find success and satisfaction at work in the web age, like I have. Please share your web working stories and ideas and questions with me at anne@webworkerdaily.com.

Contents

Foreword x

Introduction xii

1 Towards a Web Working World. 1

2 Get Ready to Web Work 33

3 Burst Your Productivity. 61

4 Rethink Your Relationship with Email 91

5 Surf Waves of Information 113

6 Connect, Communicate, and Collaborate 141

7 Go Mobile 173

8 Explode Your Career 197

9 Manage Your Money 229

10 Blend Your Work and Your Personal Life 257

11 The Future of Web Work. 279

Index 286

Foreword

To Live Is To Connect

Back in 2002, the telecom landscape was like a fertile valley, albeit one littered with the rotting carcasses of telecom companies that had blown through hundreds of billions of dollars building gigantic fiber networks that nobody was using. The bandwidth highways, in the meantime, were ready for traffic—except there were no onramps yet.

But as they say, it is always darkest before the dawn. It became clear to me then that the technology business was merely taking a pause; that technology, and broadband in particular, was going to become an integral part of our daily lives. My optimism stemmed from some core trends that were starting to emerge: Computers were getting cheaper; Steve Jobs' dream of an iPod in every pocket was becoming a reality; and we were all snapping digital photos and just as quickly sending them, electronically, to our friends.

We the people had embraced technology with a religious fervor, and there was no going back. We were the ones who told our phone and cable companies that we needed broadband. At the same time, open source tools and web technologies had matured, giving innovators an opportunity to not only tinker but bring their ideas to life.

The 1990s boom and the resulting bust had left in its wake an infrastructure that was just waiting to be taken advantage of—servers had become dirt cheap, data centers welcomed everyone with deep discounts and bandwidth prices kept falling.

Slowly but surely, our Internet highway system was taking shape. In 2003, I started to think, what would happen if half the world's population had broadband? For while we are not there yet, we are moving ever closer, and when we get there, broadband will be the platform for an always-on, always-connected life. If mobile phones destroyed the concept of location, then broadband takes away the dimension of time. And the biggest impact, I thought, would be on how we work.

Just as there is no difference between being connected to a company network over cable or an office LAN, working on your next presentation while constantly checking email or sending instant messages to colleagues is no different whether you're doing it while sitting in a coffee shop or within the confines of a dreary cubicle.

It was this changing nature of work that prompted me to start Web Worker Daily, a web site devoted to this connected future. In this book, Anne Zelenka and Judi Sohn, Web Worker Daily's co-editors, provide us with a road map for such a future and tell us what it all means. I hope you enjoy it as much as I did.

—Om Malik
Founder, Web Worker Daily & GigaOM

Introduction

In this book you'll learn how you can use the newest web tools to improve your work life. I'll tell you about the websites and services you might want to try and how to use them most effectively. I'll introduce you to the social web—the web where people are as important as corporations—and help you feel comfortable and confident participating in it in the context of your work. I'll tell you how people like yourself are working in new ways because of the web and show you how you can too. And I hope I'll convince you that web working can be a satisfying new way of approaching your professional life.

As editor at large of the *Web Worker Daily* website launched in September of 2006, I have front-row seats in the theatre of web workerhood. Every day, I get to see and hear about all the new and sometimes surprising ways people are using the web to work in smarter, more productive, and more satisfying ways. I'm excited to share what I've learned with you and looking forward to hearing from you about how the web has changed the way you work. I'm easy to find online, because I use the web each day to stay in touch with colleagues, to look for new opportunities, to learn about advances in my field, to meet new people, and always, to have fun. I don't just write about web working; I live it every day.

Isn't everyone a web worker these days? Most people working office jobs do use the web, it's true. You probably already use the web regularly during the workday: to connect and communicate with teammates and with your family and friends, to search for information, to take a break from work. But web working can be so much more than that. At *Web Worker Daily*, we think web working goes beyond merely using the web as a tool. We look at it as an exciting and welcome change in how we can make a living. The web ushers in a global, networked world where we should (theoretically at least) be able to work from wherever we want, whenever we want, on almost any information-based project we want. The reality, of course, is somewhat less revolutionary: most employers prefer on-site workers, face to face meetings may still be necessary to create trust and rapport, and cultural barriers complicate distributed work. Still, the possibilities and opportunities of a new way of working are real—and you can use them to make your work life more successful and satisfying.

The launch of the web

I can't imagine working without the World Wide Web now—but it's so young. Though it's rooted in the sixties, when academic and government researchers networked their computers across vast distances, the hyperlinked web of HTML documents only emerged in the early nineties. That's when the World Wide Web project began and when the most famous of the early web browsers, NCSA Mosaic, was built.

The developers of Mosaic wanted to provide a tool not just for finding and retrieving hypertext documents—pages linked across different computers—but also for collaboration.* They succeeded wildly if you judge by the current descendants of Mosaic, including Mozilla Firefox and Netscape Navigator. The web provides a platform for office tools like email, word processors and spreadsheets; for personal information organizers that manage to do lists and calendar events; for online meetings; and for almost anything else you might like to do in a networked web of people and computers.

When the web first started, it mainly just provided another channel for business as usual. The buzzword during those days was e-commerce, or electronic commerce, meaning taking real-world business and making it virtual. Large organizations like newspapers, department stores, and government agencies allowed us to act as their audience, their customers, and their citizens. To really see the social and professional possibilities of the web, we had to wait for broadband access, for social software and platforms, for widespread Internet phone services, and for more dynamic web user interfaces. It's the social web that radically changes work life for people like you and me.

Beyond knowledge work

In his book *Landmarks of Tomorrow* published in 1959, management guru Peter Drucker created the concept of the "knowledge worker" to refer to those who work with intangible information rather than tangible goods. The information

---

*On February 16, 1993, Mosaic developer Marc Andreessen posted a message to a number of newsgroups announcing the availability of beta versions of Mosaic. As to the purpose of the project, Andreessen said, "We are continuing to develop X Mosaic, with the end goal of making it a useful tool for networked asynchronous collaboration specifically, and global hypermedia and information system resource discovery and retrieval in general." (Available at http://www .dejavu.org/mosnew.html.)

age as envisioned by Drucker represented an advance beyond the industrial age, which itself took over from the agricultural age.

What comes after the information age? In the book *A Whole New Mind*, author Daniel Pink calls it the conceptual age: "We are moving from an economy and a society built on the logical, linear, computerlike capabilities of the Information Age to an economy and a society built on the inventive, empathic, big-picture capabilities of what's rising in its place, the Conceptual Age." Pink's conceptual age is similar to my vision of the web working age. The term "web worker" is no more specific than the term "knowledge worker" and yet it could represent just as much of a shift as the move from manufacturing to information production. This book begins to sketch a theory and vision of web work as contrasted with knowledge work. Does this mean that knowledge work becomes obsolete? Absolutely not. Just like there are still farmers and manufacturers, there will continue to be knowledge workers—but their work will certainly be changed by web ways of working, just like industrial processes changed agriculture, and like knowledge work changed manufacturing.

Are you a web worker?

You are a web worker if you use the web to reach out beyond the confines of your office, cubicle, home workspace, or seat at a wifi café to connect and collaborate with others doing the same thing. Whether you are employee, entrepreneur, or freelancer you can be a web worker.

At Web Worker Daily, we first thought about web workerhood as "going Bedouin": ditching the traditional office or cubicle setup in order to work from wifi cafés in the coolest cities in the world. But neo-Bedouins only represent a small part of the web working population, as people web work in many ways:

- **Telecommuting.** Working from home using web-based tools for connecting with people inside and outside the walls of their corporate employers.
- **Freelancing.** Choosing the ability to work from home or wherever you want, prioritizing independence over corporate benefits and posh offices, using the web to make yourself more productive and successful.

- **Distributed teams.** Working across geography and time zones to bring products to market, using the latest in technology to connect and collaborate with your teammates around the world.
- **Career mashups.** Mixing and mashing a career with a variety of income streams from advertising on a blog to online professional services marketplaces to loosely coupled consulting arrangements.
- **Cubicle connecting.** Turbocharging traditional employment using web-based collaboration tools like blogs and wikis to engage effectively with the world outside your department and company.
- **Virtual entrepreneurship.** Starting up a company that has no offices or hardware or resources of its own except a few people with laptops. You might use Amazon Web Services as your virtual hardware, software-as-a-service accounting from FreshBooks, and Google Apps for email and calendaring.
- **Side businesses.** Working at a traditional job and earning extra income on the side from an online store, ad-supported blog, or other new economy business.
- **Online career boosts.** Promoting your work to potential employers or clients with a website, making professional contacts with social networking tools like LinkedIn or Facebook, and getting feedback on your skills by sharing work for free online.

The web worker attitude

In an increasingly global economy, where jobs can move overseas and industries expire in seemingly an instant, you face uncertainty and change like never before. You can't count on conventional work wisdom to get you through, not in the web age.

Think about meeting your work life with a new attitude, an attitude that is:

- **Authentic.** The new web is about your power and responsibility to define your own way, not follow someone else's. That doesn't mean that you step all over other people or that you turn to narcissism, hedonism, or escapism. You act within a web of social and professional relationships, and your actions online may be both more visible and more permanent than actions taken offline. Kindness and respect are not any less important. On the contrary, they may be more important, given that your ideas and communications can accelerate around the globe at web speed, without the context of body language to make your meaning clear.

- **Social.** You discover and pursue your goals by interacting with other people. Your satisfaction depends critically on your relationships with others. The new web is not about technology taking over our lives but about making social interactions primary.
- **Active.** You must take action in order to discover and achieve your career goals. The web working world is too new and too much in flux for you to rely exclusively on analysis and top-down planning to guide you. Try something, and see what happens. Adjust your attitude and try again. Develop a plan, but always use action to test and refine it.
- **Open.** The web age promotes openness and transparency, but this doesn't come without a cost. Opening up your professional life online can attract colleagues and clients, but it leaves you vulnerable to critics or criminal behavior too. Seek the level of openness that works for you.

This is a book about people

The web is more a social creation than a technical one. I designed it for a social effect—to help people work together—and not as a technical toy.

—Tim Berners-Lee, inventor of the web

While this is a book about how to use the web for work, it's not primarily a technology tutorial. It's a book about people. When you have trouble getting through your email, the problem is not usually technical. The problem is that it's sometimes difficult to make decisions about how to proceed on a project, difficult to communicate effectively with work associates, difficult to keep yourself productive and motivated when the inbox overflows. When constant instant messaging breaks your concentration and flow, the problem is again, not technical—the problem is finding the right balance between availability and focus. When you need to find a new job or new clients, the web can help—but likewise, this isn't a technical problem. It's a *people* problem.

Web tools can help you with some of these human problems. They can present information more clearly for you to make better decisions, get you quickly in touch with people you need to communicate with, and keep you oriented to your project plans at the same time they inform you of changes in the world that affect your work. But even as the web helps solve some problems that are really human and not technological in origin, it introduces some new human problems such as the tension between transparency and privacy, the overload of global networked hypertext, and the constant availability no matter where you are given almost ubiquitous web access and mobile connectivity.

What's in the book

Connect! serves as both manifesto and practical guide for the working world as revolutionized by the web. I will introduce you to the trends in the working world launched by next-generation web applications and services. Then, with practical tips and tool recommendations, I'll show you how to use the web to be more productive, satisfied, and successful in your work life.

Here's what you'll find in this book:

- **Chapter 1: Towards a Web Working World.** Understand the trends underpinning the shift to web work, including the rise of the social web and the power of open thinking.
- **Chapter 2: Get Ready to Web Work.** Choose your workplace, your computer, and your browser. Then arrange it for connectivity and productivity.
- **Chapter 3: Burst Your Productivity.** Learn about new methods and tools to manage your to-do list, your calendar, and your daily activities.
- **Chapter 4: Rethink Your Relationship with Email.** Explore different ways of dealing with and relating to your email.
- **Chapter 5: Surf Waves of Information.** Find out how to manage the crush of information available to you on and offline.
- **Chapter 6: Connect, Communicate, and Collaborate.** Reach out to your colleagues online. Work together effectively.
- **Chapter 7: Go Mobile.** Take your web work on the road, whether for business travel or just for a visit to a wifi café.

- **Chapter 8: Explode Your Career.** Discover how the web can burst your work life apart, letting you work how, where, and with whom you want.
- **Chapter 9: Manage Your Money.** Manage your income, your expenses, and your taxes. Includes special tips for the self-employed, since the web makes it so much easier to earn money for yourself.
- **Chapter 10: Blend Your Work and Your Personal Life.** Mix up the elements of your life in a way that suits you.
- **Chapter 11: The Future of Web Work.** Think about longer-term trends in web work and what the future holds for you.

My goal is to help you see new possibilities then try them out for yourself. If, after reading these essays, you have doubts or questions or new ideas, join me at the Web Worker Daily website where we talk together every day about making working with the web successful and satisfying.

About the software, services, and sites listed here

I've gathered resource lists of software, services, and sites you might like to check out. But you may find that by the time you read the book, some are no longer available. Use them as a suggestion for the sort of thing that might be available rather than a definitive guide. For the latest in online tools that might help you work better, visit our website at www.webworkerdaily.com.

1 Towards a Web Working World

The web can transform your experience of work. With the web, you can reach out laterally and informally and globally, not just according to an organizational hierarchy, though it can make it easier to do that too. You can work where and when you want, to the extent your work allows it. You can define your own way instead of climbing a ladder that's set out for you. You can tap into a seemingly limitless network of people and creations online, finding possibilities you never dreamed existed.

You decide how much the web changes your work, because web work is about authenticity and individuality, not one right way of doing things. You can use the web to work better at what you're already doing, working in the same job or same business with the same people in the same office. Or you can use the web to radically revamp your entire working life, moving to self-employment or finding a new job or setting up a remote working arrangement. You can do something in the middle, adding some online income to a big company job, for example.

This chapter covers the trends that can make web working so different (and potentially so much more satisfying and rewarding) from the work that came before:

- **Web work shift.** Think of web work as the next step beyond knowledge work of the late twentieth century. Web work doesn't replace knowledge work, but complements it.
- **Those are people out there!** In the late 90s version of the web, corporate sites dominated your experience online. Now, you can come online as a three-dimensional individual—and meet other three-dimensional individuals who have come online also.

- **Work life burst.** Explore how the web allows a new style of work, burst work, in which it doesn't matter where or when you work, only that you get your work done and communicate that to the people who matter.
- **Getting rich by getting attention.** If you earn people's attention online, you can turn that into income. But attention doesn't work quite the same as money.
- **Abundance, web worker style.** Open source software, software made freely available and modifiable, shows a new way of thinking about making money and finding success. It's the source of abundance for the connected age.
- **Working together with web applications**. Online applications and other online resources bring you into a distributed network of people working online, allowing you to do more together than you could apart.

Web work shift

We've moved from an economy built on people's backs to an economy built on people's left brains to what is emerging today: an economy and society built more and more on people's right brains.

—Daniel Pink

Contrast web work with *knowledge work* as conceptualized by management guru Peter Drucker. Drucker first discussed the term knowledge work in the late 1950s, using it to refer to the manipulation of information rather than the production of material goods. The term *web worker* was popularized by Om Malik when he launched our website Web Worker Daily at webworkerdaily.com in September of 2006.

Let's see what a prototypical knowledge worker might look like compared to a prototypical web worker, keeping in mind that many people today combine some of both in their work life.

Picture the knowledge worker, a corporate employee sitting in a cubicle, working on a massive project defined by his employer or his employer's customer. He works in collaboration with other people, but almost exclusively other employees of his company or employees of the company's formal partners. He

builds upon the work of many people—mostly current or past employees of his company. He uses tools selected and maintained by his employer, many of which are choreographed into complex, difficult-to-change workflows. He produces some sort of knowledge output: software, research reports, legal documents, or a corporate website, for example. He networks mostly within his own organization, looks for new opportunities within that organization, and manages relationships up and down the hierarchy of that organization. His company sets his high-level priorities, though he largely manages himself on a day-to-day basis.

Picture the web worker, a freelancer working from home or out of wifi-enabled cafés, she works on a variety of projects across organizational boundaries. She collaborates with people she's met on the web on an ad hoc or occasionally more formal basis, sometimes with a contract and sometimes not. She creates her work by assembling and modifying pieces other people have developed; she combines ideas or photos or music or research from a thousand places across the web. She looks for new opportunities on the web; manages relationships across communities, geography, and time zones; and uses a flexible set of web-based tools in fluid workflows.

Comparing knowledge work to web work

Table 1-1 shows how knowledge work differs from web work along a number of dimensions.

Table 1-1: Knowledge work compared to web work

	Knowledge work	Web work
Who matters	The corporation	Individual people
Style of work	Busyness of step-by-step productivity	Burstiness of discontinuous productivity
Currency	Time and money	Time, money, and attention
Business model	Proprietary	Open
Information technology	Desktop-installed, often client-server, predefined workflows, heavyweight user interfaces	Web-based, software as a service, ad hoc combinations of tools, lightweight user interfaces
Priority	Knowledge	Relationships
Creative process	Building, creating	Composing, assembling

Most people and businesses mix elements of knowledge work and web work as I've described them. There's no strict dividing line between what constitutes knowledge work and what constitutes web work, but it can be helpful to think of them as two distinct work styles.

Who matters

In knowledge work, a corporation whether for-profit, nonprofit, or governmental manages projects ranging from simple to complex, marshalling people and resources to make it happen. In web work, individuals become more important and take action in their own right, even when they work for corporations, because today's web allows them to participate online not just as employees or customers or audience members.

Work style

Knowledge workers tend to use what I call a busy style of work while web workers tend to use a bursty style. You'll see more about busyness and burstiness later on in the chapter, but here are brief definitions to get started.

- *Busy work* uses step-by-step progress towards established and crystallized goals using top-down command and control management processes. It focuses on face time, standard working hours, and adherence to organizational standards. Busy work tends to focus on creating information goods and components mainly from scratch.
- *Burst work* achieves discontinuous productivity and finds new opportunities for success by connecting with the distributed network of humans and computers that make up today's web. It emphasizes results rather than attendance or face time, openness to new possibilities rather than following only traditional pathways, provisional rather than fixed goals, and experimentation rather than prediction of the future.

You'll probably use a combination of these styles.

Currency

In the world of knowledge work, time and money rule. Corporations try to achieve their goals with the minimum of both. In web work, attention can be used as currency as well. You can earn attention by sharing your work online and turn that into a job, into new clients, or into advertising revenue. And on the spending side, you must carefully manage your attention given all the opportunities and information online that could overwhelm you.

Business model

Knowledge economy era companies like Microsoft strictly control access to their operating systems and office software, selling them for license revenue. Web economy era companies like Google make their capabilities like search freely available online. Open source efforts like Apache and WordPress make software not just free but also freely modifiable, so that other people and businesses can build more value on top of it, creating an expanding ecosystem with few barriers to entry.

Open thinking and business models don't just belong to the world of technology. Other information-centric businesses like news reporting and business research must explore how they can compete with bloggers who make their writing and analysis freely available. The music business struggles with how to control access to their products. Book publishers wonder what e-books and other information available online means for them.

The web work model is fundamentally open, and this goes for your work life too. You can use open thinking to attract new opportunities, to get feedback on your work, and to make connections with people you might work with in the future. So open thinking can be a source of new profit and abundance for you, if you understand how to use it.

Information technology

In knowledge work, desktop software like Microsoft Office is installed onto local machines. Information processing using that software is choreographed into complex and hard-to-change workflows, managed by a combination of people and software. In web work, web-based collaborative applications join together into flexible and ad-hoc workflows.

You may use both heavyweight desktop applications and lighter weight web applications in your work, even creating linkages across them to interweave your knowledge work with your web work.

Priority

Knowledge workers and knowledge work teams emphasize building and recording knowledge. Web workers emphasize building and maintaining relationships, relying on social search through their networks to find knowledge. Increasingly, large companies are providing their employees with social applications that allow employees to network with each other across the organizational hierarchy. Outside the enterprise, small businesses and freelancers use freely available services like MySpace, Facebook, and Twitter to connect with each other.

Creative process

In the knowledge work era, many information goods like software or research reports are created from scratch. In the web work era, you can create many things of value by putting together pieces that already exist. For example, a web application startup developer can reassemble existing capabilities online into a new service or a blogger can link to what's already been written on a subject and add her own opinion.

Web work doesn't make knowledge work obsolete

Web work doesn't replace knowledge work but complements it. The information age didn't replace the need for manufacturing of goods and the industrial age didn't eliminate agricultural work. As each transition occurs, the techniques of the new age can change and improve the work of the older age. Manufacturing techniques made agriculture possible on a much wider and more economical scale. Information technology, statistical analysis, and computerized robotics automate many aspects of manufacturing. The web will surely transform knowledge work, though it's hard to predict how given that we're in the midst of the transition.

In your daily work life, you will likely combine aspects of knowledge work and web work. For example, my writing this book is knowledge work and yet I'm employing all sorts of web work principles to get it done—finding information and insight online, absorbing and modifying other people's ideas, collaborating and communicating using web-based tools, and occasionally making progress in bursts of insight—though more often plugging away paragraph by paragraph.

Those are people out there!

All that is valuable in human society depends upon the opportunity for development accorded the individual.

—*Albert Einstein*

Since the dotcom crash of 2000, a new web has developed within and around the old: a social and participatory web that allows people to connect with each other at the same time that businesses conduct their commerce online.

The first version of the web from roughly 1995 to 2000 was settled mostly by for-profit organizations like Amazon, eToys, and Excite. Nonprofit and governmental organizations claimed their place too, with informational websites and interactive message boards. Individuals played the role of consumer, onlooker, reader, and occasionally forum member. Individuals could join predefined communities established by the corporations, but they mostly didn't have identity or value separate from the communities they joined.

In the second version of the web, you can join in as a full participant in the negotiations, connections, and collaborations taking place online. Even though you will still work for, buy from, and form organizations of various types, you also act in your own right. Through now-ubiquitous email and instant messaging, you can connect one to one, one to many, and many to many, inside, outside, and across formal organizational boundaries. Through blogging, you can raise your voice and talk back to big media, or talk with other people without big media involved. Through social networking, you can connect for personal and professional gain. Through open source software projects and other decentralized, sharing-based value creation models you can develop your professional reputation and skills outside of the corporate world.

Comparing the corporate web and the people web

You'll see in Figure 1-1 the way the web looks to corporations (and the way it largely looked during 1995–2000). The major nodes are the for-profit websites. Each website sees its users in a particular one-dimensional way: as buyers, as the audience, as users, as community members. User accounts aren't connected so it's as though Yahoo! users and Amazon users are not the same people. Anyway, from the corporate web's perspective it doesn't matter that these are the same people—that is, unless they make a formal relationship together to somehow share customer databases.

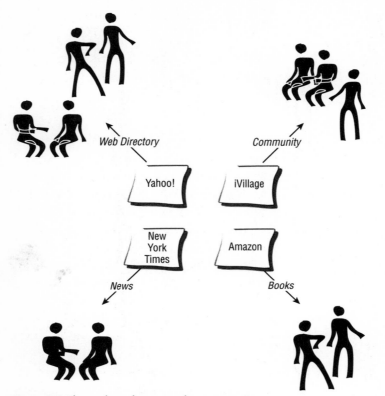

Figure 1-1: The early web, as seen by corporations

I'll use the term *the early web* to refer to the web of roughly 1995 to 2000.

From the perspective of individual people, the web is not just one-way from large websites to them (see Figure 1-2). Different people and sites on the web revolve around the individual, and many interactions are two-way. The big corporate websites are mostly unimportant to the individual, and are just used for limited interaction and transactions, as when you visit a computer hardware company's site to download a device driver or browse to a newspaper site to read one article. The sites and services that matter the most allow access to buddies—that is, to other people. Individuals on the people web also interact directly with other people via such channels as email, instant messaging, and voice over IP services.

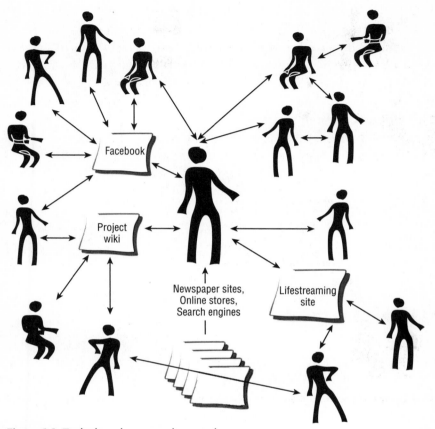

Figure 1-2: Today's web, as seen by people

I'll call the web that includes both the corporate web and the people web *today's web*. While the social web is sometimes called *Web 2.0*, the term has been overloaded—not just with multiple definitions but also with too much hype for comfortable use.

On the people web, too, you don't have an electronically unified identity, but that doesn't matter too much. By repeated interactions over time and through different services you learn who people are and show people who you are. It's the flesh-and-blood person that unifies the identity by their actions online over time. A common digital identity is not absolutely necessary, though it might make online work easier to manage if we did have one.

UNIFIED IDENTITY ONLINE WITH OPENID

While most websites today use their own user accounts, the OpenID effort offers a distributed identity scheme that should eventually allow you to log in to many different websites using the same username and password. A broad range of individuals and technology companies are working on developing and supporting OpenID.

In order to use OpenID, you register with an OpenID provider who provides account management and authentication services. Your username will be a website address or URL (for example www.janesmith.net) rather than a short handle (like janesmith). Once you have an OpenID login, you can use it to log in at any OpenID-enabled service.

You can find OpenID providers and OpenID-enabled sites listed at openid.net.

The ideal of authenticity

The rise of the people web alongside the corporate web brings the ideal of authenticity online. The individualist culture of America admires independence, personal expression, and realness: these are the components of authenticity. The ideal of authenticity calls for us to express our individuality and purpose online or off with transparency. We expect it of ourselves and we now expect it of for-profit, nonprofit, and government organizations too.

For both you as an individual worker and for corporations conducting business online, there is a three-way tension between the ideal of authenticity, the requirement to succeed financially, and the need to maintain privacy and security. There is also tension between the corporate employers who prioritize financial goals and their employees who may prioritize authenticity and self-expression. If you're an employee exploring web working, you'll have to find the right line to walk between expressing yourself and meeting your employer's needs.

Whether you're an employee or not, bringing your entire self online means you're potentially opening yourself up to criticism or worse. The information you share online becomes available to many people: to potential employers, to people you may not agree with, perhaps even to criminals. Before you act online you need to think about who might be watching. You need to protect yourself at the same time you reveal yourself, especially since it's near-impossible to pull information back once it's been published online.

Criticisms of the social web

Like any cultural and technological trend, the use of the social web comes in for ample criticism ranging from the claim that it's narcissistic to the suggestion that it's just a way of wasting time. But just as in real life, you'll find the full range of human behavior online—from the most productive to the most crude.

It's narcissistic

It's fashionable among journalists to deride social activities online like blogging as narcissistic, culture-destroying junk. They're judging social software usage online from the old perspective, the perspective of one-way information delivery from big corporation to the passive audience, rather than two-way socializing between autonomous, three-dimensional individuals.

Most people share their thoughts and their work online because they are social, not because they are fixated on themselves and their experiences. They work online not just to make money or to earn attention, but to participate in human dialogue at the same time that they fulfill the urge to contribute productively to human society.

It's addictive

Another myth of Internet usage paints web surfers as addicts and hermits, shunning normal human connection. This also ignores the fundamentally social nature of today's web. Everyone has their favorite escapist activities online, whether it's gaming or gambling or pornography or simply surfing. And some occasionally spend too much time on those activities, to the detriment of personal and work lives. But even those escapist activities can bring you into contact with others and they may provide opportunities for income too.

It's a poor substitute for real life

Some say that working virtually is less valuable and effective than working side by side physically, on the theory that only by meeting up in person can we truly trust, connect, and collaborate. But the alternative to meeting online is not necessarily meeting in person; it may be not meeting at all. Since we are working in distributed fashion around the globe, we need new ways of communicating such as those provided by the web.

The idea that online interactions are too fake misleads some companies into thinking they need to reproduce physical interaction as faithfully as possible online. For example some companies are creating advanced videoconferencing systems that seek to simulate the effects of attending an in-person meeting around a conference table. Life-sized video images of remote personnel are arrayed around the table.

But you don't need expensive systems to connect effectively with your virtual colleagues. You'll see in a later chapter the lightweight and inexpensive tools you can use to connect effectively with workmates even when they're far away.

It's populated with impostors

You may worry who you're connecting with online. How do you know they are who they say they are? Might they be pretending to be someone else in order to take advantage of you?

Actually, if you get involved with a community of web workers you will soon learn that you can't fake identity in web work for any period of time if you want to succeed. Repeated interactions over time can establish your trustworthiness or your lack of it and because web work is played out in public for others online to see, you can't hide very long. Web work relies on sharing of work and even sharing of daily life activities through digital channels.

You can operate under a pseudonym or handle without using your real name and still establish your online reputation. It's not always necessary that people know who you are in your life offline. It is important that people get to know you through multiple channels and multiple interactions and transactions online. Consistency is more important than whether the name you use is real.

It's dominated by flamers and trolls

Online message boards have attracted plenty of flamers and trolls (people who delight in making other people miserable with their acidic commentary). The social web regularly suffers from bouts of rudeness. Some people are emboldened by the shield of their computer and the Internet, saying things online that they would never say to your face.

But the majority of people online don't enjoy making other people uncomfortable—just like the majority of people offline. And if you are particularly sensitive to criticism or belligerence, there are many ways to join in the social web without opening yourself up to that.

It's only for wasting time

You can certainly waste time on the web, watching YouTube videos, playing casual games, or reading celebrity gossip. But there are many productive activities happening online too, many of which you'll read more about later in the book. You can look for jobs, build your brand, start a company, swap advice, or strengthen professional connections, among other things.

You're a social animal

By living together in groups and cooperating with each other, humans in the past were able to protect themselves from predators.* You are human, so you will seek out companionship and cooperative projects with other people. Sometimes you do it online, because it's more convenient or because it's the only way available. Today's web supports and promotes this.

In your working life, you may at times have looked to the social setting for evidence of your worth, of your talents, and of what your future direction and actions should be. The only difference in the web-working world is that now you can do it online too. The underlying rules of human engagement really haven't changed. It's still important to find challenging work, to collaborate with other people towards mutual goals, to be polite and friendly at the same time you are ambitious, and so forth. But you do it with a twist now; you can do it with people geographically distant from you much more easily than before. You can do it without meeting face to face and often without even talking on the phone. You sometimes do it without forming opinions based largely on physical appearance.

---

*"Humans Evolved to be Peaceful, Cooperative and Social Animals, not Predators," *Medical News Today* (February 20, 2006). Available at http://www.medicalnewstoday.com/medical-news.php?newsid=38011.

JOINING THE PEOPLE WEB

- **Start out by using a pseudonym** if you feel the slightest bit uncomfortable about exposing yourself and compromising your privacy online. You can always use your real name later.
- **Try social software with your friends and family** before experimenting with it in your professional life, if that makes you more comfortable.
- **Try the "Tidy Web" if you are wary of sharing too much too soon.** The Tidy Web* includes services that only share your information with people you allow to see your updates. Such services include the Vox publishing platform, Twitter for sharing short updates about what you do during each day, and Facebook for social networking.
- **Don't feel bad about lurking (observing without participating) to see how people behave in different contexts online.** Take your time and learn the etiquette before you start. But don't wait until you understand everything. The best way to learn is often to just give it a try. Be honest that you're a "newbie" and the veterans will often go easy on you.
- **Find the right social software for you.** How you bring yourself online most comfortably and effectively will depend on what your peers are doing, what profession you're in, and what jazzes you up. You can start to stretch your individuality online using a photo sharing site like Flickr, social bookmarking like Del.icio.us, blogging on Wordpress.com, or social networking on LinkedIn or Facebook.
- **Judge your efforts not on quantity (of buddies, pageviews, advertising sales) but rather on quality and connection.** It's easy for computers to count and it's easy for web page designers to display statistics like friend count, web site analytics, and advertising earnings. Yet numbers aren't going to tell you if you've made deeper relationships, discovered new ideas, or found new opportunities.
- **Choose a highly unique handle (user ID) and try to get it every time you start a new account.** This will make it easier for people to find you and easier for you to remember your account name too.

---

*I first heard of the "Tidy Web" term on Twitter, when Tara Hunt mentioned it. (http://twitter .com/missrogue/statuses/77151542). Tara also describes it on her HorsePigCow blog, crediting it to Biz Stone, one of the founders of microblogging service Twitter. Incidentally, Twitter supports a kind of tidiness by allowing users to specify that only friends can see their updates. You can read Tara's blog post here: http://www.horsepigcow.com/2007/05/25/cause-we-are-living-in-an-a-synchronous-world-and-i-am-an-a-synchronous-girl/.

Table 1-2 shows various types of social software that you may already be using or might like to consider using.

Table 1-2: Social software types

Type	Examples	Characteristics
Email	Microsoft Outlook, Apple's Mail.app, Gmail, Hotmail, Thunderbird, Kmail, Evolution	Everyone has it, and you don't have to be on the same email server to communicate. It's not time dependent, which can boost productivity by allowing you to respond on your own schedule. Used as a to-do manager and document archive by many people.
Instant messaging	AIM, MSN Messenger, Yahoo, GTalk, or aggregators such as Trillian and Adium that can access multiple accounts	Real-time, good for quick questions and quick distractions. Proliferation of incompatible messaging services has fragmented this channel.
Text messaging	On your mobile phone	Not web-based, but part of the web worker's toolkit. Short and to the point. Useful for intimate socializing as well as quick informational exchanges when you're not sure if someone is near their computer, but you know they're always near their phone.
Professional networking services	LinkedIn, Xing	Allow you to keep an online list of contacts and see the contacts related to your contacts. Provide additional features such as groups, introductions, and questions. Can be source of spammy messages.
Social networking sites	Facebook, MySpace, Orkut, Bebo, Vox	Often used by younger generations for sharing daily life, finding new friends, personal expression. Also used for professional networking.
Blogging	Hosted such as Typepad, WordPress.com, and Blogger or host-your-own such as WordPress, MovableType	Personal publishing platforms that allow you to create a very dynamic website with little work. Usually support commenting by readers and cross-blog links to allow for discussions and other social interaction.

Table 1-2: Social Software Types *(continued)*

Type	Examples	Characteristics
Photo sharing	Flickr, PhotoBucket, Smugmug	Share your photos and other digital images. Browse, comment on, and use others' photos, subject to copyright restrictions.
Social bookmarking	del.icio.us, StumbleUpon	Bookmark and share sites of interest. See what other people find interesting. Find people with similar interests. Access bookmarks from multiple browsers and computers.
Microblogging	Jaiku, Twitter, Tumblr	Allow you to issue short updates to friends, family, and colleagues. Can help maintain a sense of familiarity and intimacy even when people are distributed geographically.
Wikis	Hosted such as PBWiki, WetPaint, Open source host-your-own such as MediaWiki	Collection of web pages that can be collaboratively developed and maintained.

Work life burst

> *We used to talk about two steps forward and three steps back but today it's more like 50 steps sideways and 2000 steps forward. Networked, social-based opportunities are so explosive today that when we pursue them we're flung forward at pace.*
>
> —*James Governor*

The web isn't just a platform for geeky tools. It encourages a style of working that can lead to leaps of productivity and satisfaction: *burst working*. Sometimes new ideas, insights, and relationships can jump you to an altogether different and more rewarding place. The social web makes it much easier to connect and communicate with people around the globe, to find new and different ideas, and to experiment with different opportunities. And so it makes it much easier to burst out to a new place in your work life.

Contrast burst working with working based on busyness, which means working standardized hours in an office building, using long-range planning to decide how to proceed, and focusing closely on measures of efficiency. For well-defined projects and goals, a busy kind of work is exactly what you need. Busy and bursty styles of work can be combined together in different ways to suit your purpose.

You'll be busy and bursty

Most people will find that they need to use busy and bursty styles at different times. In uncertain and ambiguous situations, there's no way to know whether what you do is going to lead you down a useless road or not. You can't predict what might work best, so you have to take your best guess and your best shot, then step back and look at your results. That's a bursty approach.

You might use a bursty style to find a new job or a new client, but then you'll need to focus and discipline yourself to crank out the work at some point—and that will likely require the step-by-step productivity of busyness. Finding the balance between busy and bursty is not easy, especially because you might naturally lean towards one or another—and because bursty work can look and feel unproductive.

Comparing the busy and bursty styles of work

Table 1-3 compares the two styles.

Table 1-3: Busy versus bursty styles of working*

Aspect of work	Busy	Bursty
Attendance	Work standard hours in a standard place.	Doesn't matter where or when or how long you work, as long as you get the job done.
Email	Immediate response required, even during nonworking hours.	Use better ways to communicate including blogs, wikis, instant messaging, chat rooms, text messages, and syndicated news feeds.

Table 1-3: Busy versus bursty styles of working *(continued)*

Aspect of work	Busy	Bursty
Relationships	Manage the hierarchy inside your company. Leverage formal relationships.	Connect laterally outside your department and company. Leverage ad hoc relationships.
Availability	Always available during working hours.	Declarative availability—let your coworkers know when you are or are not available.
Web surfing	Web surfing is bad.	Web surfing fertilizes and seeds the soils of the mind.
Planning	Long-term planning rules.	Try agile experimentation and fast failure instead.

*When we were discussing busy vs. bursty work styles online, Dennis Howlett produced a tabular comparison that I thought was really useful. I used it as the basis for my table here. You can see his post at http://www.accmanpro.com/2007/04/20/bysiness-v-burstiness/ and my original post on busy vs. bursty at http://webworkerdaily.com/2007/04/19/busyness-vs-burst-why-corporate-web-workers-look-unproductive/.

Let's look at each of these aspects in detail to see why when you choose a bursty style you might look unproductive or outright crazy to those who mainly practice busyness.

The bursty don't use face time

Busy work relies on face time as a proxy measure of real work. Bursty work relies on *workstreaming*—sharing your hour-by-hour achievements online using a variety of web-based tools and formats. With the web, you don't need to use proxy measures like face time any more. You can see what people are doing, through their blogs, in edits made to collaborative documents online, via source code check-ins or digital to-do lists showing marching progress towards a goal.

For those still relying on face time, though, the burster who doesn't show up at normal hours looks unproductive no matter how much he produces. The busy aren't watching your workstream; they just want to know whether you showed up before 9 AM and left no earlier than dinnertime. The face time requirement isn't completely unreasonable, because employees might not work quite so hard when they're not being watched. But face time expectations can burden workers.

The bursty prefer alternatives to email

Email is the natural habitat of the busy: everything goes there, from reminders of tasks they need to do to documents they're collaborating on with colleagues to read-only announcements to an archive of project information. In a busyness-based environment, immediate response to email is expected and so workers live in their email. So much important information and communication goes through email that this makes good sense in many situations.

Bursters realize they don't need to live in their email or respond immediately because the information will find them in other ways. They look irresponsible to the busy who jump on each email as soon as it arrives. Bursters know you should try instant messaging if you need a quick answer; go with a blog post if you're announcing something, and use a wiki for archiving information useful to the entire team. Bursters know that you can use online news readers with news alerts to track all sorts of useful events from system management to code check-ins to development schedule updates to mailing list messages, and that email doesn't have to serve that role. Bursters know that the less they respond by email, the more their colleagues will seek them out using other channels.

The bursty manage lateral, ad hoc relationships

The busy prioritize good relations with their boss and their boss' boss and their boss' boss' boss. The busy spend time managing down also, by making sure their subordinates are not slacking off on showing their faces and immediately responding to email requests. The hierarchy still matters in many settings, and the busy know how to work it to their advantage.

Bursters see that opportunities to take 2,000 steps forward in one hyperleap are more likely to happen through connections with people outside the company. To the busy, bursters look uncommitted to the company because they're not playing by the old hierarchical rules. But to bursters, the busy look overly focused on internal politics.

The bursty declare what they're doing, even if it's personal

The busy wouldn't dream of announcing publicly online that they were headed to the mall on Tuesday at 10 am to stock up on underwear, because they don't advertise when they're not working during standard hours. Anyway, coworkers don't need to know anything about that, the busy think, and who would argue with that?

Bursters don't hesitate to declare what they're doing whether it's personal or professional, because this makes it easier for colleagues to connect, collaborate, and coordinate with them. It also makes teams more productive and binds them together on a human level, which is especially important when team members work remotely from each other.

The bursty like to experiment

Bursters try crazy projects and watch them flame out fast as the busy look on with smirks on their faces. "How dumb," the busy think. But it's not always dumb, because one day those bursters could fly forward at warp speed, when one of the experiments works. Meanwhile, they'll have learned all sorts of things from their failures and made good connections in the process.

Sometimes a bursty style of work, though, just shows a lack of discipline and dedicated progress. It shouldn't become an excuse for never achieving anything. The busy know that sometimes work requires long hours of step-by-step effort.

Burst work is suited to uncertain times

Busy work corresponds loosely to the kind of work we associate with formal hierarchies in established organizations performing tightly controlled projects, while bursty work corresponds to informal problem solving and experimentation across ad hoc networks. The new science of network theory suggests that many businesses facing dynamic uncertainty in today's markets are being forced to organize in more flexible ways, ways that reflect a bursty style.

In his book *Six Degrees: The Science of a Connected Age*, sociologist and network theorist Duncan Watts describes the pressures that affect businesses in times of uncertainty, echoing some themes of the busy versus bursty dichotomy.

He says, "Ambiguity... necessitates communication between individuals whose tasks are mutually dependent, in the sense that one possesses information or resources relevant to the other. And when the environment is rapidly changing, so too are the problems; hence, intense communication becomes an ongoing necessity."

New ways of working enabled by the web bring out new opportunities, but also uncertain ones. When you enter known terrain, you can proceed step by step to your destination—that's busyness. When you're exploring unknown terrain, you need to communicate and experiment—that's burstiness.

One style is not better than the other, but the bursty style is likely to be undervalued because it looks unproductive and because it can *be* unproductive. There are no guarantees that your bursty experiments will always or *ever* succeed and you may lose credibility if you become known for one crazy scheme after another. In later chapters, you'll see how you might find the right balance for yourself between busy achievement and bursty leaps. The balance you choose between the two styles will necessarily depend on your temperament, your particular field, your goals, and your tolerance for risk and for unconventional action.

Getting rich by getting attention

Tell me to what you pay attention and I will tell you who you are.

—*Jose Ortega y Gassett*

In the web economy, attention is money. If you earn enough attention online—for your website or amateur video or web application, for example—you can turn that into money. You can turn it into money by selling advertising. You can turn it into money by selling your videocast to a big media company. You can turn it into money by selling premium subscriptions.

You can also turn attention into money by raising your professional profile online. This is one of the easiest ways of using this currency of the web age. Through sharing your work online—your writing on a blog, your photos on a photo sharing site, your web design templates in an online gallery—you show what you're capable of. Potential employers, clients, and colleagues will take note. And opportunities will flow your way.

But earning attention online is only one side of using attention as currency. Just like with money, you want to use it effectively. It is a limited resource, like your time and your money. You need to take care not to use too much of your attention on ideas and information that don't pay off in increased satisfaction, knowledge, and insight. You probably only have a limited amount of time for reading and absorbing information. You should be careful to focus on information sources that offer you the highest value. In Chapter 5, you'll read about how to manage your attention in an age of abundant information.

Attention can multiply

Money can multiply in amount as it moves through our economy. The banking system takes deposits and turns them into more money by lending more than the bank takes in. If I save money at a bank, the bank doesn't hold onto all that money; it loans some of it out. If I save $100 at my bank, the bank might loan $90 of it, knowing that across all its customers, not everyone will try to withdraw money at the same time. By lending out some of the money, the bank turns my $100 into $190. Saving and borrowing result in more money in the economy.

Might attention be subject to some sort of multiplier effect too? It could be. I don't think we each have a fixed store of attention. You might have more or less depending on your motivation, inspiration, and personal demands at a particular point in time. You can have your attention piqued when you hear something intriguing. If one of your friends tells you about something of interest, you might be motivated to spend more attention learning about that.

Surely there are limitations to how much your attention can grow, but that doesn't mean that you only have a fixed and unchanging amount to spend each day.

The Harry Potter effect

J.K. Rowling's Harry Potter book series shows how attention can multiply and expand within a broad community. In the absence of this series, both children and adults would have "spent" much less attention on reading fantasy books during the last decade. Some of the time spent reading the Potter books must certainly have substituted for other attentive reading time. But some of it probably represented attention created out of nowhere. And some substituted for lesser forms of attention, such as TV watching.

Plus, the Harry Potter phenomenon created attention for similar books like Eoin Colfer's Artemis Fowl novels and Lemony Snicket's Series of Unfortunate Events. You could look at the reading boom launched by Harry Potter as a sort of global expansion of attention, similar to the case where an economy undergoes expansion due to investment and productivity growth. You could also imagine an attention recession, where attention decreases in amount and quality. Perhaps this happened after the dotcom boom; there was less money available to fund exciting new ideas and hence, there were fewer new ideas to pay attention to.

THINK ABOUT ATTENTION AS MONEY

In Chapter 5, you'll see in depth how you can best manage your attention to online and offline sources of information and ideas. For now, start observing your own use of attention.

- **Watch your attention expand and contract.** When big news happens, you might find your attention expanding. Notice how you'll spend more time reading news and learning new things when your attention has been caught.
- **Consider the different payoffs you get from spending your attention.** We're notably bad at predicting how much satisfaction we'll get from things we buy. Are we bad at predicting how usage of our attention will pay off too? Would you do better to spend your attention on a TV show or on a book that's difficult to read? Should you spend any more time attending to things you already know, or should you reach out for new ideas?
- **Think about how other people parlay attention into opportunities.** Celebrities get book deals not because of their writing skills but because people pay attention to them. They appear in advertisements for medicines not because they know anything about science, but again because people are paying attention. The web makes it possible for you to build a little bit of celebrity in your professional community.
- **Note how earning attention feels good.** Attention isn't just something you can convert into job opportunities, new clients, or advertising sales. It's also good in and of itself. People like to have the attention and respect of other people.

Abundance, web worker style

Talent is always conscious of its own abundance, and does not object to sharing.

—Alexander Solzhenitsyn

You might think *open source* means handmade hodge-podge with no support. You might consider it the best way to develop software. Or maybe you never think about it. No matter your perspective, open source does have practical importance to you if you want to use the web to improve your work life. It's not so much open source software that matters as open source style thinking: opening up access to information and ideas so as to generate new business opportunities, garner attention in a community that matters, and make a contribution to that same community.

WHAT IS OPEN SOURCE?   *"A set of principles and practices that promote access to the design and production of goods and knowledge. The term is most commonly applied to the source code of software that is available to the general public with relaxed or non-existent intellectual property restrictions. This allows users to create software content through incremental individual effort or through collaboration." (from Wikipedia)*

Open source software and open source thinking powers the web. Most of the websites and web apps you use regularly are built upon open source technologies. More important, open source style thinking—*open thinking*—can be a source of ongoing abundance wrapped up in the capitalist pursuit of naked self-interest. Bring open thinking to your work and you'll have connected with a well of ongoing, growing value.

You already use open source

Do you use Linux, the open source operating system? You probably don't run it on your personal computer—most people don't—but you certainly use it indirectly. Google's data centers run Linux, so every time you do a Google search, you're tapping into the power of Linux. Internet bookseller Amazon runs on Linux too, as do most large and small websites.* The back end of the web is not quite as dominated by one type of software as the Microsoft-controlled client side, but open source technologies including Linux, the Apache web server, the MySQL database server, and the PHP dynamic scripting language are the default choice of most website builders. When you choose web working, you can't *not* use open source.

Open source refers specifically to software whose source code—human readable instructions written in one programming language or another—is

---

*"May 2007 Web Server Survey," *Netcraft*, (May 1, 2007), Available at http://news .netcraft.com/archives/web_server_survey.html.

made freely available so that others can study it, make changes to it, and share it, crediting back the original authors. Open source software is usually built by a community of volunteers who often, in their day jobs, work with the software produced by the open source community. In addition to being built on open source software, the web is also built upon open standards like Hypertext Markup Language (HTML) for web page content and Cascading Style Sheets (CSS) for specifying page formatting and display characteristics.

What open source and open standards have in common is this: they are both informational goods that are developed and shared across organizational boundaries. People and organizations that participate in their development and use do so for private gain, but in doing so, they create a broader public benefit. That's the optimistic view of it. Before exploring that, let's consider how this looks under the old rules as practiced by the proprietary software industry.

It looks unprofitable and destructive

Open business models like that followed by Linux look unprofitable and destructive when you consider them from the old world perspective of lengthy copyrights, strict control of intellectual property, and managing information ownership as though it were like real property. Managers of software firms who have built their business on license revenue look at open source efforts that provide software completely for free and understandably consider that such a move may destroy whatever value existed in the software industry. But there is still value to be had, and companies like Red Hat, a distributor of Linux, find it in services and support around the free software. Proprietary companies like Microsoft, however, have structured themselves to unlock value using high license fees, shrink-wrapped software, licensing protections, and expensive upgrades. From their perspective, open business models really do destroy value. The value isn't gone though; it's just moved somewhere else.

Open business models unleash an incredible amount of value by creating what Tim O'Reilly calls an architecture of participation.* The web is based upon an architecture of participation, and that's where the value in information technology is migrating. Its value comes not from the efforts of one

---

*Tim O'Reilly, "Open Source Paradigm Shift," *tim.oreilly.com*, (June 2004), available at http://tim.oreilly.com/articles/paradigmshift_0504.html.

organization or person, but from the contributions of many people and the systems that index, aggregate, filter, and make accessible all these contributions; all taken up for selfish reasons but resulting in more value for everyone. We all have the opportunity to create a website and put pages written in HTML onto that website. That information then becomes available to the web population in a few different ways. First, anyone can look at the way you put your page together. All they need to do is choose View Source from their browser menu and they'll be shown the source code you used. Second, your page may get indexed by a search engine and later displayed to a user in response to a search query. Then, many websites work by aggregating, filtering, and manipulating the information they find in other pages.

If you choose an open-source style of sharing work, you don't abandon the possibility for profiting from your work, either through attention or payments of licensing fees. The nonprofit Creative Commons organization provides guidance and tools for marking your online work with various levels of protection. You decide whether other people must credit you for use of your work, whether they can use it for commercial purposes, whether they can modify and reproduce your work, and so forth, using Creative Commons licenses. For more information, check their website at creativecommons.org.

Open thinking = abundant thinking

An open approach that encourages participation and captures value created by individuals and organizations as they pursue their own interests is an abundant approach. By creating value for yourself and then sharing it, you harness a multiplier effect.

Take the example of social bookmarking. In the earliest versions of the web, you didn't share your browser bookmarks with other people. When you found a link you were interested in, you stored it for yourself for later. You might email it to a few close friends or associates, but you wouldn't share it with people you didn't know. A social bookmarking service like del.icio.us allows you to store your bookmarks online and makes them available to the entire community of del.icio.us users. Suddenly, an activity taken on for selfish reasons—storing web page locations so you can find them later—is turned into an activity of broad social benefit.

Treating information like real property would consider even a bookmark to be something to be protected. Your judgment that a particular website is worthy of being stored as a bookmark, and the additional information you add via tags and notes—that's your property, the knowledge worker might say. You should save it for your own usage and your own benefit as though it were some sort of competitive intelligence. However, if you don't share your bookmarks and no one else shares theirs, there is much less information available for everyone. The pie itself is smaller. We are all limited from building upon the value that the information contains.

You might have read self-help books that tell you to think abundantly. Well, here's where abundant thinking isn't just self-help pseudoscience. Think abundantly about what you have to share digitally. Think about how you can build upon the information goods that other people are sharing online. That's the abundant thinking of the web worker.

OPEN THINKING

You don't have to be an open source software developer to explore the abundance of open thinking. Here are a few ways to experiment with it in your work life:

- **Give away your work.** Think how you can open up your own work products and build a business around that or attract employment opportunities. Writers can share what they do on a blog or in a free ezine. Software developers can contribute bug fixes to open source projects or offer small utilities online. Website designers can share basic website templates. Attorneys can post FAQs (frequently asked question lists) on their area of specialty online. Academics can discuss their ongoing research. Artists can swap trading cards showing their work with each other or share them with potential buyers. Opening your work up this way can raise your professional profile and bring you new opportunities and clients, while giving you early exposure to potentially disruptive shifts in your field.

OPEN THINKING (*continued*)

- **Share your career progress and experiences.** This has personal benefits for you at the same time that it benefits other people. By being open about both your successes and your failures, you are setting an example for other people and helping them learn. You will be repaid in advice and in support. Try blogging or micro-blogging tools or join a social network. But be careful. Being too open about failures where other people were involved might get you in deep trouble. As always, weigh the balance between transparency and privacy.
- **Try an open-source blogging or content management system package.** If you choose to host your own website, you may want to try a personal publishing system like WordPress or, for group-oriented sites needing more advanced capabilities, a full-featured content management system like Drupal. These open-source packages benefit from a broad community that can answer your questions about usage, provide extensions that add new features, and offer themes for customizing the look of your website. You get the added benefit of joining into the community building the tools,
- **Consider the open-source LAMP stack for any website you build.** If you set up a website, consider choosing a web host package that uses open source technologies Linux, Apache, MySQL, and PHP. When it comes time to add more dynamic capabilities to your website, you'll be glad you did—because many of the most interesting backend web capabilities work only on the so-called LAMP (Linux, Apache, MySQL, PHP) platform.

Working together with web applications

Individually, we are one drop. Together, we are an ocean.

—*Ryunosuke Satoro*

Web applications support the collaborative work that's a hallmark of today's web. Web applications put sharing and connection foremost—and that's the key to success in web work. Even the most dedicated web workers still install and use some desktop software. But applications online are where many of your most important opportunities in web work lie, because they're the ones that bring you into and onto the people web.

Web-based software, however, shows serious disadvantages relative to desktop software. It has fewer features than what you install on your own computers. It can suffer from serious lag times. And worst of all, it usually requires you to be connected to the Internet to be able to use it. You need your desktop software!

Still, web-based software can be so convenient. You don't have to install it to use it. New features don't require an upgrade; they just miraculously appear the next time you log in. Web applications can be very easy to use, if they use the text and links paradigm that the web is based upon. And now, with tabbed browsers, you've got a unified way to run every web app you want all at the same time.

With typical desktop software, you and your machine work in a close partnership. Your desktop applications need to be your everything, because for the most part, they don't have access to outside capabilities (with the exception of some hybrid applications such as iTunes or desktop-installed instant messaging aggregators). Now think of the people web. Your software connects you to a bunch of other people, even if you only use it for personal benefit, and to a variety of computing services and information resources online. Your software can be lighter weight because you're tapped into a network of human and computer intelligence. You can use a wide variety of tools, each addressing a very specific feature rather than a one-size-fits-all desktop product. Standards like really simple syndication (RSS) and extensible markup language (XML) bring them together.

Table 1-4 shows some desktop applications with web application alternatives.

Table 1-4: Webware equivalents for your office software

Software	Desktop examples	Web application alternatives
Office suite	Microsoft Office	Google Apps, Zoho Office
Illustration, diagramming	Adobe Illustrator, Microsoft Visio	Gliffy
Photo editing	Adobe Photoshop	Picnik, Fauxto
Email	Microsoft Outlook, AppleMail, Thunderbird	Gmail, Hotmail

Table 1-4: Webware equivalents for your office software *(continued)*

Software	Desktop examples	Web application alternatives
Calendaring	Microsoft Outlook, Apple iCal	Google Calendar, 30Boxes
To do list	Microsoft Outlook, Apple iCal	Remember the Milk, Ta-da list
News reader	NetNewsWire, FeedDemon	Google Reader, Bloglines

Desktop software: just you and the machine

There's no question that the desktop software you have available to you now is powerful. Microsoft Word, Adobe PhotoShop, and the Eclipse software development environment, for example, contain an almost overwhelming number of features that make one person significantly more productive. But they're fundamentally about individual productivity, even when combined into collaborative workflows with other people, using their own desktop tools. Figure 1-3 shows a user working in tightly-tied partnership with her desktop software.

Figure 1-3: Desktop software concentrates value creation onto you and your machine

For concentrated individual content creation, desktop tools can't be beat by web-based tools, not yet at least. If you are a software developer, graphic designer, scientific researcher, or are in some other kind of knowledge-intensive field, you will probably find yourself using desktop tools on a regular basis, just like I'm using Microsoft Word to produce this manuscript. However, new modes of work—web modes of work—demand new kinds of tools.

The line between web applications and desktop applications is getting fuzzier all the time. A desktop email client relies on regular access to the Internet to download new messages. Apple's iTunes music player lets you download songs or listen to online radio. Instant messaging aggregators are installed on your personal computer but require an Internet connection to be useful.

The value is distributed now

Today's web supports a distributed network of individuals and organizations collaborating together to produce knowledge, works of art, analysis, and so forth, as shown in Figure 1-4. You can now participate in distributed collaboration much more easily. Whereas before most value creation was concentrated into nodes delineated by organizational boundaries, the connectedness and social features of today's web allows us to work across or without such boundaries. Web-based applications support this.

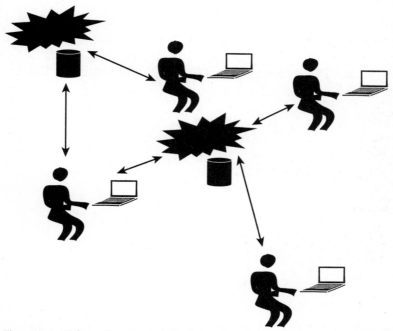

Figure 1-4: Web applications can be lightweight, because they're networked together

Web applications do not support organizationally-delineated models of value creation so well. Within an organization you can make everyone work with the same tools then benefit from standardization and tightly defined workflows. Web applications, on the other hand, make it possible for people who aren't formally related by an organization to collaborate.

You will choose a mix of desktop and web-based applications that suit your needs, depending on your employer, your team, your field, and your desire to try something new. Know that web applications don't necessarily replace your current set of desktop applications, but can complement them as they keep you connected.

Part of the point and benefit of the people web is that you don't have to do it all yourself any more and you don't have to work through formal organizations either. You can now be more a composer than creator from scratch. You can find inspiration, ideas, words, photos on the web—and then use them to create something of personal or social value (giving credit as appropriate). You can share what you create, and the cycle continues. In this world, you don't need heavyweight content creation tools quite so much as you used to.

Looking forward: Get ready to web work

It's time to get started web working. In Chapter 2, I'll talk about choosing where to work—office, home, café, other—and discuss the basic tools of the web worker.

2 Get Ready to Web Work

Even though opportunities for working online have exploded, you haven't transformed into a virtual person made of bits and bytes. You can move much of your work to the web, but you still need a physical workspace with computer hardware and an Internet connection. You need a chair to sit on and a desk or table to set your computer upon. You need a web browser and some other software too. You need access, digital or physical, to colleagues and to other people in your field.

In this chapter, you'll read about what you need to web work:

- **Cubicle, café, or castle?** Choose the work setting that suits you. Ensure you have what you need in your workspace, from the physical (a desk or other work surface) to the social (water cooler talk).
- **Plugging into the web.** Equip yourself with a computer, an Internet connection, and whatever else you need to link your physical self into the virtual world of web work.
- **Bursting free with your browser.** Your browser connects you beyond your computer and your workplace to information, services, and people online. Choose the browser that's right for you and tailor it with add-ons that suit your way of working.
- **Putting your word processor on a diet.** Try slimmed-down alternatives to heavyweight desktop word processors in an age of light-weight web publishing.
- **The myth of the paperless office.** You'll continue to use paper for the indefinite future, so equip your office with the hardware and supplies you need to work effectively across the paper/computer divide.

Cubicle, café, or castle?

> *The new guy used to be a free-ranger. Let's go watch him get broken. They say he was a photographer. Never been cubicled.*

> —Dilbert, by Scott Adams

Office environments can be noisy and overwhelming while home-based work may feel too isolated or too distracting. Cafés don't always offer the infrastructure you need: their chairs and tables aren't ergonomic, they don't have spaces for private phone calls or meetings, and you're mostly out of luck if you need to sign and fax some paperwork somewhere. Plus, though they offer the physical presence of other people it's unlikely you'll connect with those people in a way that contributes to your work.

Figure 2-1 shows a simplified version of cubicle working, each person in his or her little space. It's easy to communicate with people on the team, but not always easy to get work requiring focus and concentration done.

Figure 2-1 Before the burst: cubicles offer physical connection

Figure 2-2 shows how web work ideally lets us work from wherever we want—even, in the future, on an airplane—and stay loosely connected not just to teammates but to many people with whom we can work and socialize. Here you see how the web bursts your work life out of its familiar confines.

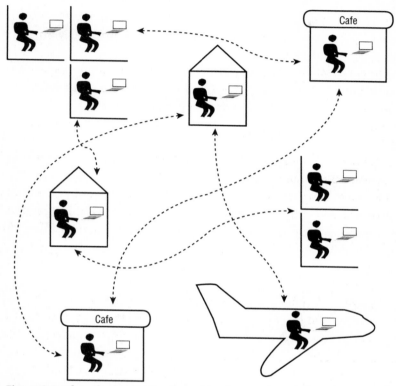

Figure 2-2 After the burst: distributed work, virtual connection replaces physical

Workspaces for web working

The neo-Bedouin web worker roams from wifi café to wifi café looking for comfort, coffee, and connection (to the Internet, that is). But most web workers work out of their employer's office or their home instead.

WHAT'S A NEO-BEDOUIN?   *"Going Bedouin" refers to companies and employees who leave traditional office buildings to work out of cafés. The neo-Bedouin or digital Bedouin only needs a laptop and an Internet connection to get work done. See Greg Olsen's blog post "Going Bedouin" at* http://www.charterstreet.com/2006/02/going_bedouin.html.

Because the Internet offers so much more connectivity than you've had before, it's much easier to work from almost anywhere. How much choice you have depends greatly, of course, on the field you work in, on your employer (if you're an employee), and on your financial situation (if you're self-employed or your employer pays for you to work from home but not out of a coffee shop). If you're an employee, you may be expected to work in whatever space your employer provides. If you're self-employed, you may feel your only option is to work from home.

But even if you feel stuck where you are, consider your alternatives. You might be able to find a situation that fits you better. Let's take a look at the pros and cons of some options.

Cubicle or office in your employer's office building

Cubicles are noted for noisiness and they don't always provide you with the most comfortable environment, since you can't usually change the temperature or the lighting. However, they give you good access to social and professional conversation and your employer pays for everything. If you have a tech problem, you can usually find someone to help. Plus, getting away from the chores of home can help you focus on work.

Home office

You can easily mix your personal and work life when you work from home, for better or worse. The dog barks, the laundry needs doing, the kids bust through your door even when the babysitter tries to stop them. You can, however, pet the dog, do the laundry, and hear about your roommate's day. In a home office, you control the light and the temperature. You pay for the electricity that turns on the lights and the heater or air conditioner though. You can take a nap in your own bed after lunch, but you may have to print and scan with your own printer and scanner that you purchase and maintain.

Café

Coffee houses can be great places to work or they can be terrible. In the best case, you listen to cool music and drink hot coffee while jamming through your work. In the worst case, you listen to bad music and drink lukewarm coffee while distracted by the cell phone conversation beside you. The wifi might be free, but those pastries are not.

Coworking

The growth in the free agent workforce has led to a new way of working called *coworking*, where independent workers share community and coffee in a workspace away from home. This can be an ideal solution for freelancers who want offline interaction throughout the workday. See the sidebar "A new kind of coworker" for more information.

A NEW KIND OF COWORKER

Working from home feels exhilarating… at first. But you might discover after a few months or years of it that you need an office space outside your home. You might miss casual chats or you might want a place that offers better focus. You can lease office space yourself—there are shared office spaces with services like an Internet connection and secretarial support—or you could look into coworking.

Coworking puts a twist on café work. Instead of a café where you can work, it's a shared office with café-like qualities. It differs from other multitenant office services in its emphasis on community and collaboration.

Brad Neuberg created the first-ever coworking space in San Francisco in 2005. He said, "I somehow wanted the community and structure of a workplace with the independence and freedom of working for myself."* Coworking efforts around the world range from nonprofit cooperative efforts to for-profit ventures. To get involved in the coworking movement, find a place to cowork, or just learn more about it, check out the Coworking Wiki at coworking.pbwiki.com.

---

*Brad Neuberg, "Moving On: Coworking, Really Simple History, and Flash Storage," Coding in Paradise, (June 7, 2007), available at http://codinginparadise.org/weblog/2007/06/moving-on-coworking-really-simple.html. See also Brad's announcement of his first coworking space at Spiral Muse, http://codinginparadise.org/weblog/2005/08/coworking-community-for-developers-who.html.

What you need in your workspace

Wherever you work—the corner office, the neighborhood coffee shop, the kitchen table—there are some things you need:

- Environmental control
- Presence/availability system
- Lightweight interaction with colleagues
- Room for private discussions
- Water cooler talk
- Ergonomic workstation
- Telephone

The web allows you to mix the physical and the virtual to achieve these things. For example, I work from home but I still take advantage of water cooler talk to keep me sane and supported. I just find it online instead of by an actual water cooler.

Let's take a look at each of the must-haves individually and see how you can arrange for them no matter where you work.

Environmental control

If you're too cold or too hot, if there's too much natural light to see your computer screen or so little that it makes you depressed, if the neighbor's running his leaf blower every Thursday when you have an important conference call, or the cubicle dweller next door blares loudly on her phone when you're trying to focus: you have an environmental control problem.

Even when you work in an office, you have some environmental control. If you're too cold, bring in a space heater and wear fingerless gloves. Too hot? A desk fan gets the air moving. Noise-canceling headphones block neighborhood and family sounds for home-based workers and work well in cubicle farms too.

Some environmental issues can't be fixed. In my first job as a software developer, I shared a windowless office. I couldn't tolerate the lack of natural light, but access to windows was limited by seniority. I changed jobs; it was that important to me. Your physical comfort is important. If your company won't provide you with an adequately comfortable space for your work, consider alternatives such as telecommuting or switching jobs if you must.

Presence/availability system

Wherever and however you work, you need to protect yourself from interruptions that keep you from getting important things done. But cutting yourself off from all interruptions isn't the answer, because part of the gestalt of web work is keeping yourself connected with people and ideas that inspire and motivate you, while you inspire and motivate others. You need to let your associates and friends know when you're available for chatting, whether in person, on the phone, or online.

Interruptions aren't always bad. In many cases, you get as much benefit from an interruption as the person who interrupted you does. However, each distraction takes you away from whatever you were working on and it's not always easy to get back to it.* When you're working on your most important and urgent projects you need some way of preventing or better yet, postponing, interruptions until you're available. You want to be interrupted—work in the connected age relies more than ever on collaboration—but at a time when it's not disruptive to your productivity.

In an office setting, you need physical means of making yourself unavailable. Some cubicles have sliding doors that can be pulled shut. You might use a do-not-disturb sign. Wearing headphones signals to those around that you're not available for discussion, and this works well in almost any workspace, home and café included. If you have something very important to do, you may need to work from home or in an out-of-the-way conference room to avoid interruptions.

When you're working remotely, for example from home or in a café, you can show your availability online. See the sidebar "Please disturb me" for ideas. This is especially important for those who don't work standard hours. If you use a bursty style of work, you might be at the grocery store at 10 AM but working at 10 PM. In that case, it becomes critical that you show your availability so colleagues know when they can reach you.

---

*Brid O'Conaill and David Frohlich, "Timespace in the Workplace: Dealing with Interruptions," *Proceedings of the CHI '95 Conference on Human Factors in Computing Systems* (1995), available at `http://acm.org/sigchi/chi95/proceedings/shortppr/boc_bdy.htm`. This study found that most interruptions offered benefits for the person who was being interrupted, but about 40 percent of the time the interruptee would not return to what he or she was doing prior to the interruption.

PLEASE DISTURB ME

As a web worker, you have many electronic means of controlling your availability. Try the following:

- **Instant messaging presence indicators**. Most IM systems allow you to specify a status (e.g., available or not available) along with a status message. When you're working on a complex project, set your presence to unavailable. If people repeatedly disturb you, you can either go offline or specifically indicate "do not disturb" with your status message.
- **Microblogging updates**. Services like Twitter and Jaiku allow you to tell your colleagues and friends what you're up to and in some cases, where you are. If you mention you're deep into coding a new feature for a web application or reviewing a hundred-page document, your colleagues will be less likely to interrupt you than if you say, "just poured myself a new cup of coffee... ah, that tastes good."
- **In/out chat room**. Teams with distributed members can create a chat room either using Internet Relay Chat (IRC) or some other service such as 37signals' Campfire. Throughout the day, team members indicate what they're working on and when they're taking breaks. Ryan Carson described this idea in his blog post "Tips for Managing Small Business Teams" at http://www.carsonified.com/biz-tips/tips-for-managing-small-business-teams.
- **Advanced presence management**. Systems like iotum (iotum.com) allow more fine-grained specification of your availability. You can make yourself available for phone calls to one or more people while specifying that other calls go to voice mail, for example.

Connection to colleagues

Cubicles offer nearly unparalleled access to your colleagues: just pop your head up and ask the next guy or gal over a question. Or walk down the hall and see your manager in the corner office. Web workers who work solely virtually on projects need to create an environment in which they have lightweight, informal interactions with their teammates or with a community of people in their field (or both). It's these interactions that can spark new ideas, solve difficult problems, keep you motivated, and remind those you work with that you exist.

If you don't work with a critical mass of colleagues in a physical workplace, you'll need to replace these lightweight interactions with their online equivalents. Many of the availability and presence options discussed in the "Please disturb me" sidebar offer channels for lightweight interactions. Social software like blogging, social networking, and social bookmarking also allows for ongoing conversation. Don't make the mistake of thinking that use of such tools represents unproductive or wasted time. In the bursty world of the web, your best chances at innovative or exciting leaps often arrive via other people that you connect with in serendipitous ways.

There needs to be a balance, of course. If you socialize all the time, you can derail your solo work projects. One of the main challenges of web working is staying connected while getting focused work done.

Room for private discussion

Lightweight, informal interactions sometimes give way to heavy-duty discussions, especially if you're working on a complex knowledge project with a number of other people. In this case, you need someplace to hold private collaborative discussions. You need a place you can talk without being disturbed and without disturbing other people. You need a whiteboard or other shared work surface.

In an office setting, you'll either meet with your collaborators in your cubicle or office or try to find an open conference room. If you're working online, the equivalent will be some sort of private chat via instant messaging or a teleconference (voice over IP, perhaps) along with a way to exchange ideas such as a virtual whiteboard. At the very least you'll use email to pass documents back and forth, but you'll probably also like to try some of the online collaborative workspace options described in Chapter 6 such as the ubiquitous WebEx for sharing PC desktops. Many new web-based systems exist for brainstorming, for sharing computer desktops across the network, for collaborative document editing, and so forth.

Water cooler talk

All work talk gets dull. You'll go crazy if you don't have casual chats during the workday. Besides, interacting on a human level with others binds you together in ways that makes work more productive and satisfying. Again, cubicle culture excels at providing this sort of thing. But you can get it even if you're working all alone in your home or in a café. Social networking sites, microblogging services, text messaging, and online message boards can all keep you connected with other people.

Ergonomic workstation

Web work doesn't have to mean flabby abdominal muscles, a spreading behind, and a back curved from hunching over your laptop. Here's another place where employees have the edge: many larger companies employ ergonomic consultants who can help you set up your workspace for physical comfort. Even if your employer doesn't offer ergonomic help, you can often browse thick office supply catalogs for exactly the keyboard tray and funky-looking mouse that suits you.

BE GOOD TO THE PHYSICAL YOU

You can get so drawn into virtual work that you neglect what your body needs. Here are a few secrets that I've learned during my years working online:

- **If you start feeling any pain at all, address it immediately.** Mild wrist pain can turn excruciating in a matter of days. The good news is that a change of equipment (for example moving from a regular mouse to a trackball) can halt the pain quickly too.
- **Use goofy mousing if necessary.** Goofy mousing—mousing with the opposite hand—can be a real lifesaver if you've let wrist or arm pain go too far. Check online for tutorials about getting started.
- **Learn keyboard shortcuts to avoid as much use of the mouse as possible.** Not only is the keyboard faster than mousing, it's also less likely to give you wrist or arm pain. You can also consider voice recognition software if using the keyboard becomes too painful, as long as you work somewhere you can use it without disturbing others.
- **Try an exercise ball instead of office chair if you're having back pain.** This can strengthen your abdominal muscles too.
- **Take frequent stretch breaks or at least do some chair exercises.** Whether you work in an office or at home, you can get so immersed in the web that you forget you have a physical body too. For some yoga exercises you can do in your chair, watch the videos available at http://www.centre4activeliving.ca/workplace/trr/tools/yoga_atdesk_en.html
- **Avoid long periods of work in awkward positions.** It's great that you can sit on your bed or slump on the couch and still get work done, but if that's your main way of working you might hurt yourself. Set up an ergonomic workstation and then use it.

Telephone service and hardware

Even if you're connected to coworkers by instant messaging, chat rooms, and email, you'll still need reliable phone service. You can choose POTS (plain old telephone service) or VoIP (voice over Internet protocol) or use your cell phone. If you take a lot of conference calls, you may want a headset that works with your phone. Some headsets can switch automatically between landline and mobile phone.

If you often work from different places, you may want to look into signing up for a single phone number that rings at all your phones with GrandCentral (grandcentral.com), now owned by Google. In addition to providing a single master phone number, GrandCentral also allows you to create rules as to which callers you want to hear from and when, giving you ample control over your availability by phone.

Plugging into the web

I do not fear computers. I fear the lack of them.

—*Isaac Asimov*

To plug yourself into the World Wide Web, you need a computer, at least one display, and an Internet connection. You may also want a headset with microphone for voice over IP calls and a webcam for video chats.

Laptop or other computer

Most web workers choose laptops. You could use a desktop system, but that not only keeps you from working at the nearest café, it also means you can't move to another room in your home when you need a change of scenery. Though professionals like graphic designers, video editors, or enterprise software developers with heavy-duty computing requirements might want the more affordable power that comes in a desktop system, many web workers will indeed find that laptops offer all they need.

Conventional wisdom may suggest, "buy the most that you can," but you should first consider whether you *need* all that you can afford. Even budget computers are quite powerful these days, and if you do the majority of your work online, you probably don't need to maximize your processor speed or hard drive size. You may be better off planning to replace your computer more often rather than buying the most you can afford. Laptops are not long-term investments. It's always a good idea, though, to load up on RAM (random access memory), because even browser-based apps run better with more memory and the latest desktop operating systems like Windows Vista demand it.

Operating system

It's no longer the case that once you choose your hardware, your operating system is chosen for you. You have three main choices in operating systems today: Windows, Mac, and Linux. If you go with Windows, you'll have to take special caution against spyware, viruses, and adware. If you choose Mac OS X, you'll be limited to Apple's hardware. If you go with Linux, you may be trading off ease of use against the philosophical and technical pleasures of open-source software.

Some web workers run multiple operating systems at the same time on one machine. Most web workers will find one desktop operating system plenty, since the browser has taken over so much responsibility for managing our workflow and running applications. But you may need to run desktop programs that are only available on one system or another. For example, my dentist neighbor recently switched over to Macs, but her business software runs only on PCs, so she either has to keep at least one PC going or run Windows on one of her Macs.

There are three ways of running multiple operating systems: dual booting, virtualization, and emulation.

Dual booting

You install two or more operating systems on your computer, and then when you turn on the computer, you choose which one to boot. For example, you can dual-boot Windows and Linux on a PC. The performance will be very good, because each operating system works natively on the hardware, but the two operating systems and programs running on them cannot interact because only one runs at any point in time.

Virtualization

The most elegant and convenient solution, virtualization supports multiple operating systems running at once on hardware that natively supports those operating systems. For example, Parallels Desktop allows you to run Windows and OS X on an Intel Mac at the same time. With this approach, you can switch back and forth between operating systems without rebooting because the systems run at the same time. If you want to do this, you'll need to load up on RAM and hard drive space.

Emulation

Emulation allows operating systems to run on hardware they're not designed for, by creating a software layer between the operating system and the hardware that emulates the hardware required by the operating system. For example, PearPC emulates the PowerPC architecture that was used by the Mac before it moved to the Intel x86 architecture. Emulation performance is poor relative to virtualization or dual booting, and is not very common these days.

LAPTOP ALTERNATIVES

You may prefer to use a desktop system in your main workspace and supplement with a laptop alternative for when you're on the go:

- **Ultra Mobile PC.** These are small tablet PCs conforming to a specification developed by Intel, Microsoft, Samsung, and others. Their touch-sensitive screens are no larger than 7″ and they are capable of running full PC operating systems such as Windows Vista.
- **Internet tablet.** These internet appliances are from Nokia, and they run Linux as well as support email usage and web browsing. They do not have cell phone functions built in, but they may be used with mobile phones acting as a modem for mobile Internet access.
- **Smart phone.** Smart phones are mobile phones with powerful computing capabilities built in, such as email and contact management, calendaring, and web browsing. Apple's iPhone qualifies as a smart phone.
- **Personal digital assistant.** PDAs are handheld devices sometimes called pocket PCs or palmtop computers. Today most PDAs are also phones. For example, Blackberries and Treos may be considered PDAs, though they could as easily be called smart phones.

Displays

In late 2006, a study sponsored by Apple suggested that 30-inch monitors boost worker productivity by over 50 percent. Not coincidentally, Apple sells just such a display, but it'll cost you almost $2,000. Do you really need one? Probably not, though you may want two medium-sized displays.

Many web workers find that two separate moderately-sized monitors are better than one monstrously huge (and expensive) one. You've already got one display on your laptop—why not use that as a secondary display when you're at your desk, and buy a decent-sized (20″ or so) flat panel to use as your main one?

You can configure your displays in a variety of ways depending on whether you're using the laptop keyboard and whether you're using a docking station that requires closing the computer (thus preventing access to its display). You may want to investigate laptop stands, which will raise your laptop to a better height for viewing and optionally tilt the keyboard for ergonomics.

Many web workers use their larger display for their knowledge work—graphic design, word processing, software development, and so on—and the secondary display for information and communications. For example, you might keep your instant messaging buddy list or your team chat room window open on your secondary monitor so you can see the coming and going of colleagues and friends.

Internet connection

Most web workers choose cable or DSL for their Internet connections. You might think you'll never need anything else, but what if your cable company decides you're using more bandwidth than you should? What if your Internet connection isn't as reliable as your work requires? What if you decide to ditch city life for a B&B in the country—and your new neighborhood has no cable or DSL?

You do have other options, but don't get too excited. There's nothing to get too excited about, except perhaps fiber optic cable to your house, and that's not widely available yet.

Satellite

If you live in one of the estimated 10 to 15 million households in the U.S. out of reach of cable or DSL, the logical choice is satellite Internet service. Satellite suffers from delays due to the long distances involved; overall performance is said to be comparable to DSL, though the speeds are usually much slower. Satellite is also more expensive than cable or DSL and usually requires a significant upfront investment for equipment and installation.

Fiber to the home (FTTH)

Those with the opportunity to sign up for fiber to the home should consider themselves lucky. At the time of this writing, Verizon offers its FiOS service to homes in select areas and claims downstream speeds of up to 30 Mbps and upload of up to 5 Mbps, depending on where you live.

Because FTTH requires laying fiber optic cable into your neighborhood and then to individual houses, it's only available to a very small subset of the population right now. Even if you do qualify, it might take a long time to get it installed and ready to go.

If Verizon isn't already providing telephone service in your area, don't count on them for fiber to your home. Some of the smaller, independent telephone companies are providing this service. Also, check with your local telephone company to see what their plans are for FTTH.

Broadband over powerline (BPL)

Wouldn't it be great if instead of having all new infrastructure put into your neighborhood, you could get web juice through the handy electrical wires that are already there? Power lines reach almost every house in America, potentially offering a solution other than satellite for the households outside the bounds of DSL and Cable Internet. But power lines weren't designed for data transmission and may never give us the speeds we need. In rural areas, a potentially important market for BPL, the economics may not make sense, due to the need to install and maintain extra equipment on the lines to support Internet traffic.

The jury's still out on BPL even as the money flows in. You probably ought not to count on it as an answer to your Internet access needs right now or any time in the near future. It might help the power companies read their meters without sending people out to your house, but it's unlikely to solve our Internet access needs, especially with our rapidly escalating demand for bandwidth-hogging videos.

Cellular 3G/EVDO

So forget the wires and cables, whether they're already there or not, and look instead at the phone in your pocket talking to that cell tower in the distance.

3G means third generation, and that's where you can get some mobile Internet access at DSL-comparable speeds. With EVDO Rev A, one type of 3G technology, you could see speeds of 3.1 Mbps up/1.8 Mbps down, as long as everyone near you doesn't decide to take the Rev A train at the same time. The 3G cards come with very stringent rules, and wireless companies frown upon excessive use of their wireless connections. You have the benefit of surfing from places that are usually inaccessible, such as trains; however, the plans can be quite expensive.

WiMAX

Yes, reader, there is a fourth generation (4G) mobile wireless solution, and it's called WiMAX. It offers greater range than wifi (up to 30 miles range for fixed stations and 3 to 10 mile range for mobile), making it of interest to cellular providers like Sprint, who has said it will offer WiMAX services in 19 cities by April 2008. We might see average speeds four times faster than EVDO service, bringing true broadband mobile wireless into our lives.

Clearwire offers another fixed wireless option; they plan to cover most of the country over the next few years. They currently use pre-WiMAX equipment but will eventually upgrade to the WiMAX standard when the gear is easily available.

Municipal wireless

Maybe you live in one of the many U.S. cities that have wifi networks across some part of their metro areas. Different cities are choosing different revenue models for citywide wifi services ranging from advertising-based to government-funded to subscriptions with tiered rate structures based on income.

If you want to use your city's wifi network for Internet access in your home, you'll likely need to buy equipment to bring the signal inside the house and perhaps sign up for a subscription to the service. If your work depends on Internet access, you might not want to put your trust in your local government or their subcontractor until they prove their reliability. Try it as a backup, maybe.

Wifi hotspot access

You can purchase monthly wifi access plans from providers such as T-Mobile and Boingo Wireless. If you frequent a café, bookstore, or airport that provides wifi under one of these plans, it can be worth your money to pay the monthly subscription fee rather than shelling out for a day pass regularly. But so many cafés offer free wifi now, it's not necessary for most people.

Choosing your Internet connection solution

Unless you can get fiber to the home, go for cable or DSL when available. Which should you choose? It depends. Cable download speeds can be up to two times faster than DSL. Cable, however, provides shared bandwidth so if you have a lot of YouTube-crazed neighbors you might be better off with DSL. DSL is distance-sensitive, so where you're located relative to the phone company switching station matters. Look for special deals, but be sure to read the fine print. You could be locking yourself into a multi-year contract.

Also, consider what your backup plan will be in case your main Internet access goes down for some reason. Is there a wifi café near your home? Is your mobile phone configured to check your email and maybe even handle instant messaging? Do you have a friend who'd let you use her kitchen table and her Internet connection in a pinch? You can't web work without Internet access, so be sure you're able to get it when you need it.

Headset with microphone + webcam

A headset functions not just as a do-not-disturb device, but also as your connection to remote colleagues and collaborators. You might look for these features:

- A mute button with mute indicator
- Bluetooth wireless connection to your computer and optionally your landline phone
- A volume control on the headset
- Noise-canceling audio (helpful for blocking out distractions in a café, even if you're not listening to anything)
- Noise-canceling microphone
- Ability to switch back and forth between landline and mobile phone
- A style that suits—over-the-head, over-the-ear, back-of-the-head, ear bud type, or an I-just-got-off-the-Starship-Enterprise ear hanger. If you use over-the-ear on one ear you can take a phone call with another phone on the other ear without removing it.

Macs come with a built-in camera and most other PC laptops can have a camera added at the time of purchase quite cheaply. If you're buying a new laptop, you might want to add a webcam for lightweight video chat. A headset plus webcam makes for a cheap videoconferencing solution.

Bursting free with your browser

Simply pushing harder within the old boundaries will not do.

—Karl Weick

Your browser is your operating system as you cross boundaries and explore new territories online. You use it to break free from working in just one place or with just one device or for just one company. You use it to join in the fun and profit that's happening online. It is the key piece of software you use for bursting out of old ways of working.

As of January 2007, around 80 percent of U.S. users chose Internet Explorer (IE) while about 14 percent of users chose Firefox, the open-source descendant of Netscape's browser.* But the number choosing Firefox is increasing while IE market share drops.

Choosing a browser is not like choosing an operating system, because it's very easy to install and run more than one. If you frequent a site that uses ActiveX for dynamic content, for example, you can use Internet Explorer for that (assuming you're running Windows for your operating system) and choose a different browser for other web surfing. However, you'll likely use one as your main one and customize it to your needs and then only use another as necessary, unless you develop web sites or web applications professionally.

---

*Eric Bangeman, "Internet Explorer loses ground to Firefox, Safari in US; holds its ground worldwide," ars technica, (February 22, 2007), available at http://arstechnica.com/news.ars/post/20070222-8908.html.

BROWSER CHOICES

We're fortunate to have many choices in browsers today:

- **Internet Explorer 7 (IE7).** Microsoft's latest version of their browser. Much improved from IE6, with tabbed browsing and better support for standards.
- **Mozilla Firefox.** An open source browser descended from Netscape Navigator that runs on Windows, Mac, and Linux operating systems. Highly configurable.
- **Safari.** The web browser that comes installed on Macs, now available on Windows also. A stripped-down version runs on the iPhone.
- **Camino.** A web browser optimized for Macs but built on top of the Mozilla platform used by Firefox.
- **Opera.** Noted for its speediness; runs on Windows, Mac, and Linux operating systems.
- **Maxthon.** A browser with tabs based on the Internet Explorer engine. Not as widely used now that IE has tabs.
- **Konqueror.** A web browser, file manager, and file viewer that runs on most Unix operating systems on top of the K Desktop Environment (KDE).
- **Lynx.** A text-only web browser useful for low-bandwidth connections or hardware not capable of rendering heavy graphics. Versions available for Unix, Windows, and Mac operating systems.

Why you might consider Firefox

Many web workers choose Mozilla's Firefox browser (available at mozilla.com) for its customizability, tabbed browsing, and other reasons described below. Firefox isn't perfect, though; some people find it runs slugglishly and uses too much memory. Since it's easy to run multiple browsers on your system, you can always give Firefox a low-risk try to see if it might suit you.

Easy to customize and personalize

Firefox's innovative add-on architecture makes it easy for you to add new capabilities to your browser, allowing you to customize it for your needs. While

IE7 and to a limited extent IE6 support add-ons, there aren't as many available. Firefox, as an open source offering, attracts community development around it, especially in the add-on space.

Offers tabbed browsing

Firefox's tabbed displays let you keep multiple websites and web apps open at once and easily switch among them using the mouse or keyboard shortcuts. IE7 has tabs, but earlier versions of Internet Explorer didn't.

Pressures Microsoft

We have tabs in IE7 now because Microsoft can't ignore the almost 15 percent and growing segment of the browser market using Firefox. IE7 is the first Internet Explorer version to offer acceptable conformance to open web standards, and again, that happened mainly because Mozilla's Firefox effort forced them into it. Unlike IE, which runs only on Windows, Firefox is truly a multi-platform browser, running on Windows, Mac OS X, and Linux. Your decision to use Firefox helps keep the browser market competitive. That wouldn't matter if it wasn't such a great browser, but it is, and this is a nice side benefit.

May present less of a security risk

Firefox is less popular than Internet Explorer, and therefore presents a less appealing target to bad guys. Also, Microsoft wove IE tightly in with Windows and this means that it's one step closer to your operating system from IE than from another browser. For example, IE has traditionally supported a number of features like ActiveX controls and Browser Helper Objects that offer entry points into your PC operating system.

Customizing your browser

Just like your computer's operating system, your web "operating system" (also known as your browser) doesn't arrive tuned to your own work style. Firefox and the other browsers offer a variety of means of customizing them so that they are more productive and useful.

Table 2-1 shows some browser capabilities you might want to tweak with add-ons, along with example Firefox add-ons available in summer 2007. Though specific add-ons come and go, this will give you an idea of what you might want to look for when you set up your browser to meet your needs.

In addition to customizing Firefox with add-ons, you can change its appearance using themes, available at `http://addons.mozilla.org/en-US/firefox/browse/type:2`.

WHERE TO FIND ADD-ONS

You can find Firefox add-ons at addons.mozilla.org and Internet Explorer add-ons at `http://www.windowsmarketplace.com/category.aspx?bcatid=834`

To find and install an add-on that I mention by name, go to the Firefox add-on site and search on the add-on name or search for the particular capability in which you're interested (for example, "downloads" or "ftp.") Before installing anything, check the bug reports and user reviews to get a read on the stability and usefulness of the add-on you're contemplating.

Stay tuned to the Web Worker Daily website (webworkerdaily.com) for updated reviews on browsers and browser add-ons as well as for tips on using your browser productively. WWD writer Mike Gunderloy shared his list of favorite Firefox extensions at `http://www.webworkerdaily.com/2007/07/20/6-firefox-extensions-for-web-workers/`.

Table 2-1: Example browser add-ons

Function	Description	Example
Tab management	Advanced management of browser tabs, including "permanent" tabs, i.e., tabs that can't be closed.	Tab Mix Plus
Downloads	Improved management of file downloads.	DownloadThemAll
File transfer (FTP)	FTP client for your browser for uploading and downloading files from sites supporting the File Transfer Protocol.	FireFTP
Panes	Split your browser window into panes to optimize your browsing experience. For example, you could compare information from two pages, keep reference information showing in its own pane, or view your email and your calendar at the same time.	Split Browser

Table 2-1: Example browser add-ons *(continued)*

Function	Description	Example
Sidebar	Display dialog information such as downloads in a vertical sidebar pane rather than in separate windows.	All-in-One Sidebar
Cookie control	Manage cookies—the little bits of data that websites leave on your computer in order to know when you visit their site again.	Cookie Culler
Script control	Allow only sites of your choice to run dynamic scripts. Some scripts can do harm, so disallowing scripts can make your browsing more secure.	NoScript
Search	Optimize your searching.	SearchWords
Ad blocking	Remove annoying ads from your web surfing experience.	AdBlock Plus
User scripts	Turbocharge your browser with a capability that allows you to install scripts customized to individual websites, to add and subtract features to make them work like you want instead of how the web designers and developers thought you wanted.	Greasemonkey

Putting your word processor on a diet

Simplicity is the ultimate sophistication.

—Leonardo da Vinci

Just like our habits changed radically from the typewriter era to the desktop publishing era, so are they changing as we move from the desktop onto the web. You no longer need a huge and bloated desktop word processor for many information and communication tasks. Instead, you can use slimmed-down online versions even if you keep Microsoft Word around for the times it's required.

Where you used to write memos and newsletters decorated with the fanciest fonts you could find, now you send quick emails, edit wikis, or post to blogs. You write more lightly formatted text for electronic publication and fewer heavily formatted documents for print. Although many workers will still find full-featured word processors or desktop publishers necessary for producing (for example) massive software specs or book-length manuscripts, it's increasingly feasible to rely on something other than Microsoft Word—or to complement Microsoft Word and its siblings with online applications like Google Docs or Zoho Office.

The content you produce with web work is increasingly:

- **Shorter in length.** Instead of writing long memos and manifestos, web workers write shorter emails.
- **Provisional and subject to change.** For example, wikis support and encourage ongoing editing and refinement. Blog posts are often offered not as the final word but as an introduction to conversation.
- **Plain text based, with formatting eliminated or stored separately.** Enterprise class content management systems and personal blogs alike allow content creators to think about and create their verbiage separate from the presentation styles.
- **Intended for online rather than print publication and consumption.** Web workers communicate mainly via email, wikis, blogs, and other electronic means, not by nicely printed memos or huge bound documents.
- **Chunked and reused.** Web standards like extensible markup language (XML) let you organize information into reusable pieces, while social media encourages sharing of parts of communications rather than communications in their entirety.
- **Conversational.** With so much communication taking place on blogs and in email and via instant messaging, writing is becoming more natural and casual, less heavily edited and spellchecked. Expressing yourself authentically and connecting in a human way takes priority.

Long documents that go through multiple rounds of revision will not become obsolete any time soon. For example, lawyers will still create contracts in Microsoft Word or Corel's WordPerfect, then go back and forth to get the details just right. Government contractors will do the same for proposals responding to RFPs. Authors will still write massive manuscripts. But the web as a publishing and collaboration platform will change many of your writing and other content creation tasks radically and thus change what you expect of your office software also.

You may very well continue to use Microsoft Word or some equivalent for many tasks. You may also experiment with online alternatives that are simpler and lighter weight, better suited to the casual conversation online. And you might like to equip yourself with a lightweight desktop text editor like TextPad for Windows or BBEdit on the Mac.

Other office applications like spreadsheets and presentation software are undergoing a similar transition from sophisticated and full-featured offline applications to simpler and collaborative online versions. For example, Excel can be replaced or augmented by Zoho Sheet (sheet.zoho.com), Powerpoint by Preezo (preezo.com), or Access by DabbleDB (dabbledb.com). These online alternatives are not necessarily one-for-one replacements for desktop office applications but can suit web styles of work.

ALTERNATIVES TO MICROSOFT OFFICE

Before you pay a few hundred dollars for a Microsoft Office license, consider the alternatives. In a time of lightweight web publishing, you might be able to get away without it.

If you have extremely lightweight document creation needs, look to the online office suites like Zoho and Google Apps. These offer word processing, spreadsheets, presentations, and more. You'll find some ability to convert back and forth between MS Office formats, but probably not enough to manage large documents.

For more serious word processing, spreadsheets, and other office tasks, look towards the open-source alternative, OpenOffice.org (sometimes abbreviated OO.o). It's available on all major operating systems and can read and write MS Office formats. Although Microsoft Office clearly dominates in desktop office suites right now with over 95 percent of the general market share, OO.o has made inroads in large organizations who wish to decrease their IT expenditures such as government agencies around the world. This commitment on the part of enterprise users means that OpenOffice.org should be with us indefinitely into the future.

You might also look at one-off substitutions for individual office applications. For example, you can use DabbleDB or Coghead for building spreadsheet and database-type applications, Fauxto or Picnik for image editing, Gliffy for illustration, or Thumbstacks for presentations.

The myth of the paperless office

By the turn of the century, we will live in a paperless society.

—*Roger Smith, chairman of General Motors, 1986*

While much of your work has moved onto your computer or out onto the web, you probably still use paper regularly despite predictions to the contrary. You sign and fax contracts. You exchange business cards. You write paper to-do lists (see sidebar "Ten reasons to use a paper to-do list"). You put sticky notes all over your workspace and homes. You read books. You manage receipts.

Accept that for the near future you will continue using paper. Then equip yourself with tools that cross the paper/computer divide: printer, fax machine or online fax service, scanner, printer paper, paper notebooks, and pens.

Printer

Most web workers will find a monochrome laser printer suits their needs. Cheap inkjets aren't suited to most office work—they're just a way for printer companies to sell expensive ink cartridges. They can be frustratingly slow too. Don't just look at the price of the printer itself: check how much it costs to print on a per-page basis. If you are going to be printing frequently, especially text-heavy documents, look to a cheap monochrome laser instead.

Fax machine or online fax service

With a printer and a scanner, a fax machine is not absolutely necessary, because you can sign up for Internet fax services to send and receive digitized faxes. If you need to sign and fax something, you can sign the paper version, scan it, and send using an online fax service. Check out eFax at efax.com, MyFax at myfax.com, or FaxZero at faxzero.com.

Scanner

A scanner offers an easy link between your analog and digital work. New scanner technology arrives all the time. Depending on your needs, you might want a flatbed, portable, or sheet-feeder scanner.

You can also use your fax machine plus an online fax service to digitize your paperwork. Just set your online fax service to deliver faxes as PDFs, fax what you want to digitize to your online fax service phone number, and wait for the digital version of your papers to come in.

TEN REASONS TO USE A PAPER TO-DO LIST

Web working doesn't mean using your computer to do everything. Though you can find nice online or desktop to-do list managers, pen and paper offers many benefits:

1. **It just feels good.** You get the tactile pleasure of writing to-do items and then scribbling them out.
2. **You can't beat pen and paper's mobility and accessibility.** Take your paper notebooks or your index cards or your loose-leaf lists anywhere and use them anywhere, even if you don't have network access, electricity, or battery power.
3. **Never hassle over synchronizing your to-do list across multiple devices again.** If you do capture items here and there on bits of paper, consolidating is easy: just write it all onto your master list when you get the chance.
4. **No application lock-in.** Tired of notebooks? Buy a set of index cards, transfer anything you need to by hand, and you've switched. No wrangling with data export and import, no operating system compatibility worries, and no software installation or configuration required.
5. **Gets you away from the computer.** It can be hard on your wrists, your eyes, and your back to work at a computer constantly. Pen on paper might be just the break you need.
6. **Gives you a reason to buy and try cool pens and notebooks.** I love Pentel EnerGel retractable gel pens with a 0.7mm tip in violet or blue ink on Mead Cambridge Limited 6″ x 8″ lined notebooks.
7. **You can doodle pictures or mind maps on your to-do lists.** Make your to-do lists fun, because you're probably going to be referring to them multiple times a day.
8. **Paper and pen don't set off the anti-electronics alarms of family and friends.** If you're putting to-do items into your PDA at dinner time or worse, sitting in your office at your computer while the rest of the family hangs in the den, better watch out. You're toast—and not the kind made with bread.
9. **It's so convenient.** There's no device to turn on, no application to launch, no account to log into. Just grab your pen and paper and go.
10. **Forces you to limit your list and eliminate what's unimportant.** It's really easy to add more and more electronic to do items; not so easy to do so with paper to-do lists. When my lists start getting messy, I rewrite them, in the process eliminating or revising tasks that no longer fit my plans.

Printer paper

Complement a monochrome laser printer with a huge box of multipurpose paper and you're ready to print anything that's not suitable for online reading or that requires a signature.

Paper notebooks

These could be the best mobile device around. A nice paper notebook that you tote with you is a good substitute for a fancy PDA. Many web workers swear by Moleskine notebooks, but don't limit yourself to those. Levenger sells a beautiful and highly recommended notebook system called Circa. Mead offers premium notebooks that don't cost quite as much as the real luxury brands.

Pens

One way to get a good discussion going on Web Worker Daily is to talk about pens; everyone has his or her favorite. If you obsess over them like I do, be thankful that they are a relatively inexpensive indulgence.

Looking forward: Burst your productivity

It's time to web work. In Chapter 3, you'll see how to get things done and make things happen in an age of connection.

3 Burst Your Productivity

If this were a book about traditional ways of working, this chapter might be called *Boost Your Productivity*. You'd read about time and task and project management, about setting objectives and priorities, and about moving step by step towards your chosen goals. But this is a book about *web* ways of working—about work in the connected age. Web work supports bursty ways of working: navigating networks of people, knowledge, software, and machines to find leaps of possibility and productivity.

The connected age encourages a new mindset around making things happen: organic rather than machine-like, bottom-up rather than top-down, provisional instead of definitive, and flexible rather than controlled. Table 3-1 contrasts the machine productivity mindset of the information age with the organic productivity mindset of the connected age. I am sharpening the difference between the two approaches to make it clearer. In practice, you may often take a hybrid approach.

Table 3-1: Machine vs. organic productivity

	Information age	Connected age
Begin with	Planning	Action
Progress by	Management control	Personal power
Productivity	Individual	Social
Project and task selection	Based on predicted results	Based on authenticity, energy, engagement

As an example of how an organic approach to productivity works, consider how experimenting with blogging could lead you to new career and money-making opportunities no matter what your profession. A personal blog might grow into an advertising-supported website, bring you freelance writing gigs, lead to a side job as a blog and PR consultant, or win the attention of a future employer. You don't know in advance where it might lead, so though you may have some preliminary objectives with respect to your blogging (or you might just try it for fun), you keep your goals flexible.

No matter what field you work in, exploring opportunities online can help you find new purpose and priorities or assist you in achieving the purpose and priorities you've already set out for yourself. Sharing your expertise, watching how others succeed, making new connections with people and with ideas are all ways you can jump to new places in your working life through the use of the web. It's not necessarily obvious, however, where these activities might lead, so you might have to feel your way forward in what seems like a dark tunnel sometimes or take two steps forward only to realize you went the wrong way.

Here's how you make things happen using the organic productivity mindset of the connected age:

- **Propelling yourself with action.** Productivity in the web age requires the same thing as productivity in any age: taking action. Get the tools you'll need to take daily action, and get yourself motivated. When you don't know what to do next, let your priorities and goals emerge from your action.
- **You are your own yeast.** In order to achieve your goals and express yourself authentically, you need to rely upon your individual power, amplified through a community, rather than solely depending on any organizational or management structures to motivate you from the outside.
- **Seeking social productivity.** Knowledge work often requires individual focus, while web work distributes knowledge and progress across people and computers, connected to each other in flexible and dynamic ways. In a web-working world, you may find that sacrificing individual productivity for group progress makes good sense sometimes.
- **Knowing when to quit.** In any kind of work, you must cut out what's not important and what's unlikely to bring satisfaction and success. But you can't always predict what will bring the best results. In times of uncertainty and ambiguity, you may evaluate based on how authentic and engaging your projects are, because you can't know up front which ones will have the largest payoffs in the future.

Propelling yourself with action

An ounce of action is worth a ton of theory.

—*Ralph Waldo Emerson*

The secret to productivity in web work is the same as the secret to productivity in any work: you must act. You may have a good idea of what you're trying to achieve. Or you may be experimenting in order to generate a good idea of what you might want to achieve. Most likely, you'll have goals and projects of both kinds at the same time: some very clear and others more ambiguous. Either way, you need to take action. Planning is helpful, but not enough, because it's only by moving forward that you can figure out what works and what doesn't, and bring yourself into closer connection with the people and information that can keep you moving forward.

In this section, you'll learn how to:

- Equip yourself with the tools and systems you need to manage your daily action.
- Get productive, busy style, based on getting your to-do list items checked off one after another.
- Get productive, bursty style, based on connecting with people and resources online.
- Motivate yourself when you're not feeling like taking any action other than a nap.
- Figure out what to do next when you're not sure what the right action is.

Tools for daily action

How you manage your daily work will depend of course on your own personal situation: your particular line of work, your place in any organizational hierarchy, your responsibilities, and your temperament. But most people will use the same basic set of tools.

No matter how you organize yourself, you'll need:

- **A goal or project tracker** to keep you focused on the big picture.
- **To-do lists** for recording and managing your everyday tasks.

- **A calendar** to maintain your schedule.
- **A reminder system** to ensure you don't forget to do anything important.
- **A personal relationship manager** (PRM), because productivity in the web age is at least as much about relating to other people as it is about getting your own solo work done.

Table 3-2 shows some possibilities online for each of these categories. In addition to considering web applications, you may also use paper-based lists and calendars or desktop software. Maybe you'll use more than one tool in each category. You may not have found a single solution that will do everything you want in all situations, and that's okay. It's not necessary to unify everything so long as you know where to find what you need, get reminded what to do at the right time, and maintain space and availability to connect with other people online and in person.

FIND PRODUCTIVITY TIPS ONLINE   *Web Worker Daily regularly provides productivity tips that get you working more productively and effectively. You might also like to check out other productivity-oriented websites, including Lifehacker (lifehacker.com), 43 Folders (43folders.com), or WWD contributing writer Leo Babauta's Zen Habits blog (zenhabits.net).*

Table 3-2: Online productivity tools you might like to try

Category	Web application	Purpose
Goal or project tracker	43 Things (43things.com)	Social goal setting
	Personal blog (for example, on wordpress.com)	Track and share your goals on a website
	Basecamp (basecamphq.com)	Project management. Free version is quite limited in features.
To-do lists	Gubb (gubb.net)	Online lists
	Remember the Milk (rememberthemilk.com)	Online to-do lists
	Stikkit (stikkit.com)	Structured notes

Table 3-2: Online productivity tools you might like to try *(continued)*

Category	Web application	Purpose
Calendar	Google Calendar (calendar.google.com)	Online calendar
	30Boxes (30boxes.com)	Online calendar
	Plaxo (plaxo.com)	Online calendar, contacts, tasks, notes
	AirSet (airset.com)	Online calendar
Reminders	Any online calendar, also the online to-do managers	May support reminders by email, text message, or by popping up on screen
	RemindMe (remindme.cc)	Schedule and receive reminders by instant messaging or email
	HassleMe (hassleme.co.uk)	Nags you by email at irregular intervals
Personal relationship management (PRM)	Highrise (highrisehq.com)	Customer relationship management for small teams
	BigContacts (bigcontacts.com)	Web-based contact management system with mobile access and tasks by contact
	Facebook (facebook.com)	Social networking platform where you can track contact information and interact with friends and colleagues
	LinkedIn (linkedin.com)	Professional networking platform where you can track people's job changes, get introduced to friends of friends, and find people's up to date contact information
	Gmail (gmail.com)	Even email can serve as a PRM tool. Gmail tracks your contacts, stores archive of interactions, and provides built-in instant messaging.

Track your goals and projects

It's okay to keep your goals only in your head, but it's better to keep a formal list. This allows you to make at least a provisional commitment to what you're focusing on at a specific point in time, while at the same time you can rule out other possible goals and projects, or at least postpone them until later. List your goals and projects on a piece of paper, track them at a social goal setting site like 43 Things, or record them in your online planner. Be willing to consider scratching one out when you decide it no longer makes sense to pursue it or if you want to put it on the back burner while you focus on more motivating and inspiring projects. Almost every project is "scratchable," though commitments you've made to other people may be more difficult to eliminate without consequences. And I wouldn't scratch "complete taxes" off my project list, much as I'd like to.

Make sure to include social connection goals and projects on your list. It's all too easy to get focused on handling administrative projects like getting those annoying taxes completed or writing that white paper your boss asked you for. Of course you need to get those things done. But you also need to track goals related to making and strengthening connections to other people.

Capture and manage to dos

Most people will keep some sort of to-do list, and how you organize yours depends greatly on your own personal situation. In web work, it's critical for you to remember to connect to other people every day, because this is the action upon which bursty web success is achieved. However you organize your to-do list, make sure it includes connecting.

You can choose from a wide variety of methods and tools for managing your to-do list, including:

- Personal information management software, either desktop or web-based, from the simplest (text files) to the most complex (dedicated project management software)
- Personal digital assistants including smart phones such as a Blackberry, Treo, or iPhone
- Notebooks, index cards, sticky notes, or other form of paper-based to-do capture

Whether to use more structured or looser approaches depends upon your style. It may be enough for you to keep a list of projects you're working on. Then, when you're deciding what to do, check the project list and go with inspiration. Some people like a very regimented approach: entering "next actions" for every current project, capturing every last to-do from their paperwork pile in their unified personal information management system, and doing weekly or even daily reviews of their to-do lists. Others choose a looser approach, leaving some to-dos as email inbox items, others as papers piled on the desk, and still others written on sticky notes stuck to their computer monitor.

WRITE IT DOWN *It doesn't matter so much how you capture your tasks as long as you don't just rely on your memory. If you don't have a PDA or smart phone that you can add tasks into while on the go, carry a notebook or pile of index cards so you can jot down reminders to yourself.*

Maintain a calendar

Both paper and electronic versions can be used successfully. Microsoft Outlook offers a full-featured calendar that many corporate employees use while Google's calendar is popular with those who prefer web-based applications. Web-based calendars provide for easy sharing with family, friends, and colleagues, which can make planning group events more convenient. They're also easy to access from mobile devices with data plans. However, they require a near-constant connection to the Internet.

Ideally, you'll use a calendar that you can add events to while you're on the move. Paper calendars or smart phones work well for this. Some online calendars also allow you to add events using text messaging from your phone. If need be, just write an event you need to remember onto a piece of paper and add it to your calendar whenever you're back to it.

Use an effective reminder system

All your to-do lists and calendars don't help if you're not nudged at the right time towards doing what needs to be done. Set up your electronic calendar to pop up reminders of events on your computer screen or send them by text message to your cell phone. Review your shopping list when you're going out to pick up milk, or better yet, keep an errands list of any tasks you need to do outside the house. Put a sticky note on the back door so you remember to take the doctor's office paperwork with you for your appointment. Have your online calendar text message you with an agenda for the day.

Your personal relationship manager

Customer relationship management (CRM) applications allow salespeople and other workers with major responsibility for managing professional relationships to keep track of people they know and people they'd like to know. With the social web, you can easily and effectively reach out to people you don't work with formally. So now it's not just salespeople who need to manage interactions with other people. If you want to make things happen as a web worker, you must manage your network of social relationships—and you may want to use something similar to a CRM application to do so. In your case, however, it might be called a *personal relationship management* (PRM) tool.

Your own PRM tool will maintain contact information for those in your professional and personal network, keep track of your interactions with those people, and even encourage you to strengthen and deepen your connections with people.

You will likely use more than one tool for relationship management, including the contacts lists in your email account and on your cell phone, social networking sites like LinkedIn and Facebook that maintain information about different people, and even a dedicated CRM-type tool like 37Signals' Highrise. Highrise and others like it will link people-related tasks to the people those tasks are related to. You don't need a specialized tool to do that, though. Just make sure that in your task manager, you keep track of those most important of to dos, the ones involving other people. I include a separate to-do list called "relate" in my task notebook that reminds me who I want to connect with, whether by phone or email or by commenting on their blog.

Productivity, busy style

It's hard to focus on connecting with other people or finding innovative connections across ideas if you're overloaded by your ongoing responsibilities. The more you get a handle on your day-to-day work, the more you can experiment and explore new opportunities online. So the first order of business—or should I say busyness—is to get your regular work done. By regular work, I mean those tasks and projects that you can get done mainly by yourself or with routine collaboration. This is the work you know how to do. You know what to do. You just need to get it done.

Try these tips to get busy.

Start out busy, not connected

Before going online in the morning—to check email or anything else—finish one or two important items from your to-do list. For example, you might have a software bug to fix, a paper or contract to review, or a phone call to make. Do that first and you'll both shorten your to-do list and create a sense of achievement.

Use a timer to get yourself to focus

Try a kitchen timer, a timer on your computer, or the oven timer. Set it for ten or fifteen minutes or only five, if that's all you can stand. Work on the task you've set out for yourself for that period of time. When the timer goes off take a break. You may find that you've created enough momentum to keep working. Or you may be ready for that break; you can always set the timer for ten minutes to relax then get back to work.

Timebox to make yourself efficient

With timeboxing, you estimate how much time a particular task should take. Then you set a timer and force yourself to finish in the allowed time. This helps you avoid perfectionism while keeping you motivated. Sometimes the time you've allocated isn't enough, but most of the time you'll find that with timeboxing, you get more done with less angst.

Cue yourself for busyness

When you need to get some focused tasks done, put yourself in the mood. Get yourself a cup of coffee or big bottle of ice water, clear off your desk, put on your headset with productive music (see sidebar), and set your IM status to busy. If you like using a timer, set the timer. And get to work.

Use a mini must-do list

Each morning, I make a sticky note with the two or three things I absolutely must get done that day. I stick it on my laptop so I'm confronted with it peripherally every time I look that way. The trick is not to add everything onto the list—just what you really, really want to get done.

Create a done list

If your energy is flagging but you still have more to do, write down everything you've already accomplished that day or that week. Seeing the fruits of your progress can spur you on to more.

PERSONALIZE YOUR MUSIC FOR PRODUCTIVITY

Can listening to music while you work make you more productive? It depends. It depends on your personality, your energy level, the kind of music you're listening to, the projects you're doing, and your music-listening habits.

Online services like Last.fm (last.fm) and Pandora (pandora.com) suggest songs based on artists, songs, and styles you say you like, on your listening patterns, and on what your friends or people similar to you like and listen to. But those services don't do any industrial engineering of the web worker mind, observing your work habits and how they interact with your music listening, then playing music designed to help you work better, faster, and smarter. If you want that kind of personalization, you'll have to do it yourself.

While we're waiting for web radio to see the possibilities of productivity-oriented personalization, try these tips for choosing music to work by:

- **Go for less distracting music when you need strong focus.** Music with low information load—with little variety and complexity, and few or no lyrics—allows you to concentrate better. I listen to SomaFM's Groove Salad ambient music station when I'm researching complex topics. Alternatively, pick music that you're familiar with when you need to concentrate. The more you've heard a piece of music, the less it will distract you. When you're cramming to get a project done and don't feel like the drone of ambient tunes, you might try old favorites from your iTunes library.
- **If you're feeling sluggish, listen to something new and different.** Music you've never heard before that introduces new demands on your brain can raise your energy level. When you're dragging, that's the time to try a recommendation service like MyStrands (mystrands.com) or Yahoo! LAUNCHcast (music.yahoo.com/launchcast/) that will play something other than what you already own. Or try Musicovery (musicovery.com), where you can enter the style and mood of music you want to hear.

PERSONALIZE YOUR MUSIC FOR PRODUCTIVITY (*continued*)

- **Keep your temperament in mind.** Introverts perform less well than extroverts when listening to background music. Choosing music for optimal productivity means getting yourself into your energy sweet spot, where you're alert and motivated but not anxious and tense. Introverts reach sensory overload earlier than extroverts, so too much sound can upset their ability to get work done. On the other hand, highly extroverted people sometimes focus better with music than without—they feel most comfortable with their senses fully engaged.
- **But don't despair if you're a music-loving introvert.** People who regularly listen to music while they work or study perform better while listening to music than people who usually work in silence. So you may be able to train yourself to work well with background music, even if you're temperamentally suited to a quieter environment.

Productivity, bursty style

Web work style (bursty) productivity looks different than knowledge work style (busy), as you've seen. Bursty productivity is about connecting—with people, across domains, to existing services and resources—rather than solo focus. Completing the solo tasks on your to-do list matters, but it's equally important that you spend time making and maintaining your relationships. And by relationships, I don't just mean with people. Bursty productivity also relies on being able to navigate informational relationships online. So you need to surf the web regularly, using the tools and techniques outlined in Chapter 5.

The tools and methods you use for managing daily productivity should recognize the fact that people can't be dealt with like to-dos. When you're alone with your keyboard, it's too easy to forget that there are distinct individuals on the other end. You don't want to isolate yourself.

To shake up your workday with some bursty productivity, think about these ways of working.

Prioritize people over other to-dos

If you are interrupted by someone, that's a chance to connect and deepen a relationship. Stay open to interactions with people instead of shutting them down. Here's where it's important to have a PRM. It will remind you of tasks related to people that otherwise might fall off your schedule as you get solo work done.

Surf the web

You can web surf productively. It's a matter of attitude. If part of your job is to be aware of new opportunities, different people, and innovative ideas, web surfing is great for that. If you tend to overdo the surfing, use a timer to limit yourself. Or use web surfing only as a reward for completing a timeboxed task.

Share your accomplishments

As you go through your day, let your colleagues and other contacts know what you're working on. What you're doing might be of benefit to them, and what they're doing might be of benefit to you. But you need to keep each other up to date to know when collaboration might be possible.

Ask questions

Don't research problems all by yourself. Ask your online contacts. Use a blog or a status updater or a social network platform to be open about what's got you stumped. You never know who might come up with a solution or a pointer to someone else who might help.

Try assembly in addition to creation

You don't always have to create everything from scratch (though you do need to abide by people's copyright statements and give credit for what you use). Before assuming you need to invent a wheel yourself, see the wheels that other people have made. Even if you don't find exactly what you want, you'll probably get some ideas from seeing how other people have solved similar problems.

"Only connect"

If all you can remember is this phrase from author E.M. Forster, keep it as your motto for those times you're web working. Connect with other people.

Connect your work to other work. Connect ideas from your field to ideas from other domains. Connect, connect, connect again. Connecting doesn't look the same as busy productivity, that's for sure, but it's your link to success and satisfaction in the web age.

Let your priorities emerge

Sometimes you'll know exactly what the next thing you need to do is. Maybe you have a contract with someone to do a project just like one you did last month. You know exactly the steps to take to complete it. Or perhaps you are writing your fifth technology book or your five hundredth real estate purchase contract. You know what to do next. You just need to keep track of where you are and continue making forward progress.

In other cases, it will be less clear what you should do next. This is especially true when you are exploring new possibilities on the web. New income opportunities arise—and you may not know how you might best take advantage of them. New relationships appear—and you can't say in advance what collaborations they might lead to. New inspiration comes to you—but you can't predict when you will find it or who might give it to you. The answer to this uncertainty is to stay flexible and to stay in the present, instead of trying to either do what worked in the past or predict the future with detailed plans.

When you don't know what to do next and you don't have a good idea of how to achieve your goals (or even what your goals are), take some small action. See what results you get and what engagement you feel, and then decide what to do next. As you keep acting, your objectives and priorities will become clearer. New goals may emerge. You will get a better idea of what longer term plan will help you achieve those emergent goals.

In situations of change and uncertainty, your task management approach needs to stay flexible. In the software development world, there's a movement currently known as Agile Software Development devoted to more lightweight and flexible development processes. Its methods emerged in the 1990s, when software development managers became increasingly disenchanted with project management approaches that used firmly fixed plans, comprehensive documentation, and supposedly deterministic processes and methods. The pioneers of agile methodologies suspected that a more human and more fluid approach might give better results.

SMALL ACTIONS TO TAKE

- **Reach out online to someone whom you find inspiring.** Send her an email, comment on his blog, or mention her in your own online writing. Don't limit yourself to just one person, because you never know who might respond. Reach out any time you feel inspired and get in the habit.

- **Try a new social web application.** Sign up for one that appeals to you and give it a try for a week or two. Don't prejudge your experience of it. Evaluate afterwards, not before. Social web applications can't be judged without trying them; you must experience them to understand their benefits. Try Facebook for sharing yourself as a three-dimensional individual, Twitter for virtual water cooler talk, Vox for sharing photos and updates with a small group of family and friends, or LinkedIn for professional networking.

- **Experiment with new ways of making money online.** Put advertising like Google AdSense or affiliate links like Amazon's on your blog, if you can (not all hosted blogs support it). Sell something on eBay. Write a pamphlet and put it up for sale online. Don't do it with the aim of making lots of money; do it to learn and to figure out what gives you the most energy.

- **If you don't already blog, start one on a hosted service like Wordpress.com or Blogger.** Create an account and write a post. See how it feels to share your words online. If that feels like too much, start by commenting on other people's blogs or try a lightweight microblogging tool like Tumblr (tumblr.com). If you are concerned about sharing too much of yourself, create a protected blog at Vox and share it only with a couple close friends. You can always venture out further later.

- **Stretch yourself offline too.** Take a class in something that interests you, volunteer for a cause that's important to you, or write a letter to the editor of your local newspaper when you're inspired or riled. Invite a neighbor for coffee, paint a picture, or plant a garden. Every time you act you learn something more about your priorities and your future.

The *Manifesto for Agile Software Development* available at ag
.org could as well apply to how you run your individual work life. In par...
ular, two Agile principles apply to individual productivity:

- Individuals and interactions over processes and tools
- Responding to change over following a plan

In ambiguous and uncertain situations, your task management processes
and tools are important, but not as important as your individual power and
your interactions with other individuals. That's the crux of the social web.
Your plans are not unimportant, but responding to ongoing change and to
social interaction is *more* important. Be willing to change direction or approach
as you learn and experience the connection of web work.

You are your own yeast

We are the yeast that leavens our lives into rich, fully baked loaves.

—*Julia Cameron*

Web work relies on the power of individuals to drive progress. But how does
that happen? I think of it organically: instead of a machine, think of your
work more like a plant (yeast is, after all, a plant, so I'm not mangling
metaphors too horribly here). Encourage development and growth according
to your individual nature rather than towards some prescribed, predefined
end. Play your part in an ecosystem of exchange, contribution, and service.

In an organic approach to making things happen, you need to:

- **Choose authentic goals**. A dandelion can't make itself into a rose,
  and a rose can't be a dandelion. Choose goals that suit your inner
  nature. Stay attuned to signs that your goals don't fit. You should
  expect to work hard to make your goals happen, but even the hard
  work should bring you enjoyment and satisfaction. If all you feel is
  stress, look for something else.

- **Increase your inner strength**. Even in the right environment, a weak plant won't succeed. Your inner resources come not just from skills but belief in those skills and an ability to effectively put those skills into use. Know how to increase what psychologists call your *self-efficacy*, your belief in your ability to achieve certain goals.
- **Let your social network boost you**. Plants rely on an ecosystem of living things to grow: earthworms till the soil, ladybugs eat destructive insects, and trees shade those plants needing shelter from sun. Likewise, you will work most productively when a supportive social network surrounds you, both on and offline.
- **Find a suitable environment**. Some plants love wet soil; others rot when their feet are wet. Some workers need the constant physical presence of colleagues while others feel drained if they don't have eight hours of quiet every day. Recognize what you need and make sure you get it.

Choose authentic goals

Make sure that your goals are self-concordant, meaning they're consistent with your own values and direction. Research by psychologist Richard Koestner and others suggests that externally imposed goals—goals you take on because your parents or your community or your peers say you should— are both less likely to be attained and less likely to be satisfying if you do attain them.* If the goals you choose are not consistent with what you really want and value, you are less likely to put in the work to achieve them or continue working towards them when obstacles appear in the path. Even goals that seem like they unfolded from yourself may have been implanted there from the outside, not from your true self.

What makes this judgment difficult is that you don't find your goals all by yourself. You define what's important to you by acting and by interacting with other people. Just because someone else thinks you should do something doesn't mean you should, but it doesn't mean you shouldn't either. Choosing authentic goals doesn't mean you don't pay attention to other people. On the

---

*Kathryn Haralambous, "New Year's Resolutions? Fuggedaboutit," *McGill Reporter*, (January 11, 2007), available at http://www.mcgill.ca/reporter/39/09/koestner/. See also Koestner's academic research articles.

contrary, your social connections will likely have a major impact on what you deem important in your work and life.

How do you make sure your goals are self-concordant? Follow your energy. Use action to generate priorities and objectives when you're not quite sure how to proceed. Interact socially with people who are important to you to define your goals in dialog with them.

You must balance authenticity against other considerations of course. At the same time that you seek self-concordant goals, you'll need to earn a living. You need to take care of the people who depend on you. And you wouldn't want to use the idea of seeking authenticity as an excuse for purely narcissistic or hedonistic pursuits. Authentic values and goals are defined within a social setting, with concern for the people and communities in which you live.

Increase your personal power

For long-term goals that take many months or even years to achieve, it helps to boost both your feelings of personal power and your sense of autonomy around those goals.

Psychologist Albert Bandura of Stanford has spent most of his career developing a theory of what he calls *self-efficacy* that explains why some people achieve their goals and others do not. The difference is in how they think of their own ability to achieve a particular goal. This is not the same as self-esteem. Self-esteem might be defined as an overall sense of your value as a person. Self-efficacy relates to ability to achieve particular objectives. It's not just a subset of self-esteem, because you could have a very high general opinion of yourself without feeling particularly capable of achieving anything.

You can boost your self-efficacy by experiencing and recalling successes related to the goal at hand. This is yet another reason why action and not contemplation matters for achieving goals. Because the web gives fast feedback in the form of website statistics, comments on blog posts, contacts in your social networks, and so forth, it's ideal for getting involved and getting positive feedback that will increase your self-efficacy.

Autonomy, a feeling that you are in control, also correlates with higher goal achievement. Again, the way to an increased sense of autonomy is through action. The rise of the individual on the web gives power to the people. Take that power and see what you can do for yourself. Reach out to someone you admire by email, create your own web app, or use a blog to get your opinion out. You'll be feeling more in control and more effective than ever.

HOW THE WEB HELPS YOU BE MORE AUTHENTIC

You can be authentic on and offline, of course, but today's web makes it especially easy to work online in a way that expresses your values:

- **Find your niche.** Chris Anderson's *The Long Tail* proposed that the web makes it possible to build a business selling to tiny niches. Theoretically, you can provide exactly what you want and use the web to find those buyers or clients who are interested in it.
- **Promote your cause.** The web provides a platform and tools for political and social activism. Use blogging, social networking, and other tools to change the world.
- **Join with people that matter to you.** The web makes it easy to join with other people who share your passions, whether they be political, environmental, health-related, or otherwise.
- **Share your creative work.** Whether you're an artist, software developer, photographer, foodie, or anything else, you can share what you think and what you create online. You can get feedback on it, attract potential employers, sell your work, and see what makes you feel like yourself.
- **Work the way you want.** Work from home, from a café, or outside in the park. Work your own hours. Work with whatever company you want no matter where they are and where you are (limited of course by that company's commitment to distributed work).
- **Build community.** Many people find that helping grow a community around a shared interest provides an authentic way of contributing to the world. The web makes possible new kinds of communities, and many of these communities need moderators and facilitators.
- **Give advice.** So your friends are sick of hearing your advice? There are plenty of people who want it online. You might feel authentically yourself when you're telling other people how to live. You can do it, for example, at an answers site like Yahoo! Answers (answers.yahoo.com), in online forums, or with a blog.

Use your online connections to boost you

You can boost your self-efficacy socially by finding role models. The web is an ideal place to do that. For example, if you dream of making money at home as a professional blogger, read blogs by successful professional bloggers. If you feel energy around open source software, then get involved in a community that appeals, and watch how other people succeed in the way you want to. If you want to find a way to share your handmade crafts, find craft sellers online and see how they've succeeded.

Sharing your goals with your peers online boosts you in multiple ways. First, if you are open about what you want to achieve, people with resources that might help can offer them to you. Second, committing to goals publicly makes you more likely to achieve them. Other people may ask you about what you said you'd do, keeping you focused and driving you forward, and you'll feel some external pressure to stick with the goals. And third, sharing your progress boosts your self-efficacy by reminding you of your progress and your capabilities.

Find the right environment

You read about this extensively in Chapter 2, but it bears repeating here: you need to find an environment that promotes your productivity and satisfaction. Don't settle for an environment that distracts you or isolates you or makes you feel physically rotten. If it makes you feel bad and you can find a better situation, leave.

Seeking social productivity

We don't accomplish anything in this world alone...and whatever happens is the result of the whole tapestry of one's life and all the weavings of individual threads from one to another that creates something.

—Sandra Day O'Connor

The web makes networked social productivity more feasible and more successful than it could be before. With the web, you can now connect with other people and with their work ten or one hundred times more easily. You can assemble intangible goods from pre-built chunks rather than creating them from scratch. You can join together with other people in ad hoc networks without always using organizations to structure your relationships.

Psychologists and newspaper columnists tell us that multitasking is bad. We need to firewall our attention, prevent interruptions, and work on one thing at a time. But what if this conventional wisdom doesn't always apply in the new world of work that the web is bringing into being? What if an alternate mode of productivity—social productivity using rapid switching between multiple tasks and maintaining near constant connection with teammates—gives better results for many connected age projects?

This could represent a new mode of achieving important goals in our increasingly connected age. I call it social productivity because it relies on connection to many human and computational resources to make progress. You could think of focused, solo, uninterrupted, disconnected work as firewall mode productivity, named after the idea of "firewalling your attention."

CAN WE REALLY MULTITASK?   *None of us truly multitasks in the sense of doing two things simultaneously. Human beings aren't like dual-core laptops, capable of running tasks in parallel. You can only do one thing at a time, but some people are better at interleaving multiple tasks and projects through the course of a day. For people, multitasking means a more rapid switching between tasks and more responsiveness to interruptions, not really doing multiple things at once.*

Is multitasking bad for individual productivity?

For many focused, complex tasks involving understanding, synthesizing, and manipulating information, multitasking almost certainly decreases productivity. If you are working on a task requiring unbroken focus and you are interrupted or you take a break to check email, it may take you 15 or 20 minutes to return to it, according to some cognitive psychologists.* This has led many productivity gurus to suggest steps such as the following to protect your productivity:

- Don't use an email notifier
- Limit your email handling to certain times during the day

---

*Some of this research is summarized in Steve Lohr, "Slow Down, Brave Multitasker, and Don't Read This in Traffic," *The New York Times* (March 25, 2007), available at http://www.nytimes.com/2007/03/25/business/25multi.html.

- Prevent instant messaging interruptions by setting your status to busy or by going offline entirely
- Don't use microblogging tools like Twitter, because they break your concentration

These steps and more can be useful ways of protecting your focus so that you can get complex projects done faster. They're appropriate for knowledge work like software engineering, legal contract review, book authoring, website development, and so forth. However, when you do web work, you might find that multitasking benefits rather than harms your productivity.

MULTITASKING FOR KNOWLEDGE WORK

If much of your day is taken up with knowledge work tasks that seem to call for single-tasking, firewalled attention, and turning your back on your professional network: don't give up on the idea of multitasking with your tech tools. Researchers Sinan Aral, Erik Brynjolfsson, and Marshall Van Alstyne found in their five-year study of executive recruiters that there are ways you can do a kind of multitasking and still get your focused work done. They discovered that an optimal level of multitasking—not too much or too little—combined with effective use of email and other asynchronous tech tools led to the highest productivity, as measured by recruiter compensation and revenue earned.*

If you want a middle ground between total connectivity and focused solo productivity, try these tips:

- **Work on more than one project at once.** In their research on executive recruiters, the researchers found that four to six projects seemed optimal. Whether that's the right number of projects for you will depend on the industry you work in and your own personal and professional situation. Too few projects and your work will stagnate and stall with the inevitable lulls that happen in individual projects. Too many projects and you'll be frazzled and fried with demands on your attention. Find the right number of projects and you can interleave tasks efficiently over the course of a day.

MULTITASKING FOR KNOWLEDGE WORK

- **Use asynchronous technology to multitask productively.** The study found that information technology doesn't increase the speed of project completion but rather allows more projects to be pursued simultaneously. This requires using technology that fills in the gaps you have available; that means asynchronous (for example, email) rather than synchronous (for example, instant messaging) tools. You may have two projects awaiting response from other people, if you have a third project going, you can send an email or query a database for information someone else created before. You don't have to wait for your busy schedule to align with someone else's.

- **Bunch your work.** The effective multitaskers in the study didn't check email every time a new message came in, but rather batch processed at certain times during the day, for example in the morning, mid-day, and evening.

- **Use short messages and quick queries in email.** Long rambling dissertations and diatribes require too much thought on the part of the receiver; they don't encourage action or quick response. The most highly productive recruiters sent short, to-the-point messages and received short, to-the-point responses in return.

- **Optimize your network of email contacts.** The researchers found that one of the biggest predictors of productivity was being able to tap into an email social network rich with information flows. This is not just a matter of creating as many relationships as possible, because if you're only interacting with people who interact with each other, you've merely found more redundant information. Instead, try to position yourself between people from different social clusters and look for diversity in your contacts.

- **Choose the right communication tool for the job.** Don't always reach for email, though. If the person you have a question or comment for is online, try instant messaging. If you know they're almost always reachable by phone, try that.

*Sinan Aral, Erik Brynjolfsson, and Marshall W. Van Alstyne, "Information, Technology and Information Worker Productivity: Task Level Evidence," available at: http://ssrn.com/abstract=942310.

Social productivity

In web work, your work is distributed across people, computers, and applications, so you have relatively less need for unbroken focus and more need for connection. This makes it possible to stay in close contact with colleagues and friends, communicating regularly with tools like instant messaging, while still maintaining high output of work products. With social productivity, you don't "firewall your attention." Instead, you open it up, and keep your attention fluid and flexible, making yourself available for interruptions and interactions with other people.

Microsoft researcher and cognitive psychologist Mary Czerwinski has found in her research on task performance that smoothly functioning groups of people can achieve higher group level productivity by remaining connected, although at a cost to individual productivity. She calls this "social cognition": distributing the work and thought over multiple people who are in constant connection.*

Table 3-3 shows some differences between firewall mode productivity suited for knowledge work and social productivity suited for web work.

Table 3-3: Firewall mode vs. social productivity

	Firewall	Social
Interruptions	Bad, should be prevented or postponed	Good, may provide just the bit of information or inspiration you need
Communication	Email	Instant messaging, text messaging, status updaters
Work mode	Creation from scratch	Assembly from components
Priority	Step-by-step progress and accumulation	Create and tap into relationships and networks
Attention	Focused	Diffuse
Workload	Concentrated, individual	Distributed, social

---

*Jon Udell, "Jon Udell and Mary Czerwinski on interruptions, context reacquisition, and spatial/temporal memory," Channel 9 Forums, (February 12, 2007), available at http://channel9 .msdn.com/ShowPost.aspx?PostID=282091.

Interruptions

With firewall mode productivity, you seek to avoid interruptions by tactics like wearing headphones in an office setting or setting instant messaging status to "do not disturb" for remote work. With social productivity, you remain open to interruptions and connections, knowing that many times the interruptions will be of benefit to either you individually or to the entire team's progress.

Communications

Social productivity uses relatively more synchronous tools for communication: instant messaging, phone calls, informal chats, and so forth. Firewall mode deflects communication to email.

New tools like Twitter, with which people issue short status updates or questions or thoughts to a bunch of people at once, allow for a lighter weight form of connectedness. No reply to a status update on Twitter is expected, but teammates can keep watch on what other people are doing or investigating and can answer if they wish. This offer a semi-synchronous way for you to stay in touch without the immediate interruption of instant messaging but with more immediacy than email.

Work mode

Perhaps the best example of social productivity's assembly-from-components work mode is the software application type known as a *mashup*. A mashup takes prebuilt services and pieces from the web and puts them together into a new system. Contrast this with building a regular software application, where you build it from the ground up, mostly with custom work. In the mashup case, much of the context of a task is stored not in your head or on your own machine, but in the prebuilt components themselves. If you make mashups, you prioritize finding the components and wiring them together, so as the prebuilt components contain more and more smarts of their own it will take less and less focus of yours to do this. In the custom creation case, your brain (and your PC probably too) store much of the context and you have to manage it.

The term "mashup" comes from music, where it refers to a song made of parts from other songs. Though music composition and other creative work has always involved building on the works of others, the web has made this style of creation much easier, because so much more content is now available in digital form.

Priority

Social productivity looks for those leaps of inspiration and innovation of the burst work style while firewall mode aims at step-by-step productivity of busyness.

Attention

With firewall mode, you take disciplined control of your attention and keep it solely focused on one project at a time. You may use timeboxing to stay on task. This is great for achieving deadlines with well-understood tasks and projects.

With social productivity, you keep your attention fluid and flexible and diffuse, open to what might happen external to your solo tasks. You remain available for interaction and inspiration.

Workload

Social productivity, when it works, can achieve better results across a group of people than firewall mode. That's because in the ideal case, work and thinking gets distributed to those team members best suited to particular tasks. No individual gets stuck for too long without the information or assistance they need to move forward, because teammates are often available to them to brainstorm or offer advice. That's in the ideal of course—in reality, getting a team to work together well, whether using something that looks like firewall mode productivity or using something that looks like social productivity, isn't all that easy.

Finding the balance that's right for you

Whether you choose firewall mode productivity or social productivity, you make tradeoffs. If you choose to firewall your attention, you're missing out on the value that ongoing contact with your professional network provides. You're missing out on the inspiration that can come from keeping your mind broadly open to new inputs. But if you choose social productivity, you may not be able to create as much original work and you may suffer from a feeling of overload.

You must choose the balance between these two modes of work according to your individual temperament, the task at hand, your chosen field, and your skill in multitasking. Czerwinski suggests that you can get better at multitasking by practicing it, just like today's teenagers have perfected the art of maintaining multiple IM conversations while listening to music and doing their homework.

When you recognize that you need to use firewall mode productivity, schedule it. Ideally, pick a time like a Saturday or Sunday afternoon when you wouldn't be interrupted anyway. Leave your social productivity projects for those times when other people are actually available.

Knowing when to quit

> *Besides the noble art of getting things done, there is the noble art of leaving things undone. The wisdom of life consists in the elimination of non-essentials.*
>
> —*Lin Yutang*

Have you heard of the Pareto principle? That's the theory that 20 percent of your work generates 80 percent of the results, while the remaining 80 percent of work only generates 20 percent of results. So, the story goes, all you need to do to get the important stuff done is to do just the 20 percent that's giving you the bulk of good results.

Maybe that might work with well-defined, well-understood projects and tasks, but how many projects and tasks are like that these days? You don't know up front if responding to an email out of the blue will lead to your best opportunity ever. You don't know whether starting a blog will be a time sink or the next great chapter of your career. You don't know which of your colleagues holds the idea that will inspire you onto your next invention. You don't know which 20 percent of your work will lead to 80 percent of results.

But that doesn't mean that you can't get ahead in web work by eliminating tasks and projects. You can. You can judge your course of action not just on what results you might get but also based on how aligned those tasks and projects are with your values. In addition to making your best judgment as to what the future holds, you can eliminate projects that don't energize you and don't engage you.

Rethink the shoulds

Examine the voice of the *shoulds* inside you. You have internalized what your parents, society, and your employers think you should do, and that can silence your individual voice. That individual, internal voice is the best chance you have at real contribution in a time when the individual really matters.

The corporate world is filled with requirements for when and where you should work, what you wear, how you behave, and what tasks you must do. Freelancing and entrepreneurship put far fewer requirements onto you. But in either case, you're forced to confront the question of should-dos vs. want-to-dos.

You may hear about the right way to succeed, but you need to define the right way to succeed for yourself. Don't think that you must make a lot of money, dress in fancy clothes, or climb the corporate ladder to find success. Find your own way: the connected age rewards individuality and authenticity, not slavish devotion to conventional notions of success or etiquette. The future is uncertain; you don't know up front whether your want-to-dos or should-dos will give better outcomes in terms of external rewards. At least if you choose what you want to do, you will be rewarded with personal satisfaction.

This doesn't mean, however, that you don't pay any attention to what anyone else thinks. You define your path and your purpose through your interaction and connections with others. Work in a connected world doesn't mean ignoring what other people think. It means ensuring that those projects and goals you take on are important to you and your connected, social self, not just important to assumed authority figures or important to the culture in which you live.

Act authentically

How do you know when you are acting from your true self? Different people will measure and sense it in different ways. Some might act out of gut instinct, others by what their heart tells them, and still others by a sense of harmony and peacefulness. I follow my energy—especially the return on energy invested. If I put a lot of effort into something and drain myself, I want to eventually be paid back with multiplied energy. If energy never follows from the investment, then those activities will soon be cut from my schedule.

For example, I've found that travel often takes more energy than it returns. Though theoretically the chance to go out and meet other people who share my interests should replenish my energy stores, in practice I've found it just leaves me worn out. Writing and blogging, however, repay me in energy and inspiration a hundred times over.

There are no guarantees that your authentic action will be your best way to make money, of course, so you need to find an intersection between what's authentic to you and what the market rewards. And in any field you can't eliminate everything that's tedious or draining. But when you do consider what projects and tasks you might eliminate, check whether what you're considering feels authentic or not. You only have a certain amount of time to work; spend that time in ways that fill up your energy at the same time they fill up your bank account.

Don't prejudge the results of your action

We may think we know what the "right" course is in a given professional situation, but do we really?

In her book *On Becoming an Artist: Reinventing Yourself Through Mindful Creativity*, mindfulness researcher Ellen Langer says, "As we search for the 'right' answer, the potential opportunities that result from many alternatives and the vagaries of our intuition are problems to be ignored or held constant." Yet those potential opportunities and alternatives that you ignore or fix in place may lead to the best outcomes—you just can't predict.

When you seek to cut back on "unimportant" tasks, then, don't judge them solely on their potential results; while you can predict some outcomes you can't know everything that will flow from one choice or another. You can try to predict what might happen from a particular path, but don't put too much weight on that prediction. The working world is far more complex and random than what you might want to believe.*

Look for intrinsic rewards

Those who seek money and prestige are generally less satisfied than those who work mainly for intrinsic satisfaction, with external rewards of limited

---

*If you're intrigued by the notion of randomness in our lives and in business decision-making, read Nassim Nicholas Taleb's books *Fooled by Randomness* and *The Black Swan*.

priority.* Ample psychological research shows that focusing on activities that are intrinsically rewarding is associated with higher levels of reported well being. So though you may think you'll be happier with a high-paying though soul-sucking job, you might be better off choosing to do what you love even if it doesn't pay as well.

Of course if you can hardly pay your bills, this will not be too helpful. You need to earn a living before you can concern yourself too much with intrinsic rewards. Most people, however, have a range of job and income options from which to choose. If you have more than you can take on and you are meeting your financial needs, consider focusing on work that brings you satisfaction and a sense of personal accomplishment.

Extrinsic rewards are mostly conferred by other people, so they're in large part out of your control. Seek instead those work activities that give you lasting internal satisfaction, and consider it a lucky fluke if this happens to bring you high social status and a fancy car at the same time.

THE NOT-TO-DO LIST

Explicitly ruling projects out at the same time you rule some in will help you deal with the plethora of project ideas that emerge from your online explorations. When you revisit your project or goal list, consider making a *not-to-do list* to get clear with yourself what you're not going to expend effort on.

Coworking inventor Brad Neuberg wrote up this idea on his blog, saying, "Every so often I look back over the projects I'm doing and take stock. I have a little inner thermometer that I check in on from time to time, and if I'm feeling stressed out and not having fun anymore it gives me information and a clue that I need to revisit what I've been doing. When I feel this, I create a Not To-Do List and figure out stuff that I need to let go of." You can see his blog post at http://www.codinginparadise.org/weblog/2007/06/moving-on-coworking-really-simple.html.

---

*Kennon M. Sheldon, Richard M. Ryan, Edward L. Deci. And Tim Kasser, "The Independent Effects of Goal Contents and Motives on Well-Being: It's Both What You Pursue and Why You Pursue It," *Personality and Social Psychology Bulletin*,Vol. 30 No. 4, (April 2004), 475-486.

THE NOT-TO-DO LIST (*continued*)

David Allen, author of *Getting Things Done*, suggests using a *someday/ maybe list* for projects you might want to do but aren't committed to working on actively yet. This allows you to keep it from distracting you in the present since you've explicitly decided not to actively pursue the goal at that point in time.

I use a variation of both of these: Yes, No, and Maybe lists. I create a list of Yes projects that I'm definitely working on, a list of Maybe projects on which I'm undecided, and a No Way list for projects or commitments I need to remove from my life. The No Way one is the hardest, because sometimes projects and goals appear there before I'm ready to take on the pain of eliminating them. Still, it's useful to confront dilemmas like that directly rather than letting my mind fester and my energy drain. And putting it down in print makes me more aware of the need to make a change.

Looking forward: Escape from email

If you can't get out of your email inbox, how will you achieve your goals? Let's get on to Chapter 4, where you'll see how you can reframe your relationship to email and make it work for you instead of the other way around.

4 Rethink Your Relationship with Email

E mail is terribly useful—one of the key tools for the connected age—with an emphasis on *terribly*. Email is both terrible and useful at the same time. Email offers complete interoperability: you need only know someone's email address to be able to contact them, unlike with instant messaging, where different services mostly won't work with each other. Email allows you to work on your own schedule while I work on mine, giving us potentially higher productivity than if we had to communicate at a time convenient to both of us. And email offers some minimal level of access control. You can decide who you want to send a message to, though you know it could get forwarded to someone else in the future.

Even with all those benefits, in the connected age you'll probably find yourself moving away from email, for many reasons. As its volume increases, people look to other tools. Younger generations find it outmoded and old-fashioned. Junk, viruses, and scams can make it unpleasant. New channels and platforms, like instant messaging and social networking, suit collaborative and connected work better.

Here's what you'll find in this chapter:

- **Remodeling your email.** Email client software hasn't kept up with the way you use email. What you can do now to address its shortcomings.
- **Is email dying?** Commitment to email is decreasing at the same time other communications mechanisms are spreading virally. Find out why.

- **Your email, your way.** Consider some assumptions about email etiquette and management. Figure out what email approach makes sense for your unique situation.
- **Escaping email.** Use alternative channels; train your colleagues to expect less by email and get more in other places; consider whether you should declare email bankruptcy.

Remodeling your email

Change in all things is sweet.

—Euripides

Email vies with search engine usage as the most popular activity online—more than 90 percent of Internet users report that they use email.* Email allows you to communicate with far-flung colleagues, get work done when no one else is available, archive documents, and track to dos. Its usefulness is its downfall. Email has been pressed into service for tasks far beyond what it comfortably supports. And so, if you're like me, you struggle with it, almost every single day—if not every single hour.

Your problems with email may be compounded by flawed ideas of how it should and could realistically be used. Let's look at the one-touch model of email usage and compare how people really use it. Then you'll see what's available now and what's available in the future that could make email suit your actual usage better.

The flawed one-touch model

Many suggestions about how you should use email base themselves on an ideal email processing pattern that few ever achieve. The one-touch model

---

*Pew Internet & American Life Project Tracking surveys (March 2000–March 2007), available at http://www.pewinternet.org/trends/Daily_Internet_Activities_6.15.07.htm.

suggests you can batch process masses of email at specific times during the day, handling each message the first time you see it, like this:*

1. If a message is just for information and doesn't require a response, read it and file.
2. If a message requires a response, respond and file.

In this model, an email is either unread or filed; nothing hangs around in the inbox.

Steve Whittaker and Candace Sidner, the researchers who identified the one-touch model, found that very few people actually followed it. And more recent research suggests the same thing: people leave a lot of email in their inbox.

The one-touch model doesn't capture the reality of everything you do with email or the complexity of some of the actions or decisions you must take when an email arrives. In addition to simply finding information or answering questions, you probably use email for much more. You may use it to remind yourself of to dos and things to think about, to move group projects forward, to collaborate on documents, and so forth. The one-touch model just doesn't fit with the way most people use email.

Some problems with email

Email has been incredibly successful in supporting distributed, anytime/anywhere work in the connected age. You can contact anyone whose email address you have. You can maintain private conversations with one person or with a group of people, even if they're all on different email systems. You can move projects forward when everyone else on the project is asleep or on vacation. It's no wonder we've pressed email into service in so many different ways.

In addition to providing for simple communications, email serves as a task list, a set of task reminders, and a personal archive. Yet it wasn't designed as a personal information manager, a reminder service, or as document storage.

Email has other disadvantages too. Incoming mail flow is largely out of your control: anyone with your email address can send something, whether

---

*This "one-touch model" is described in Steve Whittaker and Candace Sidner, "Email overload: exploring personal information management of email," Proceedings of the SIGCHI conference on human factors in computing systems, (1996), available at http://dis.shef.ac.uk/ stevewhittaker/emlch96.pdf.

you want it or not. Filing the emails you get is not an easy task, because many emails conceptually fit into multiple categories and because maintaining useful folders takes effort and time that you don't necessarily want to spend on email management. Many email clients don't do a good job of maintaining conversation context for you so you may have to reconstruct it yourself, by referencing old emails.

And the biggest difficulty you might have with your email is that it's where you're doing much of your work—and work is just complex sometimes, requiring careful thought and judgment. It can be difficult to know what next action to take on a project. It can be difficult to know how best to reply to someone's questions or comments on a document you're editing collaboratively. It can be difficult to decide whether that email you just got from someone you don't know should be answered or not. Email, because it's so useful, becomes the site of much of your work-related decisions and actions—and those decisions and actions aren't always quickly dispatched no matter whether they arrive through email or some other way.

How to address some of email's problems

You can make your email better today by choosing better tools, by enhancing your existing ones, or by working in a different way. Here, I'll take a look at the main issues you need to tackle in rethinking your relationship to email and suggest some solutions.

Email inbox not suited to task management

Too often, using email as your task manager turns you reactive. You respond to email messages and issues coming up by email because it makes you feel obligated. But you need a step between getting the email and deciding what to do. You need to make sure that you keep your own priorities in mind when you go from email message to task. So don't use your inbox as your task list.

Besides, an email message subject doesn't necessarily tell you exactly what your task is. Or the message might contain multiple tasks. Restating and unpacking tasks from email will help you manage your work better.

Use an email client such as Outlook that supports task management or install a task manager into your email application. For example, todocue (todocue.com) can add a to-do list to Gmail via a Firefox extension. Or use a to-do manager that works via email such as Backpack, Remember the Milk or Toodledo. Toodledo and Remember the Milk let you forward email to a special address where the messages are added as to dos.

Conversation context may be lost

In processing your email, you need to remind yourself of what discussion has happened before. If your email application threads conversations, it makes it much easier to keep track of conversation context, although some people find this behavior works against how they like to view their messages, preferring to see them by sender and date, not grouped according to conversation.

Filing messages is difficult and time consuming

Email researchers count the difficulty of filing email by looking for so-called "failed folders": folders that are so full or empty that you get no benefit from their presence. Making successful folders requires regular work, and the more email you have, the harder it is. So what can you do?

If your email client supports it, use tags (known in Gmail as *labels*) instead of folders. You can assign multiple tags to one message, for example, marking one message under multiple projects or with a project name and an action (e.g., "to read").

Also, find your emails by searching rather than by browsing through folders. Learn the search operators your email client supports so you can be more effective. If you use desktop email, install a desktop search such as Google Desktop (desktop.google.com) or Copernic Desktop Search (copernic.com) that will index and search your email archives.

Not always clear what to do with a message

As messages come in, you may not have all the information you need to deal with it. Or maybe you just want to give it some thought before deciding what to do. You could leave it in your inbox, where it reminds you each time you process email that you need to do something about it. Or you could file it away into a "pending" folder. Just be sure you remind yourself to check the pending folder regularly, perhaps weekly. Create a calendar reminder so you remember to do it. The biggest problem with folder schemes like "to do" and "pending" is that you may forget to ever go back and check them.

Other people generate claims on your time and attention

You have little control over the email that comes into your inbox. You can try to minimize the traffic by limiting your email address to a select few coworkers and friends, but that decreases the possibility you'll make valuable connections with people outside your current network. You can be stingy with email replies, decreasing email traffic that way. But you can't avoid all email, not if you want to get your work done and stay in connection with people.

As email comes in, it creates work for you to do. It creates to dos and to replies and to reads. But these aren't explicitly chosen; they're imposed upon you in a sense. They are not necessarily unwelcome, just a bit dangerous, in that your email could subvert your true priorities.

So respond according to your own needs and timetables, not someone else's. Separating to dos from email inbox items can help you maintain your own priorities rather than letting email define them. Don't use your inbox as a to-do list; instead, use your task manager to record a task based on the incoming email. And question carefully each to do that's generated from email.

Inboxes cluttered with many different types of messages

Your inbox might have the personal mixed with the professional, the profound mixed with the trivial, and the urgent mixed with the nice-to-know. When you go look at your inbox, you can't easily tell what you need to do or what's important.

You can use filters to direct lower-priority messages like mailing list traffic out of your inbox and into a folder or archive that you'll batch process later. For an idea of how to define useful filters, see Leo Babauta's Web Worker Daily article "Essential Gmail Filters to Unclutter Your Inbox" at http://www.webworkerdaily .com/2007/08/11/three-gmail-filters-to-leave-in-your-inbox-only-the-emails-you-need-to-see/. The ideas apply equally well to desktop email.

You could consider using multiple mail addresses for personal versus professional and for different projects or business efforts, then processing them at different times and on different schedules so that you can focus better. You might check personal mail just once a day, while checking your professional mail multiple times.

If you want help with prioritizing and organizing your Outlook email, check out add-ons like ClearContext (clearcontext.com) or MailFiler (mailfiler.com).

For more resources

Table 4-1 suggests some starting points for finding tips and add-ons that could improve your email experience. If you use Outlook, you might also like to read Samuel Dean's tips at http://www.webworkerdaily.com/2007/08/01/making-the-most-of-ms-outlook/ and http://www.webworkerdaily.com/2007/08/16/essential-tips-for-ms-outlook/.

HOW GMAIL REDEFINES EMAIL

Google Gmail has gone the farthest of any of the email clients in redefining the experience of email in a way that suits the future rather than the past of email. Let's see how it does that.

- **Search oriented, not filing oriented.** As you get better at search and search engines get better, you can dispense with time-consuming filing of email messages and just search for them. All email clients now support full-text search, but Gmail's built from the ground up assuming that you'll search. You can get messages out of your inbox just by archiving them—no moving to a folder necessary—and the search is really fast. Plus, it supports easy search of specific fields using operators like "from:<*sender name*>."
- **Labels, not folders.** Gmail has no folders, just labels. Labels are just tags: you can put multiple labels on a message and then add and subtract at will, without "moving" the message. Just as with traditional email rules, you can auto-label messages as they come in according to set criteria.
- **Conversation threading.** Gmail tracks messages that go together and displays them as a thread rather than as individual messages. This keeps the conversational context in one place, meaning you don't have to track it or reconstruct it yourself. However, this prevents you from sorting individual messages by name or date.
- **Customizable.** If you run Gmail with Firefox or another browser that supports on-the-fly user script customization like Greasemonkey, you can customize the Gmail display just by adding a new script. For example, you can eliminate display of the spam count, add a calendar agenda, or install a to-do list. Search userscripts.org with keyword Gmail to see all the things you can do (or write your own script if you're handy with HTML and JavaScript).
- **Calendar integration.** Even if Gmail doesn't get an explicit event invitation, it will check your incoming messages for potential dates and ask if you want to add them to Google Calendar. You can also add an event from Gmail that it hasn't recognized by using its Create Event function.
- **HTML document display.** View attachments as an HTML page or a Google document without the bother of downloading the file.

HOW GMAIL REDEFINES EMAIL *(continued)*

- **Online and accessible from anywhere.** Gmail isn't the first web-based email, but Google makes it extremely easy to use from whatever computer you have available. Google also offers a mobile version for use on phones with a web browser as well as a standalone mobile version that is faster and includes more features than the basic mobile web version.
- **Keyboard shortcuts.** Though most web applications treat keyboard shortcuts like an afterthought (if they have them at all), Gmail offers actions like browsing, viewing, and archiving messages with the press of just one key. You can really speed up your mail processing if you learn how to use them.
- **Automatic contact management.** In Gmail, you don't have to create contacts for the email addresses of people you send messages to. It will create them on the fly and then suggest possible email addresses as you start typing them into the To: field. Contacts are automatically added to Google Talk for instant messaging and voice calls.

Gmail isn't without drawbacks. It doesn't, as of the time of this writing, provide offline access. You can't sort messages without searching. It displays small text advertisements alongside your messages. You can fill up its seemingly generous 2GB of space if you are a heavy user who rarely deletes messages (though you can pay Google for more space). And Google's increasing knowledge of everything you do online might make you hesitate to hand your email over to them too.

Table 4-1: Resources for better email

Resource	URL	Notes
Slipstick Systems Outlook & Exchange Solutions Center	slipstick.com	Find utilities, add-ons, bug reports, and tips for Outlook
Hawk Wings	hawkwings.net	Tips and add-ons for Apple's Mail.app
Better Gmail	addons.mozilla.org/ en-US/firefox/addon/4866	Lifehacker's compilation of the best Firefox add-ons for Gmail

Filer, piler, or other?

Are you a filer or a piler? A filer keeps her inbox pristinely empty, handling and filing each email shortly after it arrives. A piler lets thousands upon thousands of read and unread messages pile up (usually in the inbox). Most people, however, choose a middle ground—keeping a bunch of emails in their inbox while filing others.

As search gets better and you get better at using it, you might find yourself moving away from filing and towards piling, whether in your inbox or tucked away into a pile you can't see, your archive. That's not a bad thing. Filing and maintaining folders takes time—if you could save yourself some of that while still managing your email reasonably effectively, why not?

Is email dying?

Email is not gone, but it is dead in the sense that it is no longer a site of deep emotional passion.

—danah boyd

In the last section, I talked about some of the problems with email and their potential solutions. Despite those problems, email remains one of the easiest and most convenient ways of connecting online with other people.

And yet for all its ease, convenience, and ubiquity, email may be a dying communications method. In fact, its ease, convenience, and ubiquity sow the seeds of its own destruction. It's too easy to use, so spammers and phishers abuse it. Even when you get mail from people you want to hear from, it may arrive in such volume that you quickly get overwhelmed and seek other ways to communicate. Younger generations find other channels like text messaging and instant messaging more immediate and less old-fashioned.

You will certainly continue to use email for the indefinite future, but much of your online social interactions may move to other places, especially as you explore web workerhood more fully. So just like letter writing, which is largely dead in our culture though still used occasionally, email may be dying, at least in terms of our emotional commitment to it and our willingness to prioritize it above other ways of connecting.

Email immunity

As email volume increases, you and others like you may become immune to it. In the paperback version of *The Tipping Point*, Malcolm Gladwell suggests that social epidemics like the use of email show an epidemic spreading period and then, later, the growth of immunity.

First, a social tool like email spreads, as people infect those close to them. Let's look at the social network Facebook as an example. I created a neighborhood group on Facebook and then invited my neighbors to join. They hadn't considered joining Facebook before, but they "caught" the Facebook virus from me.

But my neighbors have already started building up some immunity to Facebook and to social networks in general. Initially more invitations to join Facebook groups might lead them to join. But after being invited to many groups, they may start being choosier about which they join; that would show increasing immunity. And if they're asked to join a new social network, they may not, because they're already on Facebook. They may be immune to similar services, having joined one already.

Nearly everyone has caught the email virus and now people are becoming immune. The more email you get, the less each message matters to you. Each spam email you get, each request that makes you feel you must do something you weren't otherwise planning to do, each funny but irrelevant video makes you less and less likely to respond quickly and in depth to email. So you develop immunity.

Gladwell says, "The more email we get, the shorter and more selective and more delayed our responses become. These are the symptoms of immunity." Be aware that different people have developed different levels of immunity to email. If you email someone and they don't respond immediately, it might not be because they're not interested in you or in working with you. It could be they're largely immune to email at this point and you should investigate other ways of reaching them. This is something you will see more and more of in the future.

Driven away from email

A number of factors push people away from email:

- Younger people's preference for IM or texting over email
- Email's lack of ability to build trust and intimacy

- The overwhelming volume of email
- Email abuse in the form of spam, viruses, and phishing

Younger people use IM and texting instead

Teenagers these days have been heard to say they only use email to communicate with those over 30. Otherwise, they use instant messaging, text messaging, and social networks like MySpace to keep in touch with their friends. Twentysomethings and younger generations have developed some basic immunity to email because of their exposure to other communications "viruses" of the connected age.

Email doesn't build trust or intimacy

Email is well suited for crossing generational and organizational boundaries, but it's not necessarily good for building informal relationships based on trust and intimacy.* You might find that once you begin instant messaging, text messaging, or interacting with someone on a social networking site, email feels stilted and constrained, at least when used for back and forth conversation.

Email volume is overwhelming

Because it arrives in such great volume, email can feel like a monkey on your back. Online and in books, you'll find many schemes and tricks for managing the constant flow of messages into your inbox. The incredible volume of email is probably the number one reason for the growth of email immunity. If you only received ten emails a week, you will be much more likely to respond than if you receive two thousand.

Email abuse

Spam is increasing in volume, but fortunately our spam filters are getting better too. A report from May 2007 suggests that spam is bothering email users less and less over time even as it increases in volume.** Let's hope that spam doesn't follow us as we move to other channels, though.

---

*Email as tool for vertical communications across power and generational lines is discussed in Steven L. Thorne, "Artifacts and cultures-of-use in intercultural communication," Language Learning and Technology, Vol. 7, No. 2, (May 2003), pp. 38-67, available at http://llt.msu .edu/vol7num2/thorne/.
**Deborah Fallows, "Data Memo," Pew Internet & American Life Project, (May 2007), available at http://www.pewinternet.org/pdfs/PIP_Spam_May_2007.pdf.

But even if it is getting easier, dealing with spam as well as avoiding viruses and protecting yourself from phishing scams is unpleasant. Abuse of email makes people less willing to use it and contributes, over time, to people's declining commitment to it.

GET CONTACTED WHILE AVOIDING SPAM

How can you make yourself easy to reach without inviting a torrent of spam? Try these techniques.

- **Use a disposable email address**. When you need to enter your email address on a website, but are worried about how it might be used, this is a great solution. Check out Spamex (spamex.com), Mailinator (mailinator.com), and spamgourmet (spamgourmet.com).
- **Try plus addressing**. Some email services, including Gmail, support appending extra characters or words onto the end of your email address. If your regular address is jane.smith@gmail.com, you could use jane.smith+news@gmail.com and it will come straight to your regular account. If that plus address gets too much spam, use a rule to direct it straight to trash. Long term, spam senders may start stripping anything after a plus to get to your real address, but you may still find this tactic useful.
- **Offer a contact form instead of your email address**. If you're handy with web page creation or your website content management system will create one for you, do it that way. Or use a service like Contactify (contactify.com).
- **Filter incoming mail through a paid spam filtering service**. Forward your email to SpamCop (spamcop.com) or any other email service with strong spam filtering and then have it sent back to your regular email.
- **Install a client-side spam filter**. If you're running a desktop email client like Outlook or Apple's Mail.app, you can beef it up with a spam filter add-on. Try Cloudmark Desktop for Outlook or SpamSieve for Mail.app. The open source program SpamBayes runs on Windows and Linux and offers prebuilt integration with Outlook.

Pulled towards other tools

At the same time that you're getting pushed away from email by its overwhelming volume, by younger generations that prefer alternate channels, by too much spam, and by email's inability to build intimacy, you'll be pulled away from it by new tools. In Chapter 6, you'll read about the tools that might replace email and how you and your team can use them.

Your email, your way

> *If you obey all the rules, you miss all the fun.*
>
> —*Katharine Hepburn*

Email's been around long enough that there certain assumptions about how you should deal with it. For example, many office cultures assume you are checking email regularly throughout the day and expect immediate response. Email etiquette guidelines remind you how terse and curt you can come across in email even when you don't mean it. And productivity gurus promote the idea that an empty inbox is worth the time it takes to keep it clean. As you figure out how to manage your email, you'll need to examine these assumptions and expectations to see whether they work for you, especially since the rise of email immunity and the availability of new tools for communication makes email less important.

Fortunately, email is still new enough and used in enough different ways that you have some freedom to treat it the way you want. You have to take into consideration your work environment, your colleagues' preferences, and your own feelings about email, but within that context and with those constraints, you have wide latitude to find the right place for email in your life.

Assumptions about email

Here are some assumptions about email that you might reconsider as you rethink your relationship with email:

- Email stands alone
- Email clutter in your inbox is bad
- Email requires quick response

These assumptions work well within many work cultures and for many people. As your work life changes, however, and you explore new ways of connecting, you may find it useful to relax them on occasion or even more regularly. Let's look at each one in turn.

Email stands alone

Etiquette rules about email sometimes assume that email communications coming across as cold or curt will harm a relationship. But you may be communicating with your workmates and associates in many different ways now that email doesn't carry the sole burden of online relationships.

Of course, in certain situations your only contact with someone will be by email. In that case, email is carrying the weight of the relationship, so you should adjust your approach accordingly. In those situations, you can compose your email carefully, remembering the limitations of the form. Or you can establish contact with them through other means in addition to email, by phone or instant message or on a social network like Facebook.

People can learn to handle short emails and assume that as the default way of communicating by email rather than expecting some sort of mailed letter-like sensibility. In many work cultures, short and quick emails without social grooming are the norm.

I have had a number of managers who often sent curt emails; since their other interactions with me were personable and warm I had no reason to question their motives when I received short, to-the-point email from them.

Email cluttering your inbox is bad

Empty inbox rules are based on the idea that it's better to have a clean inbox than a full one. But better search capabilities in email means a full inbox is not necessarily a bad inbox. Cleaning up clutter takes time—time you could be spending doing more productive things than endlessly processing email.

Now if your cluttered inbox is keeping you from getting your important work done, then you need to come up with a different way of handling email. Perhaps you need to be careful to transfer tasks to your to-do list immediately as they arrive via email. Maybe you need to use a prioritization or labeling scheme. But if your inbox is overflowing yet you're on top of your work, you might be better off finding acceptance of your full inbox rather than worrying about getting it to empty.

You must respond to email without delay

Sometimes I will receive email replies a few days or a week after I emailed the sender; the sender may apologize for taking so long to reply. But I don't have a problem with people taking a few days to reply, because if I need something more urgently, I'll usually choose to make a phone call or use a quick instant message when I see the person online. I know that most people are overloaded by email and so I no longer expect quick response.

But the idea of immediate email response is well entrenched in many working environments. In the future this might change as email immunity increases and as people get used to connecting using other means.

Delaying your response has some advantages: it can allow time for a situation to change such that no response is necessary, it can give you time to think more about what you need to do (because many issues coming through email don't have obvious solutions), and it can give you and the sender a chance to connect synchronously through another channel and have a real-time back and forth discussion.

Email etiquette

Email is used for so many different functions and across so many different types of people that it would be impossible to come up with a set of guidelines that would work for everyone in every situation.

Different interactions require different rules. Obviously a quick message to someone you work with closely will call for a different approach than an email to a potential new employer or client. An email to your English professor asking for a higher grade probably shouldn't be written using text messaging abbreviations, but if you're using your cell phone to check in by email with your team, why not make it easy on yourself and your thumb?

Aside from that obvious problem with email etiquette, a more insidious issue is this: the more we promote a certain way of dealing with email, one that puts serious expectations on politeness and responsiveness, the more we keep ourselves from more human interactions because we're so busy dealing with email. If you share your authentic and genuine self through discussions on a blog, via a social networking platform like Facebook, in instant messaging, or an IRC channel people will come to know you—and they won't look to email for evidence of your warmth and friendliness.

HOW TO SCREW UP BY EMAIL

Though there isn't a universal email etiquette, there are a few things you'll want to avoid, especially when negotiating business deals or job offers by email, something that happens more often than you might imagine. Remember that email is asynchronous, impersonal, and only seemingly private.

Here are four ways to screw up with email.

1. **Make your emails as long as possible.** This gives you the best chance of saying something stupid or offensive. It also increases the probability that your email will not be read in its entirety, thus setting the stage for later relationship-damaging and negotiation-destroying misunderstandings.

2. **Learn to stalk, if warranted.** If you've gone days without hearing anything, take a page from the Internet Stalker's Handbook. Send email after email to your love… er… potential business partner. Tell them you can't live without them. Make sure they know exactly how you feel, down to the pain you'll suffer if you don't get to work with them. Don't, under any circumstances, send a quick and neutral follow-up note to check in. You need to escalate and suffocate, not relate and motivate.

3. **Never resort to synchronous means of discussion like instant messaging or god forbid, the telephone.** Sending an IM or picking up the phone is a bad idea. You might actually start to understand the other person's point of view and they might understand yours. Worse, you could find yourself in a back-and-forth that leads to connection and agreement. Email's strength is how it leaves long pauses between complete misunderstandings, allowing said misunderstandings to fester and grow until they kill the discussions outright.

4. **If you suspect you have been insulted, you're probably right— respond immediately in kind.** Try the Shakespearean Insult Kit (http://www.pangloss.com/seidel/shake_rule.html) if you can't come up with any good ones yourself. Calling someone a *droning crookpated footlicker* is sure to squash any chance at agreement. You probably won't ever have to hear from that *fobbing clay-brained cankerblossom* again.

For extra credit and to ensure you won't ever confront negotiation by email again, publish the entire thread on the web for everyone to read.

If you really want an empty inbox

There's no doubt that it's pleasant to confront an empty email inbox, even if you've been a diehard piler in the past. There are a variety of schemes for achieving an empty inbox, many of them described online in productivity blogs. But getting and keeping an empty inbox takes time, time that might be better spent on other work. If your inbox isn't empty, you're in good company. Research studies suggest that an empty inbox isn't very common, for all the reasons outlined at the beginning of this chapter.

If you want a comprehensive approach to clearing out your email, see Leo Babauta's Web Worker Daily article "Cranking Through Your Gmail" at `http://www.webworkerdaily.com/2007/05/20/how-to-crank-through-your-gmail/`.

I don't focus on keeping an empty inbox, but every now and then I like to process everything in my inbox and start fresh. I take a minimalist approach to it, recognizing that I don't have endless time to spend on it. I'm in connection with people in many other ways, so email doesn't bear the weight of my work world. It's not that it's unimportant; it's just one of many tools I use for communication and collaboration.

Here's how to follow my scheme:

1. Start at the most recent messages.
2. If you can archive or delete without responding, do so. I don't label most email messages in my archive because I know I can always get them back by a full text search or by searching by other criteria (e.g., sender).
3. If you can make a quick response, do so.
4. If there's a task embedded in the email, transfer it onto your to-do list and archive the email.
5. If you're not sure what to do, label it "someday" and archive it.
6. Once you've gone through the most recent email (for me, the last two weeks worth—your time frame of fresh email may differ depending on your work and your colleagues' expectations), just archive the rest. It's more important that you get back in the present than that you spend too much time with old email.
7. Now get out and connect outside of email.

Another way of getting to a place of peace about email is to drop the assumption that an empty inbox matters (if you ever had it in the first place). With better search mechanisms and with the recognition that email is less important than many other communications channels these days, you can feel just as good with a full inbox as with an empty one.

Escaping from email

A man is rich in proportion to the number of things he can afford to let alone.

—Henry David Thoreau

Get yourself ready for the future by moving away from email now. Yes, you'll still use it. How could you not? But you might be able to make your web work more satisfying if you minimize email's grip on your life.

How to do it

You have to match your email minimization practices with your own email profile: how many messages you receive every day, what your responsibilities are with regard to response, the email culture in your workgroup, and your career goals, for example.

Use alternative channels when available

Before sending any email message or replying to one, ask yourself if there's an alternative channel that might work better. If you need an answer to a question and the person who can answer it is online with instant messaging, ask by IM. You could eliminate at least two emails that way (the one you send plus at least one reply). If you're just sharing information and no reply is needed, use a broadcast mechanism like a blog post or bulletin board. If you're managing a project, use a wiki or a dedicated project management application. For socializing, use a social network or IM. Or pick up the phone.

While at first this seems much harder than using email over time, it will soon become habit and you'll decrease the flow of email among your colleagues. Plus, you'll complement email's ease and convenience with the immediacy and intimacy of other channels.

Use short, directed emails

Make it easy for people to reply the first time they read your emails. Keep each email to one subject. Ask a question directly and pose alternatives so that the person replying doesn't have to think too hard to respond. Don't ask open-ended questions if you can avoid it.

Short emails tend to generate short emails in reply too. So the more you use this technique, the more the people around you will use it too. Everyone benefits.

Train people by the way you use email

The way you use email will shape the way people try to reach you and what they expect from you. For example, immediate response to your email tends to create the expectation that you'll always immediately respond. So don't worry too much about delaying your response to non-urgent emails. Or respond by a different channel, so the person learns where to find you other than by email.

Be frugal with email replies

The more you reply to email, the more email you will get. That's fine if you like living in your email, but you probably don't. Email interactions don't have to be closed off like phone conversations, so don't feel you must reply with a "Thanks" or with a "See you soon," if there's nothing else to say beyond that.

If you're using workstreaming, sharing your regular work activities and products online to show the wider world what you're up to, email replies become less necessary because people interact with you in other ways. The social grooming that might otherwise need to happen in email can happen on Vox or in a microblogger like Jaiku or in your team chat room. For task coordination, you can update a project management application or otherwise share what's happening with your team. For back and forth discussions, try blogs or wikis.

Ignore what you can

As you do more work online, you may find people emailing you out of the blue requesting help or information. If someone sends you a personal and genuine note that resonates with you and your priorities, then you may want to respond. But if someone sends you something unsolicited that clearly reflects some sort of mass marketing campaign or doesn't fit with your purpose, don't feel you must respond out of politeness.

Cut down on mailing list email

You don't have to unsubscribe entirely from mailing lists, but you can get them out of your email. You can read the traffic in other ways; for example on the archive page or as RSS feeds in your news reader (see Chapter 5 for a discussion of RSS or syndicated news). It's easier to handle email if you can cut it down to the bare minimum. You'll have less clutter in your inbox.

You could even create a separate email address and use a different email client for such traffic and check it on a less frequent basis than your main email. For example, you could set up a web mail account on Yahoo! or Hotmail just for mailing list subscriptions.

When drastic measures are needed

Sometimes your inbox has become so cluttered and your email stress levels so high that you need to take a completely fresh approach to email—and I'm not talking about processing it down to zero. You could try email bankruptcy.

EMAIL BANKRUPTCY   *In email bankruptcy, you declare that you are unable to handle your email obligations. You clear out your inbox and start fresh, as though you had never received those emails in the first place. The idea may go back to 1999, when MIT professor Sherry Turkle conceived of it. Stanford law professor Larry Lessig popularized the term in 2004 when he used it himself, using an automated script to send a message to those senders who had yet to have their messages acknowledged, telling them he would never respond.*

If you have a blog, or some other way of broadcasting your declaration of email bankruptcy, that might be the easiest way to get the word out. If you don't have the time to deal with your email, you probably don't have the time to write a computer program to email all your erstwhile email contacts.

If you find email bankruptcy *too* drastic, here are some other tactics to try first. Of course, whether they're feasible for you depends upon your job responsibilities and your own comfort level with exploring new ways of handling email, because some of these ways might look irresponsible or impolite to some of your coworkers or your management. However, if you combine some of these tactics with reaching out to people via other channels (IM, or an announcement on a bulletin board, or a microblog update), you might find one of these will allow you to get your head above the email waters.

Delay responding to older messages

Create a folder or label named with a date in the future, maybe a week, or two days if that's the most you (and those around you) can stand. Move everything from your inbox there. Now start handling email you get going forward, but don't worry about that other email for now. When the day to check email arrives, look at the messages (set yourself a calendar reminder if you need to). Do you need to respond to them now? Many of them will no longer require a response, having been already dealt with or made obsolete by intervening events.

Direct people to other channels using an auto-reply

If you're going to impose on your email correspondents with an auto-reply, keep it short. For example, say, "I am unavailable by email at this time. If the matter is urgent, please contact me by phone or instant message." It's presumptuous to auto-reply with a long-winded description of your personal scheduling problems and proposed solution.

Think of email as a river, not a pond

The beauty of group chat like Internet Relay Chat is the ability to dip into it any time and ignore what came before and what comes after when you're not paying attention. You could treat your email the same way—by eliminating all messages older than a certain date. Try it this way: allocate an hour to deal with email. Start from the most recent and then work backwards. When your time's up, delete or archive the rest of the email. Obviously this won't work if your boss is used to tasking you by email. If that's the case, sort by sender and make sure you don't delete those. But don't assume you must reply to emails from one or two months ago. Those senders probably aren't waiting around for your reply. They may be facing their own impending email bankruptcy.

Decide for yourself

Remember, email bankruptcy or its alternatives are for the times when drastic measures are needed—when you're so behind on your email that you'll never get caught up and it's keeping you from your real priorities. And they're not rules, just ideas that might inspire you to come up with your own strategy for putting email into the place you want it in your life.

Only you can decide what will work best given your job situation and your own beliefs about email. But know that you have a lot of freedom to decide how to relate to your email.

Looking forward: Surf waves of information

How do you deal with the waves of information coming at you? Get your surfboard and hang ten! The ocean of knowledge online need not overwhelm you, if you have the right gear and attitude. Come on in; the water's warm!

5 Surf Waves of Information

The web makes available so much more information than you could access before. Sometimes it might feel like *too* much information. You might feel too connected, with access to too many questionable sources of information. Each answer you find asks more questions.

But it's a good thing to have access to more information and people. You just need the right tools and the right attitude to ensure it's a positive in your life not a negative. You don't have to feel overwhelmed by the abundance of information and communication available online. You can feel inspired and motivated by it instead.

In this chapter, I'll tell you how to take advantage of the vast ocean of information that the web makes available—and how to do it in ways that don't overwhelm you. My focus here is on exploratory and ongoing web surfing more than on comprehensive research for specific projects or on gaining a thorough grounding in a particular field, though many of the tools and tips will be useful for those tasks as well.

In web surfing, you don't have to reach some magic finish line where you've read all the right sources and learned all the right things for your particular field of interest. You will be most creative and innovative if you expose yourself to a diversity of information sources. You need to stay open to new possibilities. You need to embrace serendipity, even when you're searching for something specific. And you need to make connections, inside your own mind and across the connected and extended space of information and ideas that the web offers.

Here's what you'll find in this chapter:

- **Web surfing and searching basics.** Equip yourself with the tools you need for your web surfing. Use step-by-step searching to get where you need. Make your browser work better.

- **Striking online gold.** Learn where to go online to find sites that inform and inspire. Understand why reading a diversity of sources might make you more innovative. Embrace serendipity to be more creative.
- **Better bookmarking.** Create personal value and multiply shared value by using social bookmarking tools. Try tagging for easy organizing of information. Create a personal idea store.
- **Thinking with the online mind.** Surf the web to connect into the extended web mind. Use the quirks of your memory to surf more effectively. Move beyond information overload to information awareness, attentiveness, and appreciation.

Web surfing and searching basics

We have a hunger of the mind which asks for knowledge of all around us, and the more we gain, the more is our desire; the more we see, the more we are capable of seeing.

—Maria Mitchell

You use a wide variety of tools in finding the information you need and the information you didn't know you needed. This section tells you what tools you might want to use and how you might use them.

You browse and search the web for a variety of reasons, some of which require finding very specific information and others of which benefit from a less directed approach. You may *search* for a particular piece of information, *research* a particular topic in support of a defined project, *scan* a topic area to get an idea of its contours, *explore* a topic in more depth without a particular project or outcome in mind, or *wander* according to what attracts your attention. And you may contribute to the web as you're surfing it: commenting on articles, sharing bookmarks, and publishing blog posts that synthesize what you've learned, for example.

Is "surfing" the right name for each of these activities? Perhaps. As you browse the web, the amount of information you might be able to use is far greater than what you could absorb in a lifetime. You don't have to read entire articles. Read a line or paragraph or skim to get the gist; then use that as a springboard to the next page or next idea. You need to keep yourself above water, and you can't do it without some equipment. But a real surfer only needs her surfboard. You need more than just a browser to keep on top of the information ocean.

QUIT WASTING TIME!

Web surfing is a great way to seed your mind with new ideas, find people to connect with, and keep up to date with what's happening in the world and your profession. But some people think of it as an aimless waste of time, and sometimes it can be. Like anything else, you can surf the web too much with too little to show for it. If you tend to go overboard on your web surfing, try these tips to keep it productive:

- **Limit your surfing during times when you are most productive.** If you usually get a lot done in the morning, for example, don't surf until the afternoon, except for very targeted tasks.
- **Use web surfing as a reward after you've finished a task from your to-do list.** If you timebox tasks (estimate a specific amount of time for a task and then allow yourself only that time to do it), you know you'll get to surf in 30 minutes or an hour.
- **Try the invisibility cloak to keep yourself off of time-wasting sites at certain times of the day.** If you use Firefox and you're willing to muck around with a bit of Greasemonkey code, you can install a customization into your browser that blocks sites during certain times of the day. See `http://www.lifehacker.com/software/feature/geek-to-live-ban-timewasting-web-sites-146448.php`.
- **Focus your surfing on a specific result such as publishing a post to your blog.** Blogs originated as a way of recording someone's web surfing along with their thoughts about what they found. Turning your web surfing into a blog post or other output (like a collection of links for a specific project) will engage you better than if you surf without any goal in mind. You shouldn't always force your web surfing to produce something though—it's also useful to browse just to see what's happening.
- **Make your web surfing social.** Use a tool like StumbleUpon (stumbleupon.com) or Digg (digg.com) to share and comment on content you enjoy. Try a social surfing tool like Me.dium (me.dium.com) that allows you to see and interact with other people who are at the same places you are.

Surfing tools

These are the tools you'll need for surfing the web:

- Web browser
- Bookmarking services
- Newsreader
- Notebook applications
- Meme trackers
- Search engines
- People

Web browser

Your web browser is, of course, your most basic and useful tool for surfing the web. Later in this chapter you'll see how to customize your browser's search capabilities to suit your needs.

Bookmarking services

Your browser comes with built-in bookmarking, but you might consider using a social bookmarking service like del.icio.us (del.icio.us) or Furl (furl.net) that allows you to share your bookmarks with other people more easily as well as help you bridge references together by concept. Social bookmarking services and browser extensions are covered later on in "Better bookmarking."

Newsreader

Also known as an RSS reader, these applications bring new articles from websites and blogs right to you. If you haven't yet tried RSS, you might like to start with Common Craft's introductory video "RSS in Plain English" available at http://www.commoncraft.com/rss_plain_english. Popular web-based newsreaders include Google Reader (reader.google.com) and Bloglines (bloglines .com). Alternatively, you can try a desktop reader such as FeedDemon for Windows or NetNewsWire for OS X.

WHAT'S RSS?   *RSS stands for Rich Site Summary or Really Simple Syndication. It defines a format for news articles published online. Many websites offer their content not just as web pages, but also as an RSS feed that makes it available to RSS readers. With RSS, you don't have to go to websites to see what's new. You just open your newsreader, and it displays updated articles from the sites whose feeds you've subscribed to.*

Notebook applications

When you want to capture more information from a web page than can fit into a bookmark, try an online notebook that can gather and share snippets from multiple websites. Google of course offers one (notebook.google.com), as does Zoho (notebook.zoho.com). There are some useful offline ones too that sync with online sources.

Meme trackers

These sites aggregate blog and news conversation around specific topics and can launch a web surfing session by showing you what's newsy in your areas of interest. For example, memeorandum (memeorandum.com) gathers political discussion, while Megite's science page (megite.com/science) shows the latest news items and discussions about topics like neuroscience, global warming, and medicine.

Search engines

In addition to generic search engines like Ask.com and Google, you'll want to use specialized search engines when you're looking for a specific type of information, such as current news. For example, you can search job listings at Indeed (indeed.com), blog posts at Technorati (technorati.com), or plane tickets and hotel rooms at Sidestep (sidestep.com).

People

You'll get some of your best information from other people—through their blogs, their bookmarks, their emails to you, social networking sites, or other communication channels. The web links people with software, hardware, and information resources—this is the source of its power, so take advantage of it.

The power of search engines

One of the most useful parts of the web is the search engine. Though they use highly complex (and secretive) mathematical algorithms, massive warehouses of computers, and software components with such unappealing names as spiders and robots, they are one of the best examples of how the web knits together computational intelligence with human insight.

When you find the top hits on Google, it represents an aggregation of human votes in the form of links from one website to another. Simplified, what Google and similar search engines do is rank popularity of web pages by how many links they get from other quality, highly rated sites, which in turn are attributed authority based on links to them. Though Google's computer software gathers and combines all this information, the results trace back to human decision making and human judgment, because people create the hyperlinked web pages that the search engines process. This networking of human and computational intelligence is exactly what makes the web so amazing.

In the early days of the web, you might have used Yahoo's hierarchical, human-constructed directory of websites. You would browse through topics and subtopics, looking for the information you wanted, hoping that the person in charge of your topic did a good job finding what's important and relevant. I'm glad that we now have search, because it combines the best talents of computers and humans to give us much better and faster results, in most cases, than hierarchical directories ever did.

Beyond Google and other generic search engines, you also have available to you an array of specialized search engines ranging from people search (spock.com, for example) to academic literature search (PubMed at pubmed.gov) to book search (Amazon at amazon.com) to synonym search (thesaurus.com) to medical search (emedicine.com). Plus, a number of startups are working on search that better understands the meaning of what we're searching for rather than just the keywords (for example, Hakia at hakia.com). Such so-called "semantic search engines" will be able to do a better job of knowing when we're talking about Apple the company versus an apple to eat, for example.

Orienteering

You might think that the most commonly used way to find information online is to pop a few key words into the Google search box and go right to your target. In some situations, like when you know the exact page or bit of information you're looking for and can define it via keywords fairly precisely, that works pretty well. But for more complex searches you may use what researcher Jaime Teevan and her colleagues call *orienteering*.* In orienteering, you take small steps towards your goal, using what you already know and the context you discover as you take each step. The researchers contrast this with *teleporting*, where you go directly to what you want via keyword search.

---

*Jaime Teevan, Christine Alvarado, et. al., The Perfect Search Engine Is Not Enough: A Study of Orienteering Behavior in Directed Search, CHI 2004, (2004), available at `http://people .csail.mit.edu/teevan/work/publications/papers/chi04.pdf`. This research and conclusions are also described in an easy-to-read Powerpoint presentation from April 2005 available at `http://people.csail.mit.edu/teevan/work/publications/talks/acm05.ppt`.

Figure 5-1 shows teleporting and Figure 5-2 shows orienteering. Teleporting may seem more efficient, but orienteering provides a much richer and more engaging surfing experience.

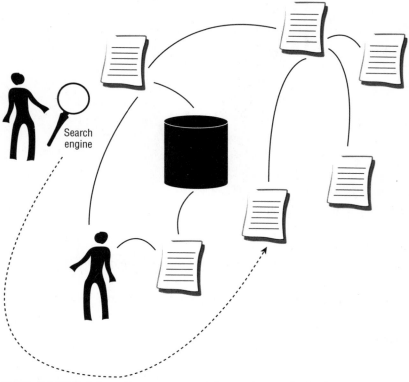

Figure 5-1: With teleporting, you go straight to what you're looking for

Most people prefer orienteering to teleporting in complex search cases for the following reasons:

- **It's easier.** You can gradually figure out how to find what you want instead of coming up with a big bang solution.
- **You get confidence in what you've found.** As you take small steps towards your goal, you find additional context that confirms you've found the right thing.
- **You learn as you orienteer.** Teleporting directly to an answer doesn't give your mind any extra food. Orienteering gives you the information you wanted plus extra useful information as well.

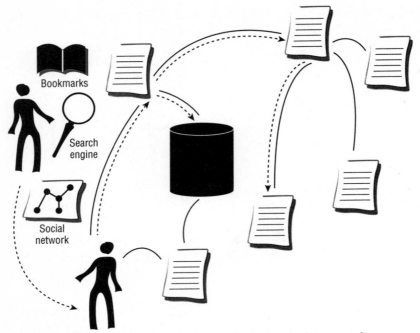

Bookmarks

Search engine

Social network

Figure 5-2: With orienteering, you take small steps towards your goal

- **Your tools may not know enough about you to support teleporting.** The same keywords mean different things to different people—but our search engines don't know enough about us to incorporate it into a teleporting search.
- **You can always backtrack.** If you're orienteering and you go down the wrong path, you can step back to your previous location and go from there. If you've gone wrong in teleporting, you start from the beginning again.
- **You can prove to yourself that something doesn't exist.** If you explore the information space by orienteering, you get an idea of whether what you're looking for even exists. If you try to teleport and don't find something, you know that your keyword search didn't work, but you don't know much about what does exist.
- **You can use people as helpers.** As you orienteer, you're not limited to querying electronic sources only. You can check with people in your extended social network. Issue a request on your blog, instant message the acquaintance most likely to know, or post a question on a forum on the topic.

ENHANCE YOUR BROWSER FOR BETTER SEARCHING

You can tune your browser to your own search needs in a variety of ways:

- **Add new search engines.** Most browsers offer a "search bar" where you can enter keywords and run a search without going to the search engine page. You can add additional search engines for specialized searches like a dictionary search or a news search.
- **Use keyword searches.** The Firefox browser supports using keywords right in the location bar (the entry box where you type in a URL to browse to it). Keywords like "dict" or "book" with search terms will run a search at a specialized search engine without your having to go to the search engine page.
- **Create and access custom search engines.** If you have a certain set of websites that you regularly search as a cluster, you can create your own search engine covering just those sites using Google Co-Op Search (google.com/coop) or Rollyo (rollyo.com).
- **Modify display of search results.** Using web page customization techniques like Greasemonkey scripts, you can make over search results pages in a way that suits your needs.

To see how to do all this with Firefox, visit Web Worker Daily's article "10 Ways to Power Up Your Firefox Search" at `http://www.webworkerdaily.com/2007/05/24/10-ways-to-power-up-your-firefox-search/`.

Better bookmarking

If you have knowledge, let others light their candles in it.

—Margaret Fuller

By bookmarking and using other social software as you surf, you can share what you find online, and at the same time you can make it more likely that you'll remember where to find it and thus put it to work for yourself. The personal benefit of these activities comes first—but the social benefits are many. So choose your tools and get involved in building and spreading knowledge online.

Social bookmarking

In the first version of the web, you probably stored your bookmarks in your browser, where you were the only one who could see them. Now you can share them with social bookmarking services: online bookmarks that other people can see, if you choose. These same tools can be used to store bookmarks just for yourself, if you want to keep them private.

Let's look at a selection representing the major categories of social bookmarking services: del.icio.us, StumbleUpon, Digg, and Clipmarks.

Yahoo!'s del.icio.us

Simply sign up for an account at the URL del.icio.us (that's the name and the URL), download the browser extension that allows you to bookmark a page with a keyboard shortcut, and start bookmarking. You specify tags—any labels that describe this page in ways you can understand—and notes if you wish. del.ico.us makes suggestions of what tags to use based on what other people have tagged the site, as well as your own tagging history. By default, bookmarks are visible to everyone, but you can make them private if you wish.

Now owned by Yahoo!, del.icio.us is the largest and most widely used of the social bookmarking services. If sharing bookmarks is a priority for you, you'll want to choose a tool like del.icio.us that has a wide and vibrant community of users. Alternatives to del.icio.us include Ma.gnolia, Furl, and BlinkList.

StumbleUpon

StumbleUpon (stumbleupon.com) injects an element of randomness into your web surfing. Using recommendations from other surfers with similar interests, it takes you to pages you might enjoy when you "stumble" through the web.

To use it, sign up for an account and choose interests from choices such as Interior Design, Geography, or Paranormal. Install the browser toolbar, then click on the "Stumble!" button to go to a new web page related to your interests and recommended by others. Click on thumbs up or thumbs down to indicate whether you like it, and write short review if you like. As you stumble upon more and more pages, specifying which you like and which you don't, StumbleUpon will personalize its recommendations.

Digg

Digg (digg.com) offers a group rating site that votes on the best articles in topics like Science, World&Business, Sports, and Gaming. Submit a link to Digg if you like it. Vote and comment on links other people have submitted. Browse popular links.

Digg is intensely popular for tech-related topics, and attracts a similarly techie crowd. It's not as useful for more general topics.

Clipmarks

Clipmarks (clipmarks.com) lets you store more than just the URL, tags, and a short note about the page. You can grab and share snippets from the page, including images. Clipmarks stands midway between a bookmarking tool and a full-featured online notebook, where you gather and format excerpts of pages into collections. Clipmarks has a relatively small community, which can feel intimate, but means you might find less comprehensive coverage than at more widely used sites.

FIND PEOPLE TOO   *Remember that there are people on the other side of your social bookmarking tool so it's not just a tool for sharing and finding bookmarks of interest but also for finding people with whom you share interests. Explore the bookmarks of people who've bookmarked the same things as you and you might find someone new to connect with.*

Bookmarking workflow

Your bookmarking must live within your browsing workflow or you won't do it. It needs to be really easy to bookmark a page and get right back to what you were doing (that is, surfing). The easiest way to do this is to download a browser extension that supports quick bookmarking with a keyboard short-cut. For example, the del.icio.us add-on for Firefox is available at `http://del.icio.us/help/firefox/extension`. Whatever bookmark capability you choose, learn how to use it efficiently.

As part of your bookmarking, you may like to publish links to a blog or allow people to subscribe to them within an RSS reader. I find it useful to subscribe to my own links in my RSS reader, because I am reminded of what interested me when I come upon it again.

Folksonomies rather than filing

Your browser bookmark system might use hierarchical file folders for organizing saved links, but most social bookmarking tools use tags instead. You can assign multiple tags to saved links and create new tags on the fly. Most bookmarking tools allow you to bundle or otherwise group related tags. Get a bunch of people tagging and pretty soon you've got a *folksonomy*.

WHAT'S A FOLKSONOMY?   *Folksonomy is a neologism for a practice of collaborative categorization using freely chosen keywords. More colloquially, this refers to a group of people cooperating spontaneously to organize information into categories." [from Wikipedia]*

Tagging is easier than filing into a folder system because you can add as many tags as you want instead of having to choose just one folder. You can use tags that express the content of the page to which you're saving a link, tags that say something about it like it's inspirational or humorous or includes research or case studies, and tags that suggest what you or other people should do with the link.

TIPS FOR TAGGING

Here are some tips to get the most out of tagging.

- **Use individual words in addition to compounds for tags.** Instead of "socialnetwork" use "social" and "network" to tag something about social networking software. This helps you see links across subjects when you look at all your tags on "social" or all your tags on "network."
- **Use a lot of tags.** There's no reason to be stingy. Using more tags makes it more likely you'll find the bookmark you want later on. You can always remove redundant tags if necessary—most bookmarking tools offer an administration tool for this.
- **Use declarative tags that say what you're going to do with this link.** I use toblog, toread, tolisten, and totry so I can remember what I wanted to do with a particular article, podcast, video, or application.
- **Use tags that tell you about the people involved in the page:** who shared it with you (use "via:<name>"), who wrote it, or who is mentioned within it. del.icio.us even supports direct sharing with people in your del.icio.us network using the "for:<name>" tag.
- **Use tags that will help you find it again.** Think about the words you would use to find this site again if you were to search for it, beyond what already appears in the title or URL and make sure that you include those words in the tags.

Your outboard idea store

In 1945, *The Atlantic Monthly* published a now-classic essay entitled "As We May Think" by Vannevar Bush, now available at `http://www.theatlantic.com/ doc/194507/bush`. Bush suggested that our society would turn its attention from war to making knowledge more accessible, and he described a tool known as a *memex* to achieve that. Now you can create your own memex—a personal idea store—online.

Your bookmarks are the start of a memex, but if you're working on specific knowledge projects you may want to store more information than just what a bookmark will hold. Also, you might want to relate the information together into documents, folders, or other structures that mirror your own projects.

You might find the following tools helpful for building your own memex:

- Online notebook applications
- Desktop information managers
- Browser extensions
- Blog
- Wiki

Online notebook applications

Tools like Zoho Notebook and Google Notebook allow you to create (and categorize) pages that gather content of various types from different sources on the web and then add your own notes. These tend to be more private than social linking sites, but you can share pages if you want to.

Desktop information managers

DevonThink for Mac OS X and EverNote for Windows capture little bits of information and then let you search them later. DevonThink even offers a semantic clustering capability so you can find information snippets similar to each other. Or try Yojimbo for Mac OS X or MS OneNote for Windows. You may already have OneNote as part of the Microsoft Office suite.

Browser extensions

The Zotero add-on for Firefox (zotero.org) lets you store links, citations, notes, and web page snapshots. This information is stored locally within the browser, so you won't be able to access it from a different machine. It's convenient because it opens in a split pane right in the browser window, making it easy to capture web page information during your surfing. Microsoft Onfolio (onfolio.com) integrates similar research capabilities into Internet Explorer via the Windows Live Toolbar.

Blog

Blogging links and ideas about a project you're working on is not only a great way to create an archive of information, but also makes it easy for other people to comment on what you're doing, offering other links and suggesting ways to improve your project. Your RSS reader may make it easy to share links or blogrolls (lists of blogs you read) directly: Google Reader offers shared links that other people can subscribe to while Bloglines can make your feed subscriptions public as a blogroll.

CROSSING THE PAPER-DIGITAL DIVIDE

In creating a memex, you may run into the problem of digitizing information from print. When electronic books or e-books become more popular, this may cease to be a problem, as it might be possible to get an electronic copy of a book at the same time you purchase the paper copy. Then you could grab the digital version of whatever information strikes you from the print.

Google's plans to digitize entire libraries of books has struck fear into the offices of print publishers everywhere, but it's yet another way we might be able to cross the paper-digital divide.

Meanwhile, in absence of readily available electronic versions of the print information you read, you may want to purchase a scanner if you regularly transfer quotes or other information from print onto your computer. Alternatively, you can hire someone to enter the information for you or type it yourself if you're quick at the keyboard.

You can also use your fax machine to get print documents into your computer in PDF format. Subscribe to an Internet fax service like eFax, and set preferences to email faxes to yourself in PDF format attachments. It's free for incoming faxes (using a long distance phone number, usually). Then fax what you want digitized to your eFax phone number, and the file will show up neatly in your inbox in PDF format.

Wiki

Wikis, easily editable websites that allow collaborative content development, are great for gathering information and then massaging it over time into the form you want it, especially when more than one person is involved. Look at PBWiki (pbwiki.com) or WikiSpaces (wikispaces.com).

Striking online gold

Our knowledge is the amassed thought and experience of innumerable minds.

—*James Surowiecki*

Now you know how to surf, but where do you start? How do you find the information sources that matter to you? How do you make sure you're not missing out on anything important? And how do you boost your chances of coming across or creating innovative ideas?

In this section you'll find out:

- Where to go to find the information sources relevant to you
- Why a diversity of sources is more important than comprehensiveness
- How to push your search into the future so that information relevant to you comes to you as it's published

WHAT ABOUT PROFESSIONAL RESEARCH? *If you do academic, market, or other professional research for your job you'll use many techniques and resources other than those listed here. My focus is on exploratory ongoing web surfing of publicly accessible information using a web working mindset. For that reason, I don't discuss specialized reference managers or offline information sources like libraries here.*

Finding information sources for your fields of interest

For best results, you'll want to get yourself equipped with an RSS feed reader (already mentioned in the first section) and learn how to recognize and subscribe to website feeds before spending a lot of time finding sources relevant

ider provides a place to store a list of the websites you like
s from those sites as they're published.

r sites that might be worth your time:

- Start with websites for the offline publications you respect in your field. Look for RSS feeds for columns you enjoy (check for an orange feed icon in your browser's location bar or on the web page). See if that publication offers any blogs. If they do, these blogs are likely to link to other blogs in the same field.
- Use Technorati (technorati.com) or Google's blog search (blogsearch .google.com) and search with keywords representing your topics of interest.
- Visit comprehensive blog surfing guides like BlogHer's (blogher.org) and check out their posts by topic, in which they refer to their own favorite blogs.
- As you find blogs you like, look to see if they have blogrolls—lists of blogs they like to read. Check out those blogs too.
- Don't limit yourself too strictly to what seems relevant to you. You can always prune back on your sources later, but you might be inspired by a new idea if you keep your options open at the beginning. No one knows that you've subscribed or unsubscribed so you can turn feeds on and off at will.

Table 5-1 offers some suggestions for additional information sources that may be relevant to you. Some charge a subscription fee for access.

Table 5-1: Information sources to try

Source	URL	Description
PRNewsWire	prnewswire.com	Press releases across every topic imaginable. Track news as it happens. But keep in mind that this is marketing spin.
Questia	questia.com	Online library of books and articles by subscription.
getAbstract	getabstract.com	Summaries of business books as PDF files.

Table 5-1: Information sources to try *(continued)*

Source	URL	Description
Google News	news.google.com	Personalizable news site. Offers email or RSS alerts based on search terms.
CustomScoop	customscoop.com	News clipping service geared towards public relations professionals that monitors a select group of news and blog sites.
PubMed Central	pubmedcentral.nih.gov	The U.S. National Institutes of Health (NIH) free digital archive of biomedical and life sciences journal literature.
Scribd	scribd.com	YouTube for PDFs and MS Word documents.
Ask MetaFilter	ask.metafilter.com	Practical, crowd-sourced advice in question and answer format.

Seek diversity of sources

In the connected age, as in earlier ages, innovation comes from making connections across different ideas and fields of thought, not necessarily from coming up with ideas from scratch. If you limit your information consumption to only sources within your own frame of reference, you are limiting your chances for fresh new ideas to burst you out of the same old thought patterns.

The "wisdom of crowds" identified by James Surowiecki in his book of the same name (and from which the quote for this section was drawn) proposes that the intelligence of groups of people comes not from their agreement and alignment, but rather from the clashing of independent perspectives. Your own thinking will benefit from a similar dynamic—and you can achieve that by reading from a diversity of information sources.

You'll note that if you start reading a bunch of blogs on a particular topic that they overlap greatly in what they produce. For example, in technology blogging you'll see the big news sites cover largely the same ground each day. Hundreds of sites may carry the same story with different words, but you'll find they're all quoting the same original source and looking at the facts from similar angles. The incremental benefit to you of reading yet one more article about the same web startup may be much lower than reading an article from a completely different topic area, like economics or marketing or graphic design.

Creativity and innovation builds on serendipity—those chance encounters with new ideas and new people and new frames of reference that blast old ways of thinking and doing apart. Your work certainly requires periods of study and learning dedicated to keeping up with the important practices of your field. But it might also benefit from an injection of the unexpected.

EMBRACING SERENDIPITY

- **Read blogs from other fields.** Pick a side interest you have and search for related blogs on Technorati. Subscribe to a couple. It's refreshing to see what worlds there are outside the fields you usually pay attention to.
- **Try multiple types of sources within the same field:** news, blogs, bookmarks, books, magazines, and Wikipedia.
- **Pay attention to people from other generations.** You'll get a completely different perspective on the world and keep your own approach from getting stale.
- **Connect with people outside your field.** You might find them through blogs or through your current contacts. Relationships that cross gaps in social networks pay off in many ways.
- **Use a social bookmarking service like StumbleUpon to find pages that other people with your interests have enjoyed.** Just sign up for an account, download the browser toolbar, specify your interests and start surfing onto random pages recommended by others.

Use prospective search

To be most productive, you shouldn't have to remember to go search for information of relevance; ideally, information will come to you as it becomes available. To make this happen, you can use *prospective search*: a search query you specify up front that is executed over various websites on a regular basis, sending you any information that has been updated since the last search.

Many search engines will allow you to turn a search into a regularly updated feed of results that match that search. Then you can get those results in your feed reader or your email. For this to work well, you'll have to define your searches with enough specificity that you don't get overwhelmed with hits.

So-called "vanity searches" can be one of the best uses of prospective search. This is where you create an RSS feed or email alert with your name, your company's name, or your company's product name as the search term. Then you can see someone's saying something about you or your company. I don't consider this as much a vanity search as a connection search, because people who are talking about you are good targets for connecting, assuming they're saying nice things. And if they're not, you still want to know about it so you can address any criticisms or misrepresentations.

Thinking with the online mind

Out of the water, I am nothing.

—*Duke Kahanamoku*

The web brings you into connection with a wide world of people and ideas that you might not otherwise meet. But it goes beyond just mere connection. The web has the potential to expand your mind. While a brief introspection might suggest that your mind is all in your head, it makes sense instead to think of it as extending out to the tools and people and other resources that help you think and create far better than you could without them. And thinking of your mind as extending out makes it easier to surf rather than try to swallow the information ocean.

With a computer connected to the web your mind can work better than it would otherwise. If you're trying to solve a sticky web design problem, you don't have to know how to do it. You can just search for how other people have solved it. If you aren't sure whether a particular idea you have quite works, you can share it online and get quick feedback on it. If you're doing a research project, you don't have to remember every source you want to use. You can store the bibliography in a desktop or online research manager.

Where does the mind end?

I'm going to take you on a brief tour of a way of thinking about the mind that works pretty well for the connectedness the web brings to us. Maybe you don't think about your mind too much; you probably just let it do its job. But given the way the web changes how you do your thinking work, it makes sense to consider what place the mind has within the web.

The mind-in-the-head view is shown in Figure 5-3. You have a bunch of ideas, you know a lot of words and concepts, and you have some belief systems that tie it all together. Of course you regularly go out into the world and learn more, bringing what's out into the world into your mind. You might use a variety of external devices to keep track of stuff—paper and pen, your computer, even a memex. But these things aren't part of your mind itself. They're just stuff out there in the world.

Figure 5-3 Mind in the head

An alternative view says that our minds expand out across the network of people and devices shown in Figure 5-2. Philosophers Andy Clark and David Chalmers suggested in 1998 that the mind extends outside our head and onto the devices and tools that participate in its thinking action. You can read about it in their paper "The Extended Mind" (http://www.consc.net/papers/extended.html) or, for a more accessible version, try Wikipedia (http://en.wikipedia.org/wiki/Extended_mind).

Figure 5-4 Connected and extended mind

The web is one of the most powerful tools ever used for extending our minds. You don't have to bring the web into your mind to expand your mind. You just have to connect out and extend out to the offerings of the web. You need to have some ideas within your head about what's out there, some links on your bookmarking sites, and maybe a personal memex that stores even more. But the vast majority of stuff that's knowable to you can stay where it is, until you need it. Then you can orienteer inside your head, across your bookmarks, through your idea stores, and around your social networks until you know what you need.

In the past, people used paper and pen to expand the abilities of their memory. You probably still do that—using sticky notes and paper calendars and to-do lists to make sure you don't forget what you need to do. Since the beginning of the PC era, you were given yet another way of extending your mind: onto your computer. And in the mid-1990s, you got the web too.

This is not just a matter of external memory—though that's one of the most obvious ways the web extends your mind. Your actual thinking can be distributed and doesn't take place only inside your head. You may have experienced something similar already in your work life, in situations where you're working with a team of people to develop a solution to a particular problem. You throw your ideas out to the team (in a meeting or in an online discussion forum) and other people change and modify and improve them. Eventually, your team arrives at some solution—but no one person created that solution. You used a distributed thought process. If this intrigues you, you will want to read Richard Ogle's book *Smart World*, which describes how the world of ideas thinks for itself.

This matters because if you think of the mind extending out onto the web—instead of the mind absorbing information from the web—you make your job during web surfing much easier. You don't have to learn and remember everything you come across, because if you remember enough about the landscape and about important landmarks, you can find what you need when the need arises.

This depends, of course, on your having learned enough of whatever subjects you use to be able to understand the information and ideas you come across online. It doesn't matter how much I surf physics blogs; I don't understand enough physics to make sense of any landmarks or landscape they offer. My undergraduate training in economics, however, is enough that surfing economics sites and blogs is useful in bringing awareness of economic thought into my work.

Becoming a better surfer

The concept of the extended mind with its distributed thought has practical importance for your web surfing and searching. If your memory and thinking extends out into the web of people and computers, it means you don't have to find everything of importance or learn or memorize it all. You can rely on the web to do much of your knowing and thinking for you. And because the web remembers for you, but only if you know how to navigate it, you need to be able to use orienteering-type search to find what you need when you need it. You can do this for a certain project if you've created enough of a mental map with landmarks about who and what exists online.

You don't need to absorb everything you read or stay on top of everything that happens in your field. You need to make connections between your mind and what's out on the web.

If you know a few things about how your memory works, you can make your web surfing more effective in extending your mind and allowing you to more fully participate in the evolution of ideas. The better you remember the ideas and people and connections you come across online, the better you'll be able to navigate the space when you need it.

Put your autobiography to work

Your memory organizes itself around episodes in your life. These episodes include your memory of who was involved, where you were, and what sorts of things were happening in your life at the time. When you find information and later want to rediscover it, you will likely use your autobiographical memory to help you rediscover the information.

You can take advantage of this effect by storing bookmarks online in such a way that they are retrievable by date or by their association with an event in your life. Blogging is the perfect way to do that, because it's organized in reverse chronology and because many people combine personal and professional information on their blogs. If you bookmark items of interest and then publish bookmarks to your blog, you'll be better equipped to reconnect with the information later by browsing your blog's archives.

You may also remember where information is stored by recalling which of your online contacts wrote about it or otherwise referenced it.

Create context by reading around the edges

You remember best when you can link a piece of information or an idea with other related information that you already know: this is called *elaboration*. You can achieve this online by reading related information as you come upon something new. The more you surf information related to a subject, the more hooks you put into your brain for new pieces of information about that subject. Unfortunately this works as well for topics like celebrity gossip as it does for digital photography.

Laugh to remember

You'll remember information better when it's presented humorously, so seek out sites that present useful information in a way that makes you laugh. Yes, watching YouTube videos can be educational, depending on their subject of course.

Seek visual displays of information

You'll remember information better if you've seen it in pictures in addition to in words instead of just in words. Though the vast majority of information online is textual, with videos and better graphic making tools, you'll find more and more opportunities for feeding your brain visually as well as verbally. Each day, make sure your web surfing includes some graphics.

Space out surfing over time

Exposing your mind over and over to information over a period of time is better than trying to cram it all in at once. Just-in-time learning for a project won't work as well as having kept up with the connecting all along. So surf regularly, even if it looks unproductive to some of your coworkers or to your manager. If you need to, set time limits on your surfing so it doesn't keep you from meeting work deadlines.

Stop in the middle of your surfing

You'll remember things better if you're interrupted in the middle of absorbing them. That's known as the Zeigarnik effect, after Russian psychologist Bluma Zeigarnik, who found that waiters remember in-process orders but not completed ones. So here's another reason to seek social productivity that allows for interruptions. It's not necessarily a bad thing to dip into the web here and there during the day, being interrupted by instant messages or your email notifier.

Take advantage of first and last effects

You will best remember the first things you come across during a surfing session and the last things, while the stuff you came across in the middle might be lost. So don't arrange your web surfing to go to the exact same sites in the exact same order each day. That way you'll probably be less likely to learn from the sites you visit in the middle even if their information is just as good. Shake things up by surfing in a different order every day.

Generate your own information

This is probably the most important tip for getting the most out of your web surfing. Don't be a passive web surfer: surf and then create your own content online from what you've learned. Generating your own words, pictures, and videos is the best way to really grasp something. It also ties your information discovery and learning better into your own personal autobiography, and you've already seen how that helps you learn better.

You don't necessarily have to share what you're doing with the world. You can blog in private for a while or just for the eyes of a few close friends or colleagues until you feel ready to open up more.

Open up your attention

More information is not a bad thing—it's a good thing, if only you can find the right way to approach it. I hope I've convinced you or at least gotten you wondering about how you can rely on the web of your online social network and the information resources you find there to do much of your knowing and thinking. Your job as a web worker is not so much to memorize and absorb everything as to bring yourself into connection with it all at critical points so that you can navigate the space when you need to.

It's at least partly a matter of attitude. Are you trying to find exactly the right information you need in the least amount of time? Are you concerned with expertise and authority? Then you might feel overloaded by what the web makes available.

If, on the other hand, you seek connection with the extended mind and idea-space that the web offers, you might see it as a river rushing by or just slipping slowly beneath you. You could find inspiration and awareness just by becoming connected to that river of ideas and intelligence.

RENEW YOUR BEGINNER'S MIND

After you've worked in a field for a long period of time, it may begin to feel tired. You've heard everything, seen everything, and worked on everything. How can you get back to the excitement you felt when it was all new? How do you get back to beginner's mind?

The information overload naysayers would tell you to take a break: stop paying attention to so many things! What if you don't want to turn off though? What if you just want to feel some excitement again?

Here's what you can try:

- **Dip into alternate rivers.** Try a new topic area or a new writer or a new political perspective. Insert some new ideas into your thought processes.
- **Read more slowly.** Don't stop reading entirely, but do it at a more leisurely pace and really absorb the material. Read a few of the newest articles in your feed reader each morning and then stop. A change of pace might be what you need.
- **Try producing information in addition to consuming it.** Write something or draw something or record something yourself. Start with how bored you are by it all if you must. Then write about what sets off even the smallest spark of interest in you. If nothing does, write about why it's boring and what might make it not boring. If you're not into writing, record a podcast or a video or visually illustrate what you're connecting with.
- **Read print publications instead of online articles.** Go to your nearest bookstore and see what headlines jump out at you from the magazine rack.
- **Take a class.** Find an online or in-person class in a subject that intrigues you. The further it is from your current field, the better. Go really deep, if you feel energy and authenticity in it.
- **Read some fiction.** Some fiction is merely escapist while other teaches while you read. Either way, words that tell a story can help you feel more human and bring a new perspective to work-related information consumption.

Table 5-2 shows two ways of thinking about the masses of information online.

Table 5-2: Old attitude versus new attitude

	Old	New
Metaphor	Drinking from a fire hose	Surfing waves in an ocean; watching a river flow by
What's out there	A little signal and a whole lot of noise	Compost for fertilizing your thought
You need to	Maximize efficiency	Embrace serendipity
You're done when	You've finished reading everything that's important and authoritative	You have something else to do—but you'll return later
Your attention is	Scarce, a fixed amount	Flowing, like a river
You should	Limit your web surfing time, it's exposing you to junk	Learn as much as you can, connect as much as you can
Look for	Information from experts	Diverse information sources that can shake up your thinking
Believe in	Your easily overwhelmed mind	Your mind's ability to extend and connect
Use the web to	Learn specific things	Build context and understanding of the space of ideas in your fields of interest

Of course sometimes you'll find the old attitude works and other times the new one does—and sometimes you combine aspects of both. Just remember that there's another way to think about web surfing than as a waste of time or as a source of information overload.

Looking forward: Connect, communicate, collaborate

In the next chapter, you'll learn the tools, techniques, and philosophy underlying using the web to work successfully with other people online. That's the key to web working: connecting productively and authentically with other people.

6 Connect, Communicate, and Collaborate

Web work allows you to connect to other people along many dimensions; that's the source of its power. But to connect and communicate and collaborate effectively across the web requires some new tools and new approaches.

In this chapter, you'll learn how to work across distances using the web:

- **Beyond email.** Use channels other than email to communicate with colleagues and other contacts for many purposes, including task coordination, information exchange, social bonding, team building, and knowledge capture.

- **Webifying your schedule.** Scheduling meetings and other events can be a huge source of overload on your email and your psyche. Try new ways of sharing and planning your schedule.

- **Getting things done together while apart.** Most projects of any significant size involve more than one person and these days, your project team is likely to be distributed geographically. Use online tools to manage projects, collaboratively edit documents, share ideas, and problem solve.

- **Finding your inner schmoozer.** You don't have to be a natural-born connector to develop a strong network of professional relationships using the web. Just follow your interests and use a variety of tools to reach out and relate.

- **Network science for nonscientists.** Got the basics of creating and building relationships down? Take it to the next level. Understand how social networks function and you'll be better equipped to create, maintain, and benefit from your own professional and personal network.

Beyond email

Let's use the web to help people understand each other.

—*Tim Berners-Lee*

While email is ubiquitous, it's not necessarily the ideal tool for all your workplace communications, as you saw in Chapter 4. Fortunately, you have a variety of other channels and platforms available that can meet your connection, communication, and collaboration needs even when you're not working in the same place as your colleagues.

When you communicate during your workday, you do so for a variety of reasons:

- Exchanging information
- Solving problems
- Coordinating multi-person projects
- Scheduling meetings and other events
- Creating and deepening relationships
- Building team spirit and morale
- Keeping in touch with family and friends

Communications aren't solely about information exchange. On distributed or virtual teams, where team members are scattered around the globe, you need to ensure you don't miss out on brief, informal interactions that move projects forward and keep team members socially connected with each other.

THAT'S PHATIC!   *Phatic communications are those that serve social purposes like relationship building and dominance signaling rather than information exchange. The urban slang word "phat" has nothing to do with the anthropologist's word phatic.*

In an office setting, phatic communications and other brief, informal exchanges take place in the hall, at the watercooler, in the kitchen, and wherever you run into coworkers. When you're working far from your colleagues, phatic communications must move to other channels like instant messaging or social networking platforms.

Researchers Steve Whittaker, David Frohlich, and Owen Daly-Jones found that informal communication in a physical workplace includes brief, unplanned, and frequent interactions without openings and closings. Conversations are left open and ongoing between face-to-face interactions.* Virtual replacements need to provide ways of reproducing this interaction when you're not geographically collocated with your teammates.

Your communications processes and tools also need to take into account the potential disruptiveness of interruptions compared to their value. Using multi-channel, multi-platform, presence-aware communications can help ensure that you interrupt people at relatively more convenient times and that you are interrupted when it suits you rather than when you are pressing to get solo work done on a deadline.

Alternatives to email

Email is convenient for many tasks: communicating asynchronously especially with people you don't know well or don't work with regularly, archiving documents, and maintaining to-do items. You can also use it with some success for ongoing communication and collaboration with your colleagues, for keeping in close touch with friends and family during the workday, for finding new relationships and deepening existing ones, or for collaborative knowledge capture. But as we saw in Chapter 4, it's not always the best choice. Let's see what other possibilities there are.

Instant messaging

Instant messaging may be the best replacement for those frequent informal interactions that you'd have with workmates if you were in the same office. You can use it for informational exchanges, problem solving, social chitchat—just about anything you'd do in person.

Unless all of your IM contacts have accounts on the same service, you'll probably want to use an IM aggregator such as Trillian (Windows), Adium (Mac OS X), or Pidgin (Windows, Linux, other Unix operating systems). These aggregators allow you to use one application to send instant messages to contacts on different networks. While you are not required to use a particular

---

*Steve Whittaker, David Frohlich, and Owen Daly-Jones, "Informal Workplace Communication: What Is It Like and How Might We Support It?" *Proceedings of CHI'94 Conference on Human Factors in Computing Systems*, (1994).

service's application to deliver messages and can use applications like Adium and Trillian, the networks are still mostly closed. You need an AIM account to send an AIM message, and a MSN account to send a MSN message, even if you're using one application to do it. Even though these are free, most are still locked to commercial entities who are free to control the service as they wish. One exception is Jabber, an open source messaging technology. Currently Google Talk is the best example of a messaging client/system that works using Jabber. Multi-service clients like Adium and Trillian also support Jabber.

Instant messaging lies somewhere in between email and phone calls in terms of its demands on attention and ability to tie people together emotionally. Stefana Broadbent of Swisscom, Switzerland's largest telecommunications company, calls it "semi-synchronous writing" and found in her user studies that people seem to prefer this (and text messaging) more and more to either email or phone conversations.*

The semi-synchronicity of IM means you can carry on more than one conversation at once, but its immediacy means you can banter back and forth in a way that's much more conversational than email. A big advantage of IM is that most clients give you an indicator that someone else is typing. You have that experience of someone else being in the same moment that you are. Plus, it's better for problem-solving or event scheduling than email, since you can explore issues or potential meeting times in quick dialog.

IM is useful as a preliminary to a phone call. You can see if someone's available and arrange for a call right then or for sometime later in the day. Some IM conversations turn into phone calls when the discussion gets too complex or lengthy. It also provides instant notes for a meeting since you now have the chat history to refer back to.

The huge drawback to instant messaging is, of course, the possibility for distraction and interruption when you're trying to get heads-down work done. To make IM work best for you, use your presence indicator liberally. Don't just say you're available; say that you're taking a coffee break. Don't just say you're busy; direct people to email or indicate when you'll be available in the status message. If you're always busy, you'll miss out on the benefits of informal, frequent interactions. But it's not unreasonable to spend a few hours a day with your status set to "not available."

*"Home truths about telecom," The Economist, (June 7, 2007), available at http://www.economist.com/printedition/displayStory.cfm?story_id=9249302.

I'M OKAY, YOU'RE OTP

There aren't any universal rules for instant messaging usage, but there are a few things you should know about using it, especially if you're new to it.

Keep in mind that IM is casual; almost anything goes. It's okay to:

- **Ignore a message, even if your status message says you're available and you're sitting right there.** You can leave the message up and respond later or not at all, depending on the situation. At the same time, don't be insulted if you feel ignored if someone appears to be available but doesn't respond. The person might have stepped away from their computer without changing their status or they might be in the middle of something else that's demanding their attention.
- **Let an IM conversation drag out with long pauses between responses.** IM works so well because you can do other things while you're doing it. Watch the "typing" indicator. If you're not getting feedback that the other person is quickly responding, they've probably moved on to something else. You can do the same.
- **Take a phone call in the middle or start a second or third conversation at the same time.** If you need to focus on the phone call, tell the other person "on the phone" or use "otp" for short.
- **Stop messaging without using a "bye" or "later" to close it off.** IM exchanges often end without an explicit goodbye. Some coworkers have quick IM exchanges throughout the day without ever closing down the communication—just like what researcher Whittaker and colleagues saw in informal communications in an office setting. It's a good idea, however, to get attention when starting a conversation with a "you there?" or "Hi Jane," then wait and see if they're available for a chat.
- **Wind up a conversation using "bye" or "later" to indicate you need to get to something else.** You don't have to use a closing, but it's helpful when you want to turn to another task. Some people use "ttyl" meaning "talk to you later."

I'M OKAY, YOU'RE OTP (*continued*)

- **Use instant messaging as a back channel during conference calls.** This is especially useful if you're in a negotiation or sales situation and need to advise a colleague of something privately. But be mindful if your keyboard is noisy. If you're typing a lot on a call and you're not the one taking notes, the parties on the phone may think you're not paying attention.
- **Turn away people when you're busy.** The easiest way to do it is set your presence indicator to busy and tell them how to reach you with your status message or an auto-reply ("please email" or "try after 3 PM PST"). But don't feel bad about telling people it's a bad time when they message you even if your status says available.

Different people have different expectations when it comes to instant messaging. For a rundown of what *might* annoy people, see my Web Worker Daily article "How to Annoy People with Instant Messaging" at http://www .webworkerdaily.com/2007/01/14/how-to-annoy-people-using-instant-messaging/.

Chat rooms

Virtual or distributed teams may find that a text-based chat room helps establish a sense of team presence while promoting ongoing communications. While IM is usually one to one, chat is usually many-to-many (often with facilities for breaking off into private chat). You can use Internet Relay Chat or a chat service like 37Signals' Campfire (campfirehq.com). IM services allow for group chat also.

WHAT'S INTERNET RELAY CHAT?   *Internet Relay Chat or IRC is an Internet-based text chat service that allows you to set up a chat room (in IRC lingo, a channel) on an IRC server and then access it using any one of many IRC clients. IRC has its own set of etiquette expectations and patterns of use; to learn more about it see Wikipedia's article at* http://en.wikipedia.org/wiki/Internet_Relay_Chat.

Your team might like to use a chat room for status updates as described in Chapter 2. You can say hello when you start working and let your teammates know when you're leaving to go out to lunch or to run errands. It's also helpful to issue a short update when you've achieved some milestone in your work. Or, if you have a question and you're not sure who might answer it, you can broadcast it via the chat room. That provides a lightweight way of asking questions without disrupting anyone's work too much.

Voice: Phone, VoIP, video chat, videoconferencing, conference calls

While each of these has its own unique characteristics, they are all about synchronous voice—that is, people talking to each other in real time. You'll read more about mobile phone usage in Chapter 7. VoIP, which was covered briefly in Chapter 2, offers free or low-cost calls transmitted across the Internet. Videoconferencing and conference calls are useful for meeting when attendees aren't in the same place. Video chat has become increasingly popular as more laptops arrive with built-in videocams. To use it effectively, though, you must have broadband with decent upload speed and low latency. Even the best computer with the best camera won't do well with video chats using dialup.

Status updaters

Sometimes called microbloggers, tools like Twitter (twitter.com), Jaiku (jaiku.com), Pownce (pownce.com), and Dodgeball (dodgeball.com) provide an easy way to keep your contacts up to date with what's happening in your work and life at the same time you keep up to date with them. For some ideas about how to use Twitter for work, see "8 Ways Twitter is Useful Professionally" at `http://www.webworkerdaily.com/2007/03/15/eight-ways-twitter-is-useful-professionally/`.

To use one of these tools, you sign up for an account and then issue short updates about what you're doing using a variety of methods such as desktop clients, web forms, text message, or instant message. The updates are sent to any of your followers by whatever channel they specify. For example, I use the Twitterific Mac OS X client to issue and receive status updates from my Twitter contacts.

While many people criticize Twitter for its inanity, narcissism, and disruptiveness, it fills a gap in the communications toolset for those of us who work mainly online. Twitter creates a space of what user interaction designer Leisa Reichelt has called "ambient intimacy" that's otherwise lacking if you work remotely from teammates and friends (see `http://www.disambiguity.com/ambient-intimacy/`). It informs your workmates when you're more or less available for discussion. And it allows you to issue questions to a bunch of people at once in a lightweight manner, without disrupting their concentration.

Twitter can be a source of noise though. Some people use it for spam or marketing and some people tweet many hundreds of times per day. Don't feel you must follow hundreds or even tens of people. As with other social networking tools, more contacts doesn't necessarily mean more benefit for you. Also, don't feel you must open up your status updates to all comers. If you prefer more privacy, keep your stream protected so that only people you allow to see it can do so.

Understanding what status updaters are good for really requires experiencing them and using them with at least a few contacts, so don't rule them out without giving them a chance.

WORKSTREAMING INSTEAD OF FACE TIME

If you work remotely from your manager (or your clients) and your colleagues, how do they know when you're working and when you're not? How can you feel a sense of connection and presence when you're working by yourself? Face time doesn't work in that case and anyway, who would want to reproduce it in the world of web work? Instead, you can use *workstreaming*.

With workstreaming, you publish your work-related activities and events to your remote colleagues so they can see what you're up to. Workstreaming is the next generation of the 11 pm email you send to your team to show them that you've been working all evening. Workstreaming is related to lifestreaming, producing an RSS feed of all the online bits and pieces of your online self in date-time order. Workstreaming, however, is aimed at professional activities, though it may include personal updates too, when they're relevant for team bonding or for updating workmates as to what you're up to.

The benefits of workstreaming include satisfying your boss (or client) that you're making regular progress towards shared goals, notifying team members of your status in case it affects their work, and even giving yourself a sense of accomplishment and progress. Because it's oriented to what you're producing and doing and not just about how much time you're spending on it, workstreaming isn't so burdensome as face time requirements. But just like face time, workstreaming could certainly be manipulated to give the illusion you're working when you're not.

WORKSTREAMING INSTEAD OF FACE TIME (*continued*)

There are a wide variety of tools that might be used for workstreaming, and which ones suit you and your team depend both on what kind of work you do and what tools your coworkers are using. It's not effective to use an IRC channel if you're the only one on the team who knows what IRC stands for, but it can be great for a techie crowd. Twitter creates a virtual shared office space that can reproduce the chatter and intimacy of a physical office while allowing team members to share what they're working on and what they've completed. RSS feeds from blogs, message boards, photo sites, and project management apps could all provide useful workstreams—especially if these are aggregated for a whole team. Source code control systems used in software development can output RSS feeds too so you can make team members aware of new features and bug fixes as they're checked in.

Of course there's always email, which has been used as a "Look, I'm working!" and "Look what I've done!" tool for years.

Social and professional networking

Social networks like Facebook or MySpace and professional networks like LinkedIn and Xing allow you to create a profile page showing your contact information and other details about you relevant to professional or personal socializing and networking. You specify your contacts or friends, other people on the service that you know in some capacity. Your contacts then can see some or all of your contact and other information, depending on how you configure your privacy settings. Different services provide different features for interacting and for publishing information about yourself.

These tools can reproduce some of the phatic communications of the physical workplace and make your remote coworkers seem more like three-dimensional human beings than disembodied brains. These platforms allow you to show who you are beyond your professional identity including who you associate with, what your affiliations are, and what you're up to in your life. They may also include status updaters and streaming feeds that create that sense of ambient intimacy you might be missing if you work from home or otherwise far away from colleagues.

If you're skeptical about whether and how you might use these services as part of your professional toolbox, see Judi Sohn's article "12 Ways to Use Facebook Professionally" at http://www.webworkerdaily.com/2007/07/24/12-ways-to-use-facebook-professionally/ and Leo Babauta's "20 Ways to Use LinkedIn Professionally" at http://www.webworkerdaily.com/2007/06/15/20-ways-to-use-linkedin-productively.

Knowledge capture and sharing: blogging, wikis, bookmarks

You can use a variety of web tools such as blogs, wikis, and social bookmarks for knowledge management. With these tools you and your team can flexibly capture and update information in a centralized or decentralized manner.

Blogging can replace lengthy and complex discussions that might otherwise take place in email or on a message board. It allows you to maintain your own information organization and set your own agenda, in contrast to how forums or message boards define those for you.

Wikis are great for knowledge management and even useful for some project management activities. They can take some document editing and archiving tasks out of your email and onto a more appropriate platform.

DO IT WIKIWIKI   *Wikis provide an easy way of collaboratively developing a website of structured online information. Using a simplified markup language and tracking edits by user, wiki platforms make it easier than ever to capture and update information online. Most include access control and change moderation features. The name comes from the Hawaiian word "wikiwiki" meaning quickly. Online encyclopedia Wikipedia is the most well-known example of a wiki. It uses MediaWiki, an open source wiki platform, as its back end.*

Instead of emailing links, sharing bookmarks using a social bookmarking tool can be more convenient while lightening the load on your inbox. Different bookmarking tools such as del.icio.us, BlueDot, Ma.gnolia, and BlinkList support varying levels of access control (for example, limiting bookmarks only to yourself or to a specified set of friends), so choose one that meets your own or your team's privacy and security requirements.

But how do I get people out of email?

Even when there are better channels and platforms available, many teams revert back to email. It's convenient, it's ubiquitous, and it provides one place to go for so many communication and collaboration needs. For some ideas on how to encourage adoption of alternate tools, see Judi Sohn's article "The Challenge of User Adoption with Small, Remote Teams" at `http://www.webworkerdaily` `.com/2007/01/21/the-challenge-of-user-adoption-with-small-remote-teams/`.

Webifying your schedule

As for the future, your task is not to foresee it, but to enable it.

—*Antoine de Saint-Exupéry*

If you work regularly with lots of different people at different organizations rather than focusing on solo tasks, your inbox might get filled up with event-scheduling traffic. It's hard enough to find a convenient time for just two people to meet; get a third person involved and it can become nearly impossible.

The web makes it easier. If you're willing to open up your schedule a bit, you can take some of the pain out of meeting scheduling. Let's see how.

The problem of scheduling meetings

The problems of scheduling meetings include these:

- You have to find a time that works for everyone.
- People's calendars are changing as you go back and forth.
- As you look at your own calendar, you need to not only consider the times you have available, but the times you'd prefer.
- The communications are often mixed into other email traffic.
- If attendees are distributed across geography, time zones can be confusing.

Some solutions for easier scheduling

You can't take all the pain out of meeting scheduling, but you can make it a bit easier. Make your calendar available to colleagues and other people you might be meeting with and explore alternatives to email for scheduling.

WHAT TO DO ABOUT TIME ZONE DEMENTIA

Do you suffer from TZD? That's Time Zone Dementia. It happens when you work virtually and physically across so many time zones that events on your calendar confuse you completely.

You might have TZD if you show signs and symptoms like these:

- **Early morning wakeups.** You get up at 6:45 AM to dial into a conference call scheduled for 7 AM Mountain Standard Time. But you live in New York.
- **Midday confusion.** You go for lunch with a friend on Tuesday at noon, trusting the open space on your calendar. You miss an important online developer chat because you didn't convert the time properly when recording it.
- **Self-centered meeting planning.** You ask your colleague in Sydney to call in for a mandatory 8 AM PST meeting, forgetting that it would be 3 AM to her.
- **Disorientation when traveling away from home.** You diligently record the details of an important webinar onto your calendar, but miss it anyway, because while you're traveling your calendar still reflects your home time zone.
- **Socially inappropriate behavior.** You plan a springtime brunch, only to be surprised in your pajamas by the guests who remembered to "spring forward" for daylight savings time.

What can you do about Time Zone Dementia? Here are a few suggestions.

- **Put a world clock on your start page or dashboard with the most important time zones for you.** Besides making it really easy to see what time it is where your colleagues are, this ups your time zone awareness because every time you look at your start page, you are reminded of the time offsets between you and the geographic locations that matter to you.

WHAT TO DO ABOUT TIME ZONE DEMENTIA (*continued*)

- **Take advantage of the time zone support your calendar software provides.** In the Mac iCal program, you can turn on advanced time support in Preferences > Advanced. This allows you to specify a time zone other than the default for a particular event, useful if you know the event time elsewhere but not for your current location. It also supports floating events which occur at the same time no matter what time zone you switch your calendar to. In Microsoft Exchange, you can display two time zones at once; you might want to try that if you travel regularly between two cities or work remotely from a company headquarters.

- **Try The World Clock Meeting Planner** (`http://www.timeanddate.com/worldclock/meeting.html`) **when you're planning a meeting.** You enter the cities for each person attending and it will show you what time it is in each place at a given time. Then you can pick something that's reasonable for everyone.

- **Put the time zone right into your event names on your calendar.** If you'll be traveling but need to take conference calls on the road, include the time zone right in the event header (for example, "call Rick 10 AM EST"). Even if you check your calendar from your Blackberry or a start page that shows only the barest of event data, you'll be reminded of the actual time of the event.

- **Include the time zone in all email communications about meetings.** Even if you know the recipient is in your same time zone, they may forward your email to another attendee. If you get in the habit of always being clear about the time zone, you won't forget to be clear when it really matters.

Share your calendar with colleagues

Desktop and web-based calendars allow you to share your calendar with whomever you want. Do that, and it's a lot easier for one member of your team to schedule a meeting. This option is best for those closest to you, as you probably don't want random strangers knowing when you have a doctor's appointment.

You may want to use your calendar program to create multiple calendars: personal, by project, and so forth. That way you can share your work commitments with colleagues without also sharing the Saturday afternoon soccer game you have scheduled.

Publish a free/busy calendar

If you regularly schedule meetings with people you don't know well, you may be able to publish just free/busy information online so that those people can pick from available times on your calendar. For example, Google Calendar supports that.

Use a wiki

If you have a specific chunk of time where you'd like to allow other people to schedule your time instead of setting up plans yourself, you can publish a wiki for that. Amazon Web Services evangelist Jeff Barr has used that approach when he travels so that those who want to meet with him can do self-service scheduling You can see the wiki he created at `http://s3.amazonaws.com/s3wiki/wiki/JeffBarrLondonMay2007`.

Try a web-based scheduling helper

A number of startups are aiming at solving the difficulties of scheduling. These services use polls, embedded chat, and other ways of softening the pain of event scheduling. Check out Renkoo (renkoo.com), Doodle (doodle.ch), and Planypus (planyp.us).

Getting things done together while apart

Coming together is a beginning. Keeping together is progress. Working together is success.

—Henry Ford

Whether the people you work with are sitting in the neighboring cubicles or in a country around the world, you need to coordinate and collaborate. Distributed teams have become the rule rather than the exception, as some employees choose telecommuting, employers create remote worksites, and virtual teams launch without any headquarters offices at all. Even teams with all members in one place often work in partnership with consultants or employees of other organizations who are not nearby.

Effective virtual teamwork

Although every virtual team faces unique challenges, there are some practices that would help almost any team to collaborate more effectively. Here are a few habits I've seen practiced by successful virtual teams.

Management shows thorough commitment to virtual work

It's not enough for managers to merely allow team members to work remotely. They should support it both philosophically and financially, perhaps even working remotely themselves. Managers who try to make virtual work look as much as possible like office work (establishing standard hours, expecting employees to make do with the bare minimum of tools for remote collaboration, and treating remote team members as second-class citizens) won't get long-term productivity from their teams. Managers who themselves enjoy the benefits of remote work will be more likely to do whatever they need to make it succeed.

Team members check in with each other frequently

In an office, you can always "prairie dog"—pop up out of your cube and ask the guy in the next cube over something—to make sure little issues don't turn into big problems. With instant messaging and chat rooms, even with email, it's possible to let your coworkers know what you're up to or get a quick answer to something you're wondering.

Don't rule out the telephone either. Let them hear your voice, hear you laugh, and pick up another side of your personality from time to time. Don't let yourself turn into an avatar, someone who exists seemingly only in digital form.

The team shares a view of their work

You can accomplish this with a variety of tools, and what works best for each team depends on the kind of work that team is doing. You may want to share calendars, project plans, status updates, work in progress, and so forth. Virtual team success requires more than the usual degree of openness, since casual information exchanges can be less likely to occur than in office setups.

The team leverages the diversity of team members

I don't just mean a demographic mix by gender, age, and race, although that helps. Teams benefit from the contributions from people of different temperaments, from different geographic areas (think of a software development that achieves 24-hour productivity by passing off code around the world), and from people with different professional skills and experience.

Team members get to know each other on a human level

One thing you miss with a virtual team is getting to know about each other's lives. Telephone calls offer a good opportunity to learn a bit more about each other. A group chat room can provide a virtual water cooler for teammates to swap stories about what they did during their vacation or over the weekend. Quick instant messaging lets you learn little bits about another person's life and know them more as a whole person. Social networks, blogging, or microbloggers can show three-dimensional personalities too.

Trust and respect are assumed, not earned

Does trust-at-a-distance need to be earned, or should it be assumed instead? I'd argue that you are better off using a "trust, but verify" approach rather than a "you must earn our trust first" with new team members. New teammates have already been vetted through some sort of hiring process (though not necessarily the standard resume-and-interview approach of yore). If you want remote team members to feel both accountable and authorized to work independently towards team goals, you need to trust them. Saying, "I trust you" to a new colleague is a powerful way to make them feel both competent and committed. Taking a "prove you are worthy" stance will make them more likely to doubt themselves and consequently less likely to take risks for the team.

Tools for collaborative online work

Office tools have moved online as web-based, collaborative applications that provide for more sharing and new usage patterns. These offerings aren't necessarily direct replacements for desktop-based office software like Microsoft Office, as you saw in Chapter 2. If you judge them on a feature-by-feature basis, the web-based applications may look inferior. Consider them instead on their own merits and as potential complements to your desktop software:

- **Online document editing** like Zoho Writer (writer.zoho.com) and Google Docs (docs.google.com) allow for review and editing of the exact same version of the document at the same time.

- **Do-it-yourself development tools** like Coghead (coghead.com) and DabbleDB (dabbledb.com) let nonprogrammers create online database applications for workgroups.
- **Web-based project management applications** like Basecamp (basecamphq.com) and GoPlan (goplan.org) makes it easy for a team to have a shared view of project progress.
- **Presentation sharing services** like SlideShare (slideshare.net) make PowerPoint and other file formats easily shareable and viewable across the web, with no download required by the viewer.
- **Collaborative mind mapping** like MindMeister (mindmeister.com) provides a shared workspace for brainstorming and organizing ideas.

In each case, you aren't limited to sharing information and interaction only with those in your own organization or those who have access to your organization's computer network. Because they're web-based, these applications promote sharing and real-time collaboration across organizational boundaries. Many of them also provide new ways to access information created within the applications. For example, some online spreadsheets provide RSS feeds as output and some project management applications offer reminders via email, instant message, or text message.

Introduce new tools slowly and watch to see people's reactions. You might want to wait until you have a lull in deadline work to try one out; right before a major demo to your CEO or most important customer is probably not the right time. And be aware that these tools change often, may go offline with no notice, and may not offer the privacy and security your company requires.

Virtual meetings a.k.a. conference calls

When the team's distributed, it doesn't mean meetings are unnecessary, though if you stay in regular contact with instant messaging and other semi-synchronous channels you can get a lot done without them. When you do need to have one, you'll probably arrange for a conference call.

Meeting using a conference call instead of a conference room presents its own challenge. Here are all the things you'll need to know for ensuring those you organize run smoothly and for getting the most out of those you attend.

Set up the dial-in

If you're leading the call, it's your job to make it easy on the people calling in by setting up a dial-in or otherwise getting everyone together on the phone. You can use a variety of online services including foonz, FreeConference.com, and LiveOffice. These services and others like them allow you to set up a conference dial-in for free, but long distance charges will apply. They also provide premium services such as toll-free numbers for US and Canadian callers.

You can try VoIP if all the callers are internet-savvy. Skype, Gizmo, and other voice over IP services provide a completely free alternative for conference calls if all your attendees are equipped with the software and hardware required to make the call. For those who don't have VoIP capabilities, you can always use the call-out service, usually at a reasonable cost.

Or you can use your phone's flash button for a three-way call. If your landline service supports three-way calling, you can use the flash button to put your first caller on hold, dial another person, and hit "flash" again to join parties together. This is handy for small spur-of-the-moment calls.

Preparing for the call

Consider distributing an agenda. If your conference call is a one-off meeting to discuss a specific subject, you may not need one. But if you are running a regularly scheduled call, it's helpful to have an agenda so that the meeting doesn't devolve into idle chitchat or witty banter at the expense of covering important topics.

You might want to use a headset for conference calls. A decent speakerphone might be all you need for your conference calls, but a headset with microphone that plugs into your phone (or into your computer if you're using VoIP) provides some great benefits. It keeps other people from hearing the other side of your phone conversation, overrides the annoying mute button beep that so many cheap speakerphones make, and eliminates the speakerphone cave effect.

If you're the conference organizer, you'll probably need to arrange for a web conferencing setup to share presentations or desktop demos. Adobe Acrobat Connect gets good marks for its flexibility and ease of use, but there are many options to choose from including GoToMeeting, Microsoft Office Live Meeting, and WebEx. You might want to check out Glance at glance.net. It's simple and reliable, though it doesn't offer comprehensive collaboration features.

You might want to record the call, for archive purposes or to turn it into a podcast. If you've got some interesting people on the phone who are willing to go on record with their opinions, it's not too hard to record it and then publish it for everyone on the Internet to listen and learn. Or maybe you might need to refer to it again yourself, so a recording would come in handy. Of course, you'll need to get everyone's permission before recording it.

Dialing in etiquette

Whether you're the leader or just an attendee, you should dial in on time. Be careful of other people's time, and get on that call when you said you would. If you have to be late for some reason, IM or email another participant if possible and give them an estimated time for when you'll be on.

Identify yourself when you get on the call. No, you don't have to actually say your name if the conference calling service demands it—in fact, you might not want to, because some of those same services will replay your name if you want to surreptitiously hang up. But do announce yourself upon joining, as soon as there's a break in the chitchat or someone asks, "Who just joined?"

State up front if you'll be getting off the call early. That way you don't have to interrupt the call if everyone's heatedly discussing some important topic. It will also give the organizer a chance to make sure any topics needing your input can be addressed before you have to hang up.

Get the call going

If you're the leader, especially of a regularly-scheduled conference call, make it a habit to start on time. Stragglers will soon learn they should be on time if they want to know what's going on. You can even give participants forewarning of your punctuality in the email invite to the call: tell them "the conference call is scheduled for 10 AM and begins promptly at 10:02." Then keep your word.

Know when you should cancel and reschedule due to no-shows. Ten minutes is reasonable unless the person in question is very important. Ideally, shoot off a quick email or IM to the laggard and see if they're still planning to attend. You should probably stay on the call for the fully-scheduled time and perhaps even longer if you're waiting for the CEO of a Fortune 500 company.

Before launching into discussion, review the purpose, agenda, and duration of the meeting. This keeps the meeting focused and notifies the attendees that you care about staying on track.

Use the mute button appropriately and judiciously

How could we live without a mute button? But it's not entirely a good thing either. If everyone's on mute while one person is talking, the presenter might not get any feedback in the form of "mmm hmmm" or "that's right" because everyone's just nodding their heads... mutely.

Be careful what you say even when using the mute button. It's so important to have a mute indicator on your phone or headset because before you yell at your spouse or say something cynical about one coworker to another, you need to know that phone is on mute. Better yet, try to avoid saying anything even on mute that you'd be embarrassed to have heard. It may not be worth the risk.

Be productive and focused during the call

If you're on the call as a sort of "just-in-case" advisor as opposed to being a central participant, you'll want to find something to do that allows you to keep track of the conversation while moving your own projects forward.

Have a ready-made excuse in case you do get distracted. You are checking your email, aren't you? And you don't know what they're talking about when they asked for your opinion.

Be ready with a likely-sounding excuse. "My secretary just came in and asked me something" is not very believable for the home-based web worker but it might work for a corporate attorney. How about, "I had to pick up an urgent call on my cell phone" or "Sorry, I was just looking up a blog post that I thought would be relevant to the discussion." And then add, "What did you want my comment on?"

If you do find yourself daydreaming and losing track of the discussion, try taking notes. I use a simple text editor. Some people like to do mind mapping. Pen and paper can be fun, if you like the tactile sensation of writing and the ability to doodle, though doodling can be distracting too.

Use instant messaging as a backchannel

It's not rude to instant message your colleagues while on a call. It can be a good way of checking out things before saying them (if you're a subordinate member of the team) and also a way of letting the organizer or the person who talks the most know that you want to say something.

Don't use a "clicky" keyboard if you're going to IM during the meeting. Sometimes you'll need to use the backchannel and talk at the same time. If your keyboard is too loud people will hear you typing, which is not ideal (though it's not necessarily rude either, because taking notes during a call is always acceptable).

Getting the most out of the meeting

Don't be afraid of interrupting. The conversational dynamic of conference calls can be difficult, lacking as it is in body language cues as to who wants to talk or who might have some disagreement with what's being said. Though ideally discussion will take place with regular turn-taking you'll sometimes have to talk over people to make your point. Wait for a pause, if you can, but if the discussion is moving on, speak up—add an "excuse me" if you need to—and make sure your mute button is off, or you'll feel really frustrated.

Know when to take things offline. If a particular discussion goes off on a tangent or gets heated up with emotion, suggest that it be dealt with in a separate call or meeting. This is especially important when there are people on the call who aren't interested in whatever tangent or conflict has come up. Don't waste their time.

Closing the call

Close with a summary of action items. If the conference leader doesn't do this and you are a bold sort, you might want to summarize what happens next before everyone hangs up.

And finally, follow up. If you might want to connect with these people in the future, send a quick thank you note or ask a clarification question after the conference call to make the relationship more real.

Finding your inner schmoozer

> *The biggest mistake is believing there is one right way to listen, to talk, to have a conversation—or a relationship.*
>
> —*Deborah Tannen*

No longer is networking and schmoozing required only of salespeople and politicians. In the web age, everyone must build a social network in order to succeed. Fortunately, with web-based tools it's never been easier or more rewarding. You're not limited to interacting just with those close to you geographically or by virtue of profession. You can use the tools and techniques that suit your temperament. And you can do it from almost anywhere you want.

Remember those are people out there

A hazard of focusing solely on professional networking is you might start to think of the network as the important thing and think of only what it can do for you. Don't be a user. The social web is about fully-formed people coming online, and that means fully formed human relationships between people too.

Be sure you connect on a human level. Here's how.

Use social communications to strengthen relationships

Use instant messaging, status updaters, chat rooms, email, text messaging, phone calls, and face-to-face meetings to bond with people. Facebook and other networks will show you when a connection has an upcoming birthday or other special event. Don't be afraid to connect with people on a personal level, even if they are a work connection.

Don't look to connect just because someone can do something for you

Look for people that you want to associate with. You can find them by blogging about topics important to you, joining groups on social networks that appeal to you, and so forth. Build up a network of people you genuinely like—mutual support and assistance flows out of that. Ask yourself: If this person were in town for the weekend, would I invite them to dinner? If the answer is yes, that's a good sign you should pursue the relationship.

Sheer numbers are not important as diversity and depth of connections

It's easy to get caught up in the contact count since so many online social sites display it prominently. But the most useful and satisfying social network isn't always the biggest one. Don't pay too much attention to how many contacts you have.

Seek to understand people three dimensionally

Many people work online using a variety of channels and platforms so you can get to know them in more than one way. Take advantage of this to know them as people. If there's someone you want to get to know better, read their blog and check out their Flickr pictures, if they have those. Follow them on Twitter or befriend them on Facebook. If they share any of their work online, become familiar with it.

COMMUNICATIONS PREFERENCES

Pay attention to how your contacts like to be reached. Some people publish their contact preferences online. For example, see Sean Bonner's preferences at `http://seanbonner.pbwiki.com/PreferedMeansOfContact` and Tantek Çelik's communications protocols at `http://tantek.pbwiki.com/CommunicationProtocols`.

Most people, however, don't publish preferences so you have to pay attention to what they do and use some common sense:

- **Email is always a reasonable first try for contacting someone you haven't already met.** Keep your email polite but brief. You don't need to give out your life story.
- **If someone replies to your email with a very short response, it doesn't mean they're rude.** It may mean they receive a lot of email. Tailor your emails accordingly; make them short and to the point. If they don't respond, and you don't already have a business relationship with them, don't send them more email asking "did you get my email?" Try another contact method or assume that they are not interested in communicating with you and move on. Alternatively, try again a few weeks later. You may have reached them at a bad time.
- **If someone publishes a bunch of IM accounts on their blog, it may mean they live in IM.** Give that a try, but don't feel bad if they don't respond. You may need to make yourself known to them by other channels before they feel comfortable chatting with you by IM.
- **Use the conversational power of blogs.** If you want to get someone's attention without going through email or IM, you can leave a comment on their blog, if they have one, or write about them on your own blog. Realize, however, that it takes time to get to know people this way. One comment does not a relationship make.
- **If the person you're trying to reach is a celebrity of sorts, you might want to have a mutual friend introduce you.** Email introductions work well for this sort of thing. LinkedIn offers specific support for getting introduced to a friend-of-a-friend.

Present yourself authentically

You need to balance authenticity with privacy and caution, of course, but the more you can show who you really are, the more you can connect with people in a genuine and sincere way.

Pay attention to other's preferences

Especially with those you work with closely, you can learn a lot about how a person likes to work even if you're working out of different places. You can understand their daily rhythms, see how they like to communicate, and get a sense of the up and downs of their moods. Tune your communications and interactions to that.

Don't be afraid to say you're sorry

There will be times that you will type without thinking and you may type or say something that hurts someone else's feelings. Don't be afraid to admit when you've been wrong, and apologize just as you would if you hurt someone "in real life."

Tools for managing your relationships and your network

Managing all your contact data can be a major hassle, especially if you get good at expanding your professional network. You have a variety of tools at your disposal; the main problem is getting them all to work together.

In addition to recording contact data like email addresses and mobile phone numbers, you will probably want to make your own contact information available online in a way that people can find you yet still protect information that needs protecting. This may take the form of multiple accounts on different services. You might use LinkedIn to reach one set of people while using Facebook to reach another set. The varying professional and social networking services attract different types of people, so to make your professional network as effective as possible, don't limit yourself to just one.

Some tasks you'll want to accomplish include these:

- Store contact information so you can reach people
- Keep track of interactions you've had with people

- Maintain a task list of people you need to call or email or otherwise get in touch with
- Make yourself available for other people to find you
- Publish your contact information and possibly your communications preferences
- Join into services that allow for social grooming and bonding

Table 6-1 shows some tools you may wish to use as part of an overall network, relationship, and contact management approach.

Table 6-1: Contact and relationship management solutions

Tool	Description
LinkedIn	Professional networking tool that allows you to record your professional relationships and find "friends of friends" in order to be introduced. You can also ask questions of your network and recommend people for professional work.
Plaxo	Online address book that syncs with many email contact managers and your mobile phone. Provides auto-update of contact information for people in the network and aggregates social networking updates.
Xing	Professional networking platform with contact management capabilities.
Facebook	Social networking platform for presenting yourself as a 360-degree human being and getting to know others as full people.
Twitter	Status updater that provides for lightweight social interaction with your professional and personal contacts.
Email contact management	Store your contact information in your email client, whether it's web or desktop based.
BigContacts	Another online contact management solution; includes support for shared contacts for work teams.
Highrise	Customer relationship management brought to individuals and small workgroups. Contact management plus tasks by contact plus history of interactions.
Pen and paper	Store your contact information offline, in a paper notebook or on index cards.

Network science for nonscientists

> *The world is shrinking because social links that would have died out a hundred years ago are kept alive and can be easily activated.*

> —*Albert-László Barabási*

Physicists, social scientists, and mathematicians have been studying social networks and coming up with all sorts of interesting results that have practical importance for how you conduct your professional networking online. You don't have to have a Ph.D. in network science, though, to put these results into action in your own professional life. Popular science books like *Six Degrees: The Science of a Connected Age* by Duncan J. Watts, *Linked: How Everything is Connected to Everything Else and What it Means* by Albert-Laszlo Barabasi, and *Smart World: Breakthrough Creativity and the New Science of Ideas* by Richard Ogle present recent theories and findings in network science for a general audience. If you want to thoroughly understand this new way of thinking, you'll want to pick up those books.

If, however, you just want a quick primer on what this means for your work life and your professional networking, you can find that here.

Social networks in the web age

Understand these nine basic concepts in how networks work and you'll be ready to do some advanced professional networking:

- **Homophily.** People like to hang out with others who are similar to themselves.
- **Clustering.** Homophily leads humans to cluster into groups of people similar to one another.
- **Multi-dimensional identities.** But people have many ways of being similar to one another.
- **Small worlds.** Multiple identities allow networks of people to show both clustering and smallness (that is, short paths of only a few intermediate relationships between people).

- **Innovation through cross-pollination**. Innovation occurs not when one genius comes up with a never-before-conceived idea but rather when ideas and patterns are translated and applied from one domain to another.
- **Stagnation**. Clusters can be too connected. If people in a cluster associate mainly with other people from the cluster and align their thinking to one another, new ideas can't diffuse in.
- **Dilution**. Clusters can be underconnected, lacking enough relationships to diffuse ideas and thinking and professional support.
- **Social problem-solving**. Problem-solving under uncertainty and ambiguity can be undertaken with local social search and social problem-solving.
- **Weak ties**. Some of the most important help you'll get when you're trying to achieve some goal in your work life will come not from people you know well but rather from casual acquaintances and friends of friends—people with whom you have weak ties.

In the following sections, I go into more detail on each of these, describing what practical impact they might have on your own networking activities.

Homophily

Homophily means that people like to hang out with people like themselves. You'll probably seek out people like yourself to work and socialize with. You'll tend to spend time with people who are similar to you demographically, because you'll come into contact with them most frequently. Children are grouped by age level in school. Adults tend to do activities with others of their same age and economic status.

Homophily can make the world seem more homogeneous to you than it actually is. Because most of the people you spend time with are similar to you in some way, you will have more exposure to those like you than those unlike you. All other things equal, you will not be regularly exposed to ideas radically different than your own.

Homophily can be a source of connection and a source of stagnation. It's a source of connection because it allows you to find people with whom to work and socialize. It can be a source of stagnation if it means you don't expose your thinking and your work to different opinions and perspectives and information.

Clustering

Homophily leads to clusters of people who know each other. For example, I work within a cluster of people who blog about enterprise software development. Many of us know each other or at least know of each other.

The principle of clustering means that if you know one person in a cluster, you are very likely to know or be able to be introduced to someone else in that cluster.

Within a cluster, information and ideas are shared and in many cases opinions become aligned to a certain way of thinking. The clusters to which you belong do some of your thinking for you, which can be both good and bad. It's good, in that you don't have to come up with frameworks of thought all by yourself. It's bad if it keeps you from seeing other ways of thinking that might bring you more success and progress.

Multi-dimensional identities

Your multi-dimensional identity means that you can be a part of many clusters at once. You can be similar to people demographically or geographically; by virtue of group affiliations, political beliefs, or religious practice; through your professional work or personal hobbies; and on and on. You belong to more than one cluster.

So even if you find one cluster stagnant in its thinking or approach, you always can connect with other clusters. Your homophily need not be a source of staleness if you are willing to connect along other dimensions of your identity.

For example, you might be professionally interested in social media online while pursuing knitting as a hobby. You might find that connecting with people on knitting blogs brings a whole new perspective to your social media work because many of the knitters come from an entirely different background and can share new ideas that might be relevant to social media.

Small worlds

Big worlds are made small by multi-dimensional people joining with clusters along their many dimensions. If each person only joined one cluster, the clusters would be isolated from each other. But people join many clusters and so we don't fragment into independent caves ignorant of each other.

The small-worlds principle is sometimes called "six degrees of separation" which says that each person in the world is within six steps of every other person in the world. Whether the number is six or something else, this idea has been shown to have some basis in both empirical results and theory.

What does this mean for you? It says that you make the world a smaller and perhaps more collaborative place when you join into different clusters based on your multi-dimensional identity. Diffusion of innovation and the practice of collaboration benefits from your creation of short paths between different people in a small-world network.

Innovation through cross-pollination

Creative and innovative value lies in translating ideas and assistance across different clusters: this is sometimes known as *brokerage* but can also be thought of as cross-pollination. Its opposite *closure* occurs when many people in a cluster interact regularly and align their thinking and ideas with each other. Brokerage occurs when people bring new ideas from one cluster to another. Innovation usually occurs when ideas or patterns are transferred from one cluster to another during brokerage.

If you want to find creativity and innovation, find new clusters to join by exploring your many dimensions of identity. Practice brokerage as much as you practice closure.

Stagnation

Networks can be too highly connected, leading to stagnation. If everyone in a particular cluster is associated only with people from that cluster and inter-act mainly with people from that cluster, new ideas can't diffuse in. Network science suggests that hubs with high numbers of connections are highly unlikely to be influenced, because each relationship they have means very little to them. When hubs in clusters can't be influenced and everyone only rein-forces each other's thinking, new ideas are never given a chance. This can lead to stagnation.

If you want to bring fresh ideas, seek clusters that aren't overconnected and closed. For example, the blog community tracking Web 2.0 startups is so connected that it's very hard for a new web startup to get much meaningful attention. If you have a shiny new web service that you'd like to make a splash with, you might be better off looking to some other community. You could introduce your service as a vertical offering targeted at a specific industry, thereby reaching a community that is more susceptible to new ideas and new services.

Dilution

Networks can suffer a dearth of connectivity, leaving too few relationships for ideas and information and support to move. Clusters without adequate numbers of relationships and people will be ineffective in making anything happen.

If you want to spread fresh ideas or make progress using your professional network, seek clusters that have enough connectivity.

Social problem-solving

Ambiguity and uncertainty demand navigation and search on social networks, because you don't know who might have access to the information or ideas you need.

In times of uncertainty and ambiguity and change, check with the different communities to which you belong for help. Don't focus only on the cluster in which the problem arose.

Weak ties

You might think that your best help will come from people you know best, but empirical research and theory in sociology suggests otherwise. In the seventies, sociologist Mark Granovetter suggested that weak ties between people (casual acquaintanceship and friends of a friend relationships) enable access to opportunities and possibilities that otherwise wouldn't be available.*

When engaging in social problem-solving such as creating a successful business or finding a new job or solving a thorny problem at work, your ability to navigate weak ties leading to a variety of clusters is crucial. Keep in mind the necessity both of having the weak ties available and of taking advantage of them when you need to. Activate weak ties to find new opportunities, stretch your thinking, and exchange the professional support that makes web work successful and satisfying.

---

*Mark Granovetter, "The Strength of Weak Ties", *American Journal of Sociology*, Vol. 78, Issue 6 (1974), available at http://www.stanford.edu/dept/soc/people/faculty/granovetter/documents/TheStrengthofWeakTies.pdf.

PRACTICAL NETWORK SCIENCE IN SHORT

Boiled down into the practical, here's what the new network science says you should do to take best advantage of your professional network:

- **Connect to other people based on multiple facets of your identity, not just based on profession or geography.**
- **Look for innovative ideas in domains other than where you're trying to innovate.** Think brokerage or cross-pollination.
- **If you want to disseminate new ideas, choose domains that are just connected enough.**
- **Use social problem solving to deal with situations of uncertainty or ambiguity.** Consult your social network for help; don't try to solve something all on your own.
- **Look to friends of friends and casual acquaintances in your social problem-solving.** Because they connect you into new clusters, they are the source of rich opportunity.

Looking forward: Going mobile with web work

Web work promises the ability to work from almost anywhere you want. Charge up your mobile phone, put your laptop in its bag, and let's get moving.

7 Go Mobile

Today's workers are connected all the time, checking email from their smart phones, calling anyone and everyone, talking loudly and bothering everyone around them, right? They're working from cafés or airports or hotels or their cars, right? They're hypermobile, right?

Not necessarily. Most people don't do much work on the go, even web workers. Though web workers may be hyperconnected by the Internet they're not necessarily hypermobile. Many work in just one or two places: maybe an employer's cubicle and their own home office, for example.

And, despite the media's fascination with Blackberry addiction and Blackberry thumbs, the vast majority of mobile phone users around the world use a "feature phone"—that is, a basic cell phone optimized mainly for voice and text messaging. Most people don't have vast numbers of contacts on their phones; they use them only to communicate with a select few relatives, close friends, and key coworkers.

Of course, you may be one of those who have mastered mobile work, carrying a smart phone that gives you high-powered email and web browsing wherever you are, knowing exactly what to carry in your laptop bag, and jumping online whenever and wherever you need to.

Mobile guru or not, you'll get out of your usual workplace at least occasionally. The web hasn't removed the necessity of meeting face to face or of traveling long distance to do so. You need to know how to work effectively and comfortably when away from your home base, whether it's a real home or not. That's what this chapter is about: staying productive and connected while you're on the go.

You'll read about what you need to know when you're away from your usual workplace:

- **Bagging it.** Choose a laptop bag and fill it up with the gadgets and supplies you need.
- **Online and in touch, whenever and wherever.** Find Internet access on the road and use it safely and securely.
- **Let's get this phone on the road.** Choose and use a cell phone that suits your mobile needs. Learn about text messaging and mobile web apps that you might like to use.
- **Real life rendezvous.** Is meeting face to face necessary for virtual teams and remote partnerships? Maybe. Make the most of your in-person time, whether at a worksite, a conference, or other meeting.

Bagging it

Travel and change of place impart new vigor to the mind.

—Seneca

Getting out of the house so you can work somewhere else sometimes feels as hard as getting ready to leave when you have a baby. Just like with a baby, you need a big bag. Just like with a baby, you need equipment and hygiene supplies and maybe even some food and drink. Just like with a baby, you need to be prepared to handle the unexpected whether it's a lack of power, an urgent request from a coworker, or a serendipitous meeting with someone you might like to work with in the future.

In Chapter 2, you read about choosing a laptop. Now you'll find out what else you need and how to carry it all around.

Choosing a laptop bag

If you're out and about regularly, you need a good laptop bag. It's got to be the right size: big enough for your laptop and everything you want to put in it but not so big you can't maneuver while you're carrying it. It needs to be comfortable to carry. It needs to look good too.

You might choose from four main styles: messenger bag, briefcase, backpack, or tote. Most men in professions with casual dress (software development, web design, and writing for example) choose messenger bag style. It's conveniently easy to carry without making you look like a grad student, as a backpack might.

Women have more choices available to them. A backpack keeps you from knocking someone in the head as you maneuver through a plane aisle or a crowded coffee house, but it looks very casual for better or worse. Messenger bags offer convenient carrying with a more formal look than a backpack. A tote bag fits easily under your arm but maybe you want to carry your purse that way instead.

If you will be traveling by airplane regularly, consider the size of the bag carefully. Some bags won't fit beneath the seat in front of you, and if you like to keep it there for easy access during the flight, you'll want one small enough to fit.

When choosing a material, think of how formal you want to look. Leather is attractive but might seem overly professional in many settings; many men choose heavy-duty nylon instead. Women can choose from a variety of attractive fabrics such as pretty jacquards or colorful cotton prints. These fabrics, however, probably won't be as durable as ballistic nylon.

You may want to look for the following:

- **Laptop sleeve.** You don't want your machine sliding all around inside the bag. Look for a padded compartment with a strap or zipper to hold your computer in place. If the bag you want to carry doesn't come with one, you can always buy a separate sleeve, which has the added benefit of slipping out easily if you need to remove your laptop when going through airport security.
- **Specialized compartments.** You might like a magnetically-closing pocket on the outside that gives you easy access to pens, business cards, plane tickets, and other things you need to get to without unzipping the whole bag.
- **Luggage attachment.** It's nice to hook your bag onto your rollable suitcase if you travel a lot. Some laptop bags come with straps and connectors that make it easy.
- **Room for power cord and additional hardware.** If you can, try out the bag beforehand to see how your laptop plus extra hardware fits in. You might have trouble squeezing in the humongous power brick on the cord or an extra battery. But you can't leave home without that! You may also want to allow room to carry an iPod, external hard drive, portable speakers, and so forth.

BUYING A BAG ONLINE

It's a bit risky to buy a bag online; you can't try it on to see how it looks, touch the fabric to see if you like it, or stick your laptop in to ensure it fits. But you'll find a great selection online and you can get it ordered during your workday.

If you love to shop online and are looking for a laptop bag, check these online stores:

- eBags (ebags.com) has the widest selection along with user reviews.
- Timbuk2 (timbuk2.com) allows you to design your own messenger bag or backpack.
- Kolobags (kolobags.com) has a nicely selected set of designer laptop bags categorized conveniently by color, laptop size, style, and brands.

For more on choosing a laptop bag, see Web Worker Daily's posts at `http://www.webworkerdaily.com/2007/01/10/in-search-of-the-perfect-bag/` and `http://www.webworkerdaily.com/2007/03/06/in-search-of-a-perfect-laptop-bag-womens-edition/`.

What to pack

Whether you're going away from your regular workspace for a couple hours or a couple days, make sure you're equipped.

Mobile phone

Even more important than your laptop, your cell phone offers you a lightweight and easy connection to your online work. Even if you don't have a smart phone, you can accomplish a lot more than just making phone calls. Most mobile phones today support basic web browsing and text messaging; between these two you can get quite a bit of work done without getting out your laptop. Later on in this chapter, you'll read about choosing and using your phone to get work done on the road.

Laptop or ultraportable

Still, if you're going on a business trip or spending the day working at a café, you'll want your laptop with you. Make sure to bring your power cord or an extra battery. If you're not handy with your touchpad or other pointing device, bring a mini-mouse along.

Also, consider bringing your system restore or other emergency boot CD. If you power up the computer and get a blue screen or other error, you'll want to be able to troubleshoot. Make sure you have the computer's help line number in your cell phone, just in case you need to call in for support.

Headphones

Headphones serve two purposes: letting you listen to what you want while blocking out noise you don't want to hear. If you travel regularly or like to work in busy wifi cafés, invest in a good pair of noise-canceling or noise-reducing headphones. You might like a stereo microphone headset that can allow you to listen to music and take calls via VoIP, which can be easier than using your cell phone in public.

Camera

You never know when you might run into someone you'd like to capture for your online photo account or when you might see the perfect sign to turn into a banner on your blog. If your phone has a decent camera, that might be all you need, but if you're into photography, take a nicer camera with you.

Toiletries

Three cups of coffee and no food could make your breath smell terrible. Bring a toothbrush, toothpaste, and mints with you on the road. And since you'll be seeing people in person rather than online, you might need some other beauty or handsomeness support as well. Bring a comb, hairspray, lipstick or lip balm, and whatever you need to present yourself at your best. Screen and disinfecting wipes can keep your computer hygienic too.

Pen, paper, and printed reading material

Don't assume you'll have an Internet connection or get a cell signal every-where you go. Bring a book, magazine, or printed documents to review. Carry a notebook so you can jot down reminders of things you need to do or ideas that come to you.

Online and in touch, whenever and wherever

Television is not real life. In real life people actually have to leave the coffee shop and go to jobs.

—*Charles Sykes*

In his book *Dumbing Down Our Kids*, Charles Sykes said people have to leave the coffee shop to go to their jobs, but he didn't foresee the rise of the digital Bedouin class, working wherever they can find a good cup of joe and a decent Internet connection. Now you don't have to leave the coffee shop to get to your job. You can work from almost anywhere... a café, an airport, a hotel, your house, or the nearest park, for example.

But you do need to find an Internet connection to get your work done. Find a good spot to work, plug into the Internet, and you're set.

Choosing a good spot to work

Sometimes you need to get out of the house or the cubicle. Or maybe you're on a business trip. Whatever the reason, you need to find an alternate spot to work. What should you look for?

- **Internet access.** Ideally free or already paid for.
- **A power outlet.** Look for one before you need it because when you start to run low on juice, all the seats close to one might have been taken.
- **The right noise level.** This varies by person, because some people like to work with lots of ambient noise while others prefer total quiet. If you bring your noise-canceling headset along, then any place might work for you. Light levels matter too; some cafes are too dark to read printed material comfortably.
- **A sturdy table to work on.** Yes, you can balance your laptop on your legs, but if you're working for a significant period of time, you'll want something more comfortable. If you use an external mouse, you'll need room for that.

- **Screen viewability.** That means not too much sunlight, or some way of seeing your screen even if there is. Web Worker Daily's Mike Gunderloy offers a few tips for working outside at `http://www .webworkerdaily.com/2007/07/17/how-to-use-your-laptop-outside/`.
- **Food and drink.** But don't spill your coffee into your laptop keyboard.
- **Easily accessible bathrooms.** Some cafés require you get a key from the barista. Think about whether you can trust another patron or employee to watch your stuff while you take a break, otherwise you may have to pack everything up, possibly losing your seat.

If you do visit the same café every day, treating it as your regular office, be sure to buy more than just a small cup of coffee when you visit. Buy meals, tip generously, and talk the place up to your friends. If the coffee house owners are giving you Internet access, a place to sit, and electrical power you need to repay them by being a good customer. You may not be able to deduct these costs on your taxes (though if you have the nerve, go for it and establish a precedent for the rest of us web workers), but it's the right thing to do anyway.

Also, be respectful of other people in the café. Don't speak too loudly while on the phone, take up multiple tables to spread out paperwork and equipment, or hog the power outlets for eight hours every day.

Finding free hot spots

You can buy a cheap wifi detector that might help you find the strongest signal in a café, but that assumes you already know where you want to work. How do you know where to find wireless Internet access? And better yet, how do you know where to get it free?

Many cafés offer free wifi in order to compete with Starbucks, which at this time offers wifi by daily fee or monthly subscription through T-Mobile. Some public libraries offer free access also. Check Table 7-1 for resources for finding wifi hotspots near you and see Judi's article "Franchises that are the Web Worker's Best Friend" at `http://www.webworkerdaily.com/2007/06/19/franchises-that-are-the-web-workers-best-friend/` for more ideas of where to go.

Table 7-1: Ways to find wifi

Service	URL	Notes
JiWire wifi directory and hotspot finder	jiwire.com	Search for hotspots using location.
Hotspotr community-driven directory	hotspotr.com	Search by city or zip code. Includes reviews and ratings.
Forbes wipod wifi field guide	forbes.anchorfree.com/wipod/	Download list of hotspots in your state into your iPod notes.
4INFO text message search	4info.net	Text "wifi <your zip code>" to 4INFO (44636).

If you're looking for wifi right near you, you can find it in a number of ways. You can buy hardware wifi detectors for less than thirty dollars so you don't even have to open your laptop. On your computer, you might want to install a utility like NetStumbler (netstumbler.com) for Windows, WiFi Radar for Linux (wifi-radar.systemimager.org), or the Mac dashboard utility AirTrafficControl (http://www.apple.com/downloads/dashboard/networking_security/airtrafficcontrol.html). These utilities make it easier to see what wireless networks are available, where the signal strength is strongest, and whether you need to enter a password to get on the network or not.

THE CELLULAR SOLUTION *If you're on the go regularly and you have the money, you might want to look into cellular broadband (for example, Verizon EVDO or AT&T 3G) for your Internet access. You'll have to pay a steep monthly fee in addition to your voice contract, but this can give you much wider coverage than relying on wifi hotspots. You can either use your phone as a modem (tethering it with hardware or wireless technology like Bluetooth) or buy a dedicated cellular broadband card.*

STAY SAFE WHILE OUT AND ONLINE

Most wifi hotspots you use at cafés don't use any encryption. That means much of the information going to and from your web browser is sent in clear text. A criminal could intercept the traffic and get sensitive data like your usernames and passwords. Or he could see the instant messages, emails, and online documents you're using for communication and collaboration.

How can you protect yourself? Take these steps.

1. **Make sure you're connected to the right access point.** Check with the barista to see what SSID (access point name) you should be using. Bad guys can set up their own wifi hotspots and track everything you do.

2. **If you have to enter a password to connect to the hotspot, it means the hotspot is using some sort of encryption.** Of the two basic types, WPA is far preferred as WEP can be easily decrypted. The vast majority of public hotspots, however, don't use anything. Note that using a T-Mobile hotspot doesn't require you to enter a password to connect to the hotspot but prompts you for a login before you can actually surf the web; this is different, and doesn't mean that your surfing is encrypted.

3. **Use encrypted versions of web sites, where available.** You know a web page is using encryption via secure sockets layer (SSL) if the URL starts with "https://" instead of "http://"—but not every site offers a secure connection and those that do may not advertise them very well, given it requires more work for their servers to handle SSL traffic.

   Be aware that as of this writing, Google's Gmail only uses SSL for login and not for your incoming and outgoing email. If you don't want your email getting sent out in clear text, use the CustomizeGoogle add-on for Firefox (customizegoogle.com), which allows you to use SSL for all Gmail traffic. Or just make sure each time you access Gmail, you put "https://" before the address. Other web mail like Yahoo! and Hotmail only uses SSL for login, not for sending and receiving your email.

STAY SAFE WHILE OUT AND ONLINE *(continued)*

4. If you use desktop email via IMAP or POP3 and SMTP, make sure your email provider supports SSL or other encryption for both sending and receiving email. Your email may contain information you don't want to become public, like usernames and passwords for web application accounts.

5. Don't enter usernames, passwords, or other sensitive information over http:// links. If you must, think about using a virtual private network solution to encrypt all your network traffic (see how below).

6. Protect your instant messages. IM aggregators like Trillian, Pidgin, and Adium support encryption. You'll probably need to enable it, though, so if you're concerned about other people seeing your instant messaging, turn it on.

7. Configure your firewall software to disallow unwanted incoming connections—like file sharing—which could allow access to your hard drive. The built-in firewall in Mac OS X does a good job. As of the beginning of 2007, many experts recommended against relying on the basic firewall in Windows Vista, so you may want to look at a third-party alternative such as ZoneAlarm Internet Security Suite or Norton Internet Security 2007.

If you still feel unprotected—and if you regularly deal in sensitive information over public wifi—think about using virtual private network software to encrypt all your network traffic. Most larger companies use VPNs to protect employees' network traffic, but you don't have to work for a big company to use one. And even if your company offers one, it may not encrypt traffic that doesn't involve your company's network (for example, your personal web mail traffic).

See Web Worker Daily's two-part series by Samuel Dean on free and low-cost VPNs that individuals can use at http://www.webworkerdaily.com/2007/08/17/free-vpn-solutions-for-securing-your-public-wi-fi-sessions/ and http://www.webworkerdaily.com/2007/08/15/keeping-your-public-wi-fi-sessions-secure/.

Let's get this phone on the road

Tell me about yourself—your struggles, your dreams, your telephone number.

—Peter Arno

For some people, the mobile phone is a lifeline. For others, it's a necessity but by no means the main way of reaching people. Consider what kind of phone suits you and how you should use it for maximum effectiveness.

Choosing a phone

Since you'll probably use your phone for both work and personal needs, you need to think about your overall lifestyle when choosing one. Some people need a high degree of connectivity. Some people only use their phone occasionally. Some people want an all-in-one device to minimize weight and inconvenience. Some people choose two devices: a feature phone for easy calling and texting along with a smart phone for email and web browsing.

THE HYPERMOBILITY MYTH *Swisscom researcher Stefana Broadbent says research shows that mobile workers communicate on the road but do the bulk of their work back at their desks. See* `http://www.economist.com/printedition/displayStory.cfm?story_id=9249302` *for more.*

You have many choices in mobile phones, but you can simplify the process of choosing by thinking of them in just three categories:

- **Feature phone.** This is any phone without smart phone or PDA capabilities and is ideal if you use your phone mainly for phone calls and text messages. Many support limited web browsing. Most run third-party applications via the Java platform, though Verizon Wireless phones use BREW instead. You'll usually find these as candybar, flip, or slider-style models.
- **Business-oriented smart phone.** This is the choice for people who need to stay in close touch with work while on the go. These smart phones provide convenient access to email, calendaring,

and more advanced web browsing than you'll get on a feature phone. Blackberries fall into this category, as do Treos and phones that run Windows Mobile.

- **Consumer-oriented smart phone.** Although other handset makers have aimed smart phones at the consumer set, the iPhone has received the most attention and hype. These devices are not necessarily good for access to corporate email, but provide solid web browsing and multi-media playing features. Others in this category include the Blackberry Pearl and the Palm Centro.

Locked and unlocked cell phones

In the United States, most phones are "locked," meaning they will only work with one wireless carrier. This is in contrast to the cell phone market in other parts of the world such as Europe, where you can buy an unlocked cell phone and then swap the SIM cards (the small circuit board that identifies your phone to your carrier) depending on which wireless carrier you use. Phones are usually sold locked in the U.S. because carriers subsidize the cost of the phones in return for getting your loyalty as a customer. Also, as in the case of the iPhone, there is profit for the phone manufacturer in their agreements with exclusive carriers. Of course, the carriers also ensure your loyalty by selling one or two-year contracts with hefty cancellation fees.

If you have a locked mobile phone, you likely won't be able to switch carriers and use the same phone. There are third-party services that will unlock phones for you and sometimes the wireless carriers will do it, but there's no guarantee it will work. Also, you may lose support from your carrier and phone manufacturer if you have your phone unlocked.

You might not need a smart phone

If you need access to email, especially corporate, while you're on the go (for example, you're a parent of kids with lots of after-school activities and you'd like to check in with your work while hanging out at soccer practice or tae kwon do) you'll probably want a smart phone. While basic feature phones do have some ability to check email, they're not usually suitable for composing anything but the simplest of messages.

If you don't need access to corporate email but would like to occasionally check into your web mail, you can do so from a web browser on your phone. It may already have one installed on it and all you have to do is activate it and start browsing. If you don't like the basic browser that comes on your phone, you may be able to use the Opera Mini browser, if your phone supports Java applications. Opera Mini, available at operamini.com, uses a remote server to modify and compress web page content so it suits mobile phones. Note that Verizon Wireless customers can't use it, because those phones run the BREW platform, not Java.

Check if your favorite sites offer mobile versions. For example, you can access Gmail optimized for mobile phones at m.gmail.com. Gmail also offers a downloadable Java client that makes doing your email on your phone even easier. Go to gmail.com/app to get it.

Be aware that your carrier may charge you airtime or data transfer charges for any web browsing you do from your phone, in addition to any monthly web access fees. These fees can add up fast; be sure to check with your carrier before doing any web browsing.

Choosing a smart phone

Smart phones run one of a number of operating systems: Windows Mobile, Blackberry, Symbian, Palm, a downsized version of Mac OS X, or Linux variants. Which suits you depends upon your need for access to corporate or web mail, your past history with smart phones and PDAs, your desktop computer if you plan to sync data, and whether your employer specifies what you should use.

Around the world, the Symbian operating system is most popular, but in the U.S., Windows Mobile and Blackberry rule. Windows Mobile is not as good as you might think at handling email, but it is strong in synchronizing data with your Windows PC and supports a wide range of third-party applications. Blackberry rules when it comes to email. The Palm operating system is easy to use and has many third-party applications available but may not be a viable contender long-term. Palm was the original smart phone OS so it has loyalty through legacy, but it's getting dated and has had limited success reinventing itself. The Treo devices made by Palm, the purveyor of the Palm OS, are now offered in Windows Mobile versions as well as Palm OS.

Linux appeals to mobile phone makers because it's free for them to use and offers a vast community of dedicated open source developers who could create applications. There are too many variants of mobile Linux, however, making it impossible to develop one mobile Linux application that runs on all the Linux smart phones.

Which smart phone you choose may be driven by your laptop operating system. Macs work best with Palm and iPhone right out of the box, but third party tools allow Windows Mobile and Blackberry handsets to also work well with Macs.

Some smart phones include wifi support, so if you're in range of a hotspot you can get much faster access to the Internet. Most also provide Bluetooth support for wireless accessories such as headsets. You might like to look for media playing capabilities, if you like to listen to music and watch videos, and a built-in camera.

A smart phone could replace a laptop, depending on how much work you do while on the go. They can read and work with Office and PDF files, store your calendar and task data, and let you take notes.

Text messaging

If you don't choose a smart phone or even if you do, you might want to take the time to learn how text messaging (also known as short message service, or SMS) could help you stay connected and productive on the go. With SMS, you can send and receive short text messages of 160 characters or less to and from your cell phone. This is a good way to keep in touch with colleagues and friends but you can do a lot more than that.

If you do decide to use text messaging, be sure to buy a text messaging bundle to go with your cell phone plan. Individual text messages might cost only 15 cents a piece, but if you start using them heavily, that can add up. On the other hand, a bundle of 250 for a month might cost just $5.00. Note that you will be charged for messages that you receive as well as the ones you send.

If you've never sent a text message, it can be a bit daunting your first time. It's not hard, but it may be unfamiliar. Give it a try anyway. You just use the "new text message" function on your phone, enter a mobile phone number with area code (for a person) or a short code (a sequence of five numbers to access an SMS service), and then type out your message.

QUICK PRODUCTIVITY WITH TEXT MESSAGES

You don't have to have a smart phone to stay productive while on the go. You don't even have to fire up your web browser. Warm up your thumbs and see what you can do with just a few 160-character messages.

- **Get quick shots of information.** You can get weather reports, locations of nearby wifi hotspots, stock quotes, directions, and more. Services like 4INFO (http://4info.net/howto/index.jsp?tag=fr_hp_btm_nav) and Google Mobile's SMS search (http://google.com/intl/en_us/mobile/sms/) make it easy. For example, text "wifi 80222" to 4INFO (44636) for hotspots in zip code 80222 or "flight UAL 696" to GOOGLE (466453) for United 696 flight status.
- **Add an item to your to-do list or calendar.** Set up a to-do list on Gubb (gubb.net) and you can add items by SMS. Add events to your 30Boxes (30boxes.com) or Google Calendar (calendar.google.com) by just texting the details to the short code, like "8/8 8am meet with John."
- **Check your daily agenda.** Google Calendar makes it easy to find out what's on your schedule. Text "next" to GVENT (48368) to get your next appointment, "day" to get that day's agenda, or "nday" to get tomorrow's agenda.
- **Remind yourself.** Online calendars will send you text message reminders of upcoming events. Remember the Milk to-do lists (rememberthemilk .com) will remind you by SMS too. You can also use a dedicated reminder service like PingMe (gopingme.com).
- **Read your voice mail.** Get the gist of a voicemail message by SMS, with CallWave's Vtxt service (http://www.callwave.com/widgets/ureg.aspx). You won't get an exact transcription—less important comments like "hello" and "ummmm" will be left out—but that keeps the message down to about the size of a text message.
- **Get email by text message.** All the carriers offer email gateways to SMS; check the list at http://www.tipmonkies.com/2005/09/22/sms-to-e-mail-the-complete-guide/ to see what yours is. Figure out what yours is and you can forward selected email to your phone. If you want to get certain urgent emails, you can tell the senders to put a code word into the subject and use a filter to send only those messages to SMS.

Real life rendezvous

Really great people make you feel that you, too, can become great.

—*Mark Twain*

Conventional wisdom suggests that the brave new world of ultraconnection doesn't make face to face meeting obsolete. But what does the empirical research say? Do colleagues need to meet face to face? And if so, how can you make the most of your time when you do meet in person with colleagues and associates?

Why face to face meetings still matter

Even in the time of the social web and hyperconnection, many workers and managers believe in the importance of face to face meeting and geographically collocated work. Though teams and projects may be distributed around the world, team leaders and teammates seek opportunities to get together in person.

Face to face meetings allow people to build rapport and trust, creating social ties that can then be used profitably and successfully when the people return to their home bases. Regular in-person meetings help the team to create shared norms and understandings about how they work together. You can do this with online tools, but it's not as easy.

Face to face meetings offer a chance to deal with problems that are too thorny for online solution. Personal conflicts, complex procedures for completing tasks, and technical obstacles can be tackled in a way that provides for the rich and deep communication that might be necessary for their resolution.

Also, in a time when many workers don't devote themselves only to one project or one company or even just one career, an in-person meeting can get multiple members of the team focused on the team's projects all at the same time. Travel away from home, for those who come from afar, can lessen personal distractions too. You can't get away with checking your email or folding your laundry in the middle of a face to face meeting.

For all these reasons, face to face meetings are desirable. But are they entirely necessary? Getting together in person can be expensive and disruptive. Many people find traveling tiring and annoying (see Table 7-2 for some sites that can make it easier). This means that managers and team members need to be careful to weigh the tradeoffs against the benefits.

Table 7-2: Websites that make travel easier and more social

Site	URL	Notes
TripAdvisor	tripadvisor.com	User reviews help you choose a suitable hotel.
Kayak	kayak.com	Travel aggregator for finding plane tickets and hotel rooms.
Farecast	farecast.com	Tracks and predicts fare prices over time to ensure you get the best deal.
SeatGuru	seatguru.com	With seat layouts and amenity information for airplanes from all the major carriers, helps you pick the best seat.
FlightAware	flightaware.com	Comprehensive air traffic data allows you to see all traffic into and out of specific airports.
Unthirsty	unthirsty.com	Find happy hours wherever you are.
Plazes	plazes.com	Let people know where you are. Find out who else is close by.
Dopplr	dopplr.com	Share your upcoming travel plans with your social network.
Upcoming	upcoming.yahoo.com	Find concerts, conferences, and other happenings you might like to attend while in a different city.
TripIt	tripit.com	Automatically organizes travel plans: you email plane, hotel, and car reservations to the service and it compiles them into a unified itinerary.

To read more about these and other online travel services, check out Samuel Dean's articles "Top Sites for Easing Travel Woes" (http://www.webworkerdaily.com/2007/08/06/top-sites-for-easing-travel-woes/) and "Click-and-Drag to Save Travel Dollars and Avoid Hassle" (http://www.webworkerdaily.com/2007/08/23/click-and-drag-to-save-travel-dollars-and-avoid-hassle/).

Social tools make face to face less important

While ample research shows the benefit of face to face meetings for distributed teams, some research shows that virtual collaboration tools can work just as well for day-to-day problem-solving.* The tools you have available for working together online increasingly offer many ways to build the social connections that successful teamwork relies upon. Social networking tools like Facebook allow teammates to see each other as three-dimensional people. Blogs embed knowledge transfer in a personal view of the world. VoIP, video chat, and plain-text IM let colleagues exchange ideas almost as easily as peeking over the cubicle wall. See Chapter 6 for all the tools and practices you can use to work effectively when your colleagues are far away.

Making the most of face to face meetings

You will work most effectively with other people when your social ties with them are strong. The virtual teams who work best together show high degrees of trust and rapport. Face to face meetings can promote that trust and rapport.

But getting the most out of your in-person meetings, whether you're just attending or you're organizing it for an entire team, requires work beforehand and afterwards to make the meetings pay off.**

When planning a face to face meeting, think of doing the following:

- **Engage people socially beforehand.** Make sure teammates are connected by group chat, IM, or social networking. Figure out which platform (or platforms) works best for your team and then use it consistently to develop a team habit.
- **Encourage people to participate in planning.** Start an online discussion thread about what people would like to discuss or achieve or resolve. Think about web-enabling the schedule by creating a wiki that everyone can edit and comment on.
- **Schedule formal activities.** Don't underschedule, because people may just find an available power plug and do solo work the whole time they're there if you don't have useful meetings and activities and plans.

---

*See, for example, David H. Jonassen and Hyug Kwon II, "Communication patterns in computer mediated versus face-to-face group problem solving," *Educational Technology Research and Development* (2001).

**Julia Kotlarsky and Ilan Oshri, "Social ties, knowledge sharing and successful collaboration in globally distributed system development projects," European Journal of Information Systems 14 (2005), available at http://www.juliakotlarsky.com/user/image/kotlarsky_and_oshri_ejis_2005.pdf.

BUSINESS CARDS

When you're out and about, you will definitely need business cards. They provide a link between the in-the-flesh you and the online you by specifying your email address, your IM accounts, your phone number, and your website.

It's not difficult to get business cards. Order them online at some place like OvernightPrints (overnightprints.com) if you're on a limited budget, try a copy center like Copy Max for nicer card stock at a moderate price, or go with a full-service printer like Sir Speedy for luxury cards at a price to match. Of course web working zealots may already have Moo minicards from Flickr (available at moo.com)—they're cheap, they're fun, and they're high quality, though not at all traditional, since they're about half the size of traditional business cards.

The hard part might be deciding what exactly to put on your card. If you're mashing up your career from a variety of income streams and skillsets (such as web development, web design, and search engine optimization) it's not so obvious what to call yourself—especially if you work for yourself. If you're a freelancer but haven't incorporated your business, you might not know whether to list a business name, and if so, what name to use. If you write or work in multiple places online, you may not know which, if any, to list.

If you run your own business, you can call yourself anything you want from "Ubergeek of the Universe" to "Lazy Genius" to "Chief Executive and Janitor." Corporate employees can get creative with job titles also, if their employer allows. Subject to space constraints, you can put any combination of phone numbers, IM and VoIP contact names, URLs, photos, avatars, and mottos on your business cards. To make it even more complex, you can design any number of business cards for the different facets of your work life.

There are things you may leave off your business cards: mailing address and fax numbers, while still used, aren't the primary means of reaching web workers in a time of email, IM, and follow-you-anywhere phone numbers. Of course, what you put on your card will sometimes be dictated by the norms of your industry as well as your employer.

- **But leave time for ad hoc meetings too.** Face to face meetings are a great time for team members to undertake informal training or join together to plan for the future. Mealtimes may be a great way for getting to know each other better on a personal level.
- **Be careful with people's time and energy.** Just because team members come in town for a face to face meeting doesn't mean you own them from early morning to late at night. Each person needs down time to reconnect with their personal lives, rest, and possibly do work that couldn't get done during the day.
- **Follow up afterwards.** Check in with coworkers to see what they thought of the activities. Take care of any action items you took on. Use the momentum you've established to keep the team closer together.

For ideas on what to do if you are a remote worker visiting headquarters, see Sabra Aaron's Web Worker Daily article with tips on making the most of an on-site visit at `http://www.webworkerdaily.com/2007/06/28/5-tips-for-making-the-most-of-an-on-site-visit/`.

A conference survival guide

One of the best ways to get out and meet people in your field is to attend conferences. If you can get your employer to give you time off from work and pay for your pass, that's great, but even if you're going on your own dime it can be worthwhile to attend one or two or more each year. You will meet new people that might make good partners or clients or friends, rekindle relationships that you've been keeping up online, and refresh yourself with new ideas.

These are Judi's tips for surviving and thriving at conferences. You might also like to read Mike Gunderloy's thoughts on conferences for web workers at `http://www.webworkerdaily.com/2007/08/23/conferences-for-the-web-worker/`.

Ease the financial burden

If you're self-funded, these things can be expensive. You have round trip airfare, ground transportation, nights in a hotel, conference registration and you may want to eat something every now and then. To top it all off, if you're a sole proprietor, this might as well be vacation time as work won't get done if you're not doing it. Here's how you might make it work:

- **Get the cheapest flight you can.** Use Farecast at farecast.com (my favorite) or a similar travel site to book your travel. Be flexible. If you're willing to catch a 6 AM flight instead of an 11 AM one or make multiple connections, you might save a lot of money.
- **Find a roommate.** Monitor message boards or blog posts where folks are talking about the conference. You may hook up with another solo traveler and cut the hotel expenses in half.
- **Decide early.** Conferences typically offer an early bird rate if you register well in advance.
- **Try and get a press pass.** Do you blog about the industry that is covered by the conference? That may be enough to apply for and get a free ride.
- **Apply for a scholarship.** If you work for a nonprofit, are a full-time student or can demonstrate financial hardship you might be able to apply for savings off the regular conference rate.
- **Speak at the conference.** Submit a breakout session idea. Some conferences are more open to these kinds of submissions than others. Some actively solicit speakers. Speakers can often get all the expenses covered.
- **Combine the conference with another meeting.** If the conference is in Chicago, and you have a client in Chicago, how about you suggest meeting before or after the conference? If you can't charge the travel expense directly, you will at least have an easier time writing it off.

Before the conference

Okay, so now your budget is set, your flight is booked, you have registered for the conference and you have a place to stay. What's next?

- **Pack for comfort.** Even if the dress code is business, make sure your shoes are comfortable. You can handle anything if your feet don't hurt.
- **Plan for the swag.** You're going to come home with trinkets, do-dads, brochures, CDs and more pens, mugs, keychains and mousepads than

any human being can use in their lifetime. There will be shopping bags available on the show floor, but those are uncomfortable to carry around and then you're stuck with that bag at the airport. Nowadays, more and more conferences are giving shoulder bags to attendees, but to be safe pack your own. Get one of those lightweight shoulder bags that folds into itself. Takes very little room in your suitcase going to the conference, and then you can check the bag with your other luggage going home. It's also far more comfortable when walking around the show floor.

- **Make a game plan.** Look at the list of exhibitors and note the booths you really want to get to. Figure out the keynotes, sessions, break-outs, and special meetings you want to attend. There will always be changes when you get there, but having a rough idea in advance is very helpful. You may even be able to download a show guide in advance to your phone or PDA.

- **Figure out who you want to meet with.** Don't wait until the day before the conference to email a friend or colleague to say you'll be in town. Be realistic. You're going to have very busy days. Don't plan for hours of socializing. Maybe plan to meet for coffee in the hotel lobby. For meetings with others attending the same show, same rules apply. They'll be running around just as much as you will be.

- **Talk about it.** If you have blog, talk about the fact that you're going. You may find out about a meeting or event, or be able to arrange a chat with someone that's off the beaten path.

At the conference

Once you're there, make the most of it:

- **Pace yourself.** My 8-year-old daughter gets a certain look in her eye when she walks into a toy store. I know how she feels. You want to see and do everything. You can't. If you've planned well, you know where your priorities are, so stick to it.

- **Plan for the wifi.** If you're going to need Internet access while at the show (and who doesn't?), don't count on the "Internet Cafe" the show organizers will provide. It may work, it may not. You'll never know for sure. Try and get in to a hotel that provides wired Internet access in the rooms. That will be more reliable than the wifi. Even better, use EvDO or 3G for your Internet access and skip worrying about 802.11 connections all together.

- **You can eat well or on a budget, rarely both.** If you think you can have lunch for under $10, then you haven't been to an expo hall. You're hungry, you're tired, you want to get off your feet so that $5 can of soda and $15 sandwich look just fine. Buy a big bottle of water and carry it around with you on the show floor, refilling from a fountain when necessary. Some conferences do provide some meals...which is fine if rubber chicken is a favorite of yours. I will always request vegetarian meals, which tend to be more edible.

- **Take lots of business cards with you.** It's a currency. You don't get 'em unless you say, "...let me give you my card" and then they do the same. It's all about the talking and the people. Some of the best connections I've ever made in my business were people I met at conferences and trade shows. Make a habit of writing some notes on the back of the card as soon as you take it. Some little cue that helps you remember why that person was important enough to take their card. Trust me, when you get home you won't have a clue why you have that card without it.

- **Sort through your swag before you leave.** Take the time in the hotel room to go through everything, making notes on the materials you want to follow up on while it's still fresh in your head. Throw out those things you know you'll never touch again. Do you really need 56 more pens?

When you get home

After you've crashed for a while, it's time to ease back into your regular web working routine. But before you do that, you need to get the most of your trip with a few wrap-up tips. Chris Brogan had some excellent suggestions on his blog at http://www.grasshopperfactory.com/cbc/things-to-do-after-a-conference/, which I'll summarize:

- **Deal with your business cards.** Don't let them pile up. Enter them into your contact database and get it over with.

- **Send emails.** I have a colleague who will send a "was great to meet you" email to every single person she spoke to at these things. I'm not sure you have to go that far, but this is where the networking really begins. Take advantage of it while your conversation is still fresh in their head.

- **Fulfill your promises.** If you said that you'd send them a sample from your portfolio, or a copy of that great article you talked about, then do it. Now.
- **Connect your network.** If you're on LinkedIn or Twitter, this is certainly the time to increase your connections.
- **Search blogs and add comments.** People are talking about the conference. Add your perspective and further expand your connections based on the common experience. And post your media. Write your wrap-up about the conference for your own blog, and post your pictures. If you were a presenter at the conference, then this is a must.

Looking forward: Explore career possibilities

You've been reading all about your day-to-day work life, from getting your office set up to managing daily tasks and email to collaborating with teammates. Now it's time to take a broader view. How might the web transform your career?

8 Explode Your Career

Explode your career? What? Aren't careers supposed to be serious, linear, planned, and carefully carried out? Aren't they what you build your life upon, at least the pragmatic and financial and responsible part of your life?

Not necessarily. Not after what the web has done to work lives and work trajectories. Before the web, careers were supposed to follow well-trod paths, usually up a corporate ladder or into a solid profession, like medicine or law or accounting. The web explodes the pathways and possibilities, in a good way.

In the introduction, I described all the ways you can web work, from telecommuting to remotely connecting with colleagues to adding online side income to promoting your work online to virtual entrepreneurship. In each case, it's become much easier to combine where you want to work, who you want to work with, what kind of work you want to do, and what hours and ways you're available to do it. It looks like an explosion of old ways of working or maybe, in less drastic terms, a network of new possibilities. You don't have to commit to narrow paths that go one way only. Before, you chose a geographic location and the kind of work you could do might be limited to only those industries in that location. Or you chose a particular career path—technology, maybe?—and had to go to where the action was (in the case of technology, Silicon Valley or some other major high tech city). Or you chose to have a couple kids and thought you might have taken yourself out of the workforce permanently.

So now it's much easier to flexibly combine different jobs, different income streams, different plans, different workstyles, and different people into productive work and into an authentic and rewarding career over a lifetime. It's easier, but it's not altogether easy. I can't tell you exactly what to do, because today's web is about individual possibility, not standard operating procedures.

I can, however, give you some tools and techniques for making transformative career decisions that work for you:

- **Leaping off the ladder.** You don't have to climb the corporate ladder. Use a multi-metaphor approach for thinking about and planning your career.
- **The digital you.** Bring yourself online in ways that suit you. Create a personal brand that uniquely expresses what you offer.
- **Making more money, the web way.** Explore new ways of making money online. Think about whether leaving traditional employment for freelancing or entrepreneurship is right for you.
- **Flopping without folding.** No one succeeds all the time, and if you take an experimental approach to your work, failure is every bit as expected as success. That doesn't mean that failure feels good—so learn how you can cope with it.
- **Sharing your work to share in success.** By sharing your work freely, you can attract opportunities and relationships. Learn how. And see what other secrets web workers follow for career success.

Leaping off the ladder

Is the system going to flatten you out and deny you your humanity, or are you going to be able to make use of the system to the attainment of human purposes?

—*Joseph Campbell*

You don't have to climb the career ladder. That's an old-fashioned way of looking at career progress and planning. Try some alternate metaphors for framing your thinking about your career. Build a toolkit of career metaphors that keeps you flexible and engaged with work-life decision-making.

A multi-metaphor toolkit works whether you want to use the web to work better or not, but it particularly suits web work because the web can make traditional career metaphors like the career ladder obsolete. You can't navigate a network with a ladder; the web is not hierarchical or directional and it doesn't often suggest definitive stepwise progress.

A multi-metaphor toolkit

When you evaluate or plan your career, you may do so through the lens of some metaphor or another. If you are aiming at eventually becoming a vice-president of a Fortune 500 company, you might think of yourself as climbing a ladder. If you are a creative sort, you might think of your career as a story. If you've left a cubicle job behind in favor of freelance work or other entrepreneurship, maybe you think of your career as a rebellion.

Metaphors can enlighten you when they guide you towards productive action or when they motivate you. But metaphors can limit you too, if you get stuck thinking you have to act in a certain way because that's what the metaphor suggests. For example, the metaphor of the career ladder demands regular upward movement. If you're not getting promoted, what are you doing up on that ladder? That can keep you from taking lateral or apparently lesser positions that might suit you better. The ladder metaphor assumes that one way is up (and better) and that everyone wants to go that way.

Try not to get trapped in any one particular metaphor and don't just let metaphors choose you. Be aware of what metaphors you are using and what metaphors might be more or less useful at a given point in your work life. Use multiple metaphors, adopting one or another depending on where you are and what you need.*

There are five career metaphors that work especially well in the web age: career as living thing, career as corporation, career as portfolio, career as narrative, and career as kaleidoscope. You will as well find other metaphors that suit you at different times.

Career as living thing: Your life as a tree

In Chapter 3, I introduced an organic approach to discovering your priorities, goals, and purpose and set it against a view of work as machine-like. These two metaphors work well in different situations. Treating your work as a machine helps when you are fairly certain of what you want to do and you know how to do it. It's just a matter of creating a plan, gathering resources (fuel for the machine), and making step-by-step progress toward your goal. I

---

*For a discussion of key metaphors in career thinking, see Kerr Inkson, "Images of career: Nine key metaphors," Journal of Vocational Behavior 65 (2004), available at http://www.cvmbs .colostate.edu/workshop/Inkson.pdf.

could use a machine metaphor when writing this book, because the goal and the outputs along the way are well-defined.

Treating your work as a tree or other living thing, on the other hand, works when you are less certain what you want to achieve and which direction you should go. If living according to your inner nature—living authentically—is important to you, you might use the organic metaphor. As I described in Chapter 3, you need to make sure you have the right environment with plenty of sun, water, and food. You need to put yourself into a healthily-functioning ecosystem. And then you need to be patient waiting for the growth to occur.

What does organic career decision-making look like? Here are some examples where people allow their work to grow naturally towards success and satisfaction rather than taking a top-down, machine-like planning approach:

- An artist turns a painting hobby into a business, when her family and friends want to purchase her artwork. She explores online art communities and serendipitously discovers a way to promote and sell her art online.
- A college graduate takes a job as an online community manager for a health-related nonprofit, because he cares deeply about the mission of the nonprofit, not because he knows exactly where the job will take his career in the long run.
- An attorney starts a blog under a pseudonym, writing humorously about the legal profession. She attracts the attention of a publisher, who offers her a contract to write a book with funny advice for lawyers and law students.
- A software developer contributes bug fixes and feature additions to an open-source project because he needs them for a project he's doing at work. He attracts the attention of that open source community and eventually leaves his job to become a paid evangelist for that open source software project.

Like all metaphors, the organic metaphor has its limitations. It can turn into an excuse for laziness or for shirking your commitments. It can make you complacent, waiting for the next spurt of growth that may never come if you don't make it happen.

But the organic metaphor suits uncertain and dynamic times in which you want to find your own best place, so it's useful to keep in your toolbox of metaphors, as long as you're aware you're using it, and you choose a different metaphor at times and situations when the organic approach doesn't serve you.

Career as corporation: You, Inc.

You can conceive of your career as a business unto itself no matter whether you are employed by someone else or choose self-employment. The career-as-corporation metaphor makes you aware of the importance of strategic planning across all your endeavors and of making your work financially profitable and sustainable over time. It also reminds you to craft a coherent and compelling marketing message for the fields in which you work.

The corporate metaphor, however, can limit you because people are not the same as corporations. A for-profit corporation maximizes profits within the bounds of its mission while a person may put more emphasis on personal satisfaction, community contribution, or finding a comfortable and supportive work environment.

You'll read later in this chapter about building your personal brand online. The idea of a personal brand comes from the career as corporation metaphor.

Career as portfolio: The slash career

The web makes it easier than ever to create and maintain multiple income streams. If you think of your work as a portfolio of different fields of expertise or of different projects, you break yourself out of the conventional idea that success always comes from one prestigious, high-paying job.

If you're feeling stagnant and wanting some new challenge, you could ditch what you're doing and start something altogether different. But that's disruptive and scary. Author/speaker/coach Marci Alboher suggests an alternative in her book *One Person/Multiple Careers*: add a slash. Don't stop what you're already doing. Add something alongside your current work. You can have more than one occupation at once, Alboher suggests, and there are many good reasons to do so.

Creating a slash career allows you to personalize your work to your skills and interests, explore different facets of your personality with lowered risk to your wallet, and take advantage of today's increasingly flexible and fluid workplace. Some slash careers add up to more than the sum of their parts, each mutually reinforcing the other and bringing new opportunities to each other.

The web offers many opportunities for profiting from and promoting your slash work: you can open an online store, create a website that shows off your work and your skills, or find freelance contracts in an online marketplace.

Career as kaleidoscope: Many-colored patterns

In their book *The Opt-Out Revolt: Why People Are Leaving Companies to Create Kaleidoscope Careers*, Lisa Mainiero and Sherry Sullivan propose a kaleidoscope metaphor for careers. With this view, if you make one change to one aspect of your life, everything else changes, as the pattern of a kaleidoscope changes completely when you turn the tube even slightly.

In the kaleidoscope metaphor, all aspects of your life—work, family, relationships, hobbies—are interlinked, and you can't change one without affecting the others. You also don't know what the next pattern is going to look like. You make a change and see what happens. You step back and see the beauty of the whole, as everything drops into place.

The kaleidoscope metaphor, like the organic metaphor, suits uncertain times when you don't know what results your efforts will bring. It helps you understand that different aspects of your life are interlinked and that you often can't change one aspect without changing another. It can break you out of career and life ruts, by helping you focus on the beauty of the whole rather than the detail. You see that you are in control—you turn the kaleidoscope—but you accept that by making certain decisions you are forcing others.

But the kaleidoscope metaphor can limit you by leaving you feeling like you have less control than you really do. With a kaleidoscope, all you can do is turn the tube. You have some control over every aspect of your work and life, even though the kaleidoscope metaphor might suggest otherwise.

Career as narrative: The hero's journey

Perhaps my favorite career metaphor is that of career as story. Most people engage in storytelling about their lives in order to make sense of them and to create hope for the future. Seeing your career as an ongoing narrative can motivate you at the same time it relieves stress over obstacles and failures. For example, if bad things happen because that's part of your story of triumph, they become challenges you will overcome rather than pain to dwell on.

Joseph Campbell's hero's journey provides the template for many stories and myths. It can be a template for your own career progress too. The hero's journey includes the following stages:

1. A call to adventure that removes you from ordinary society.
2. A series of trials or challenges.
3. Achieving a goal or "boon," a treasure to bring back to society.
4. A return to the ordinary world.
5. Using the boon to improve your society.

You can interpret your career story as a hero's journey. This works especially well for those times when you're suffering a feeling of disengagement or rejection or failure. You can interpret that as leaving ordinary society. Now you need to find new meaning, the "boon," to bring back to society. Finding the boon requires that you face and overcome challenges during your adventure away from society. Finally, you return to the world you knew, but you return changed. And you return with something of value for the people in your community.

The story metaphor could of course be used with the other metaphors already mentioned—a sort of meta-metaphor that guides you and supports you as you confront inevitable obstacles. There's no reason you can't use multiple metaphors at once; in fact, you probably should in order to keep yourself flexible.

The hero's journey is one of the most hopeful and motivating ways I know of to think about career. It can be overdramatic and not disciplined enough for some career situations, of course. But it might be something that you'd like to use to frame your actions as you carry out your purpose in life.

Other metaphors

These are not the only metaphors you can use in helping plan your career and move it forward. If you're a dentist and so was your father, you might consider your career an inheritance. If you go out to Alaska (or to some place or profession that seems like Alaska) to make your way, like psychologist Judith Kleinfeld describes in her book *Go For It! How to Find Your Own Frontier*, you are exploring the frontier. If you like to take on many projects, each very meaningful and beautiful to you, perhaps your career is like a tapestry or a stained-glass window.

The networked web of people and ideas online suggests some metaphors more than others, but the ones that work for you of course depend upon you. Table 8-1 gives some example situations and applicable metaphors to give you an idea of how multiple metaphor career management might work.

Table 8-1: Examples of metaphor usage in career planning

Situation	Metaphor	Why
Starting a blog for the first time	Organic	You are planting a seed and you don't know how it might grow.
Building up readership on an advertising-supported blog when you've gained experience as a successful blogger	Machine	Successful income-earning blogs require regular updates, a defined niche, and comprehensive promotion plans. The process of building an ad-supported blog is fairly well understood, though it's not necessarily easy to succeed.
Creating an online presence for your offline work	Corporate or Organic	Depending on how comfortable you feel online, you may proceed with a detailed plan for personal branding (corporate metaphor) or take a more experimental approach (organic metaphor).
Telecommuting after spending years working in an office and commuting	Kaleidoscope	Many things about your life will suddenly change, in ways you can't always predict.
Dealing with a layoff	Story	You have just received a hero's call to adventure, if you can interpret it that way.
Wanting to explore a different career	Portfolio	See if you can explore the new field while keeping income from your existing job or business.
Launching a startup to provide an online web application or service	Organic	Many web startups these days start with a vague idea, and then let it grow naturally.
Making your freelance work your main source of income	Corporate or Story	Build your personal brand online. Or take your own hero's journey, leaving the comforts of employment to strike out on your own.

The digital you

Nobody can be exactly like me. Sometimes even I have trouble doing it.

—*Tallulah Bankhead*

The media may focus on how online missteps can hurt your career, but they rarely mention how a digital you can help you succeed. What you do online can show your value to potential employers and clients, make you more visible in your field, and give you experience you need to create the career you want.

Yes, it's true that you might harm your career (or at least change it radically and suddenly) with your online activities. Posting drunken pictures of yourself on MySpace might prevent you from getting that first job out of college. Sharing outrageous views could make potential clients look in other places. Writing about your employer in negative terms—or any terms at all—on your blog could get you dooced.

WHAT'S DOOCED?   *Heather Armstrong, who blogs at dooce.com, was fired from her job for blogging about her workplace. She went on to become a famous blogger and "dooced" entered the lexicon as a term for getting terminated from your job for blogging about it.*

But the opportunities for improving your career are just as great as the opportunities for limiting it. If you build your professional profile online, you might be able to skip resume writing and interviewing when looking for a new job or new clients. A strong and consistent online presence can sell you better than any one-page summary or two-hour meeting. Your social connections online can lead to opportunities and partnerships. Online, you can explore new ways of working and relating; you can find the direction that's right for you.

The downside to having a very public professional or personal presence online may be facing rudeness or worse as you open your thoughts and other work to public feedback. The vast majority of people online are polite and friendly, but the few who aren't can make online work intolerable sometimes. Still, on balance, you are likely better off having this additional way of showing off your talents and connecting with those you might work with productively.

Besides, you can choose how visible you are online. Some people will video-cast every aspect of their lives. Most would rather keep their lives a bit more private though. It's up to you how much of yourself and your work life you open up online.

How to build your online persona

You can use the web to connect just with people who already know you—by email, instant messaging, and other tools with access and privacy control. But once you've done that for a while you might be ready for more. If you'd like to create a digital you that's visible online to potential colleagues, employers, and clients, try these steps:

1. **Check your Googleability.** When you plug your name into Google, where does any information about you appear? If you're one-of-a-kind and show up on the first page and every page thereafter, you can probably skip step 2.

2. **Consider making your name more unusual.** If you have a very common name or you share a name with a celebrity, you may want to start using a variation on your name that makes it unique. You can add a middle initial, use a nickname, or, for women, choose between your maiden and married names. You don't have to do this, of course, but some people care enough about their visibility online that they do.

3. **Choose a unique handle too.** You can use your full name without spaces for usernames on various services or choose something else meaningful to you and unusual enough that you'll be able to use it when you create new accounts online. I try to get "annez" on every service. It's unusual enough that it's almost always available. Then people who know me on one service can find me on another.

4. **Buy your domain name.** Ideally, get your .com address (that is, <yourname>.com). You can think about getting additional addresses also, including those with .net and .org suffixes. You can buy a domain name and not do anything with it for under $10 a year.

5. **Write a blog under your own name at your domain.** Search engines love blogs because they're updated regularly and they tend to be more link heavy than simple marketing websites. Use the name you chose in step 2. Be sure to include a biography.

6. **Spread your name across the Internet.** Create accounts on multiple services using your chosen name. Consider creating accounts on

LinkedIn, Flickr, MySpace, del.icio.us, and Twitter. Use the handle you chose in step 3 and the name from step 2.

7. **Remove incriminating material.** While search engine caching and the Wayback Machine at `http://www.archive.org/web/web.php` means that you can never really take anything off the Internet, you can make it less available. Delete those drunken photos and sarcastic blog posts. Along with creating fresh and happy content on your blog, this will help bury anything you don't want potential employers, clients, and partners to see. And think before you create anything online—a sarcastic or negative comment on someone else's blog will be around long after you've forgotten about it.

TRADING OFF TRANSPARENCY AND PRIVACY

Protecting your identity online requires two seemingly opposed strategies:

- Keeping sensitive information secret.
- Consistently and regularly appearing online as yourself.

The first strategy protects you from identity theft. Make sure you never share your social security number, financial account information, or home address online. When you buy a domain name, register it as private for a few extra dollars a year. That way people can't find your address by looking at the Internet domain name registry. If you have other information about yourself you'd like to protect (a particular health condition, for example), make it a rule not to discuss it online using identifying information.

The second strategy, consistently and regularly appearing online using your real name, ensures that you have the ability to present yourself the way you want, and protects you from those who might try to sully your reputation. The best way to make sure that you are presented online the way you want is to act online—via a blog or other website, on social networking platforms like MySpace or Facebook, and by sharing your work in the forums that make sense for your particular profession.

The actual risk of having your reputation harmed online is quite low, so most people without highly visible online or offline identities don't need to worry much about it.

Personal branding

Soloists and employees alike can benefit from being known for specialized expertise and a particular way of doing business—this can be captured in a personal brand. You don't *have* to create a personal brand, even if you're self-employed. You can just be yourself without any marketing veneer. This works just fine for many situations. If, however, you want to take more disciplined control of how you come across online, it can be helpful to think in terms of what value you offer to potential customers or employers and how you weave that into a coherent vision and story—to think in terms of brand.

A personal brand incorporates many elements, including your personality, style, skills, services, and anything else that makes you unique. Taken altogether, your personal brand expresses in a memorable way what differentiates you from other people who do the same thing you do.

You don't have to hire a branding consultant. Building a personal brand is something you can do for yourself, over time, letting it evolve as you discover what works and what doesn't.

Take your time

Let your branding emerge over time as you act and interact online. You don't have to figure out the perfect way to express your business value up front. Keep notes as you discover what's important to you and what your main contribution to your professional community is. You might not remember if you save it all up for later.

Remember you're human

Companies may need slick brands, but too much slickness in personal branding is a turn off. You still need to connect person to person. The brand is helpful for communicating about yourself, but the ultimate offering is you, a person, not a consumer packaged good.

Be authentic

If you choose a personal brand that doesn't go with what you really like to do, you're going to make yourself unhappy. Find a way to express yourself as you really are and the opportunities that will come to you will be satisfying and rewarding.

YOU, IN SHORT

The explosion of new ways to work online means it's not always easy to describe what you do to other people. You may even have trouble sometimes knowing exactly what you're about. Take some time to capture the essence of what you do. Here are a few ways you might do that:

- **A personal elevator pitch.** Entrepreneurs create a 15 or 30-second description of their company that they can use in case they find themselves in an elevator with a potential investor or client. You can do this for yourself too. Try 15 Second Pitch's (15secondpitch.com) pitch wizard if you need help coming up with one.
- **A blog or business card tag line.** Can you summarize what you're about in one or two sentences? Put it on your blog or on your business card. For some interesting blog tag lines, see `http://vaspersthegrate.blogspot.com/2005/05/blog-taglines-experiment-1.html`.
- **A motto or mantra.** Similar to a tag line, but focused more on values and principles rather than a particular subject. Your motto or mantra should be short and full of meaning. You can use it to remind yourself what you're about and to get it across to others. Read more on the difference between mantras and mission statements at `http://blog.guykawasaki.com/2006/01/mantras_versus_.html`.
- **A personal mission statement.** You can publish one on your blog or keep it to yourself. Try Franklin Covey's mission statement builder for help (`http://www.franklincovey.com/fc/library_and_resources/mission_statement_builder`). If that's too serious for you, use Dilbert's instead (`http://www.dilbert.com/comics/dilbert/games/career/bin/ms.cgi`).

Build upon your uniqueness

The key to a memorable brand is that it should differentiate you from others with professional profiles similar to yours. Even traits that seem initially like drawbacks can be turned into an element of your brand with a little bit of cleverness.

Seek consistency

As you figure out what your brand should be, apply it with consistency across your various on and offline activities. If you're having trouble being consistent, realize that you may have gotten off track. Focus on authenticity again.

But let it evolve

Even as you act consistently according to your brand, you'll find ways in which it needs to change. Don't get stuck on consistency when you discover a better way of presenting yourself. Your brand is a help to you in communicating about and promoting your work, not an end in itself.

Making more money, the web way

> *Imagination is the beginning of creation. You imagine what you desire, you will what you imagine and at last you create what you will.*
>
> —*George Bernard Shaw*

You can take your existing work and extend it in new ways online. Or you can try altogether new ways of making money, made possible by the web. You can become your own boss or keep your boss but start up a business on the side. Let your imagination run wild, and then let your work life follow.

Basics of making money online

There are many ways to make money online, but the most basic ones come down to these three: marketing yourself or your business online, selling things online, and publishing content in order to earn advertising income.

Market yourself and your services

Whether you are a satisfied employee who wants to make yourself available for other opportunities, a business owner who wants to reach out to potential clients, or a freelancer who wants to show off your talents, web publishing is a great way to market whatever you're offering. Depending on your goals, you could consider the following ways of marketing yourself and your services:

- **Create your own website.** A static website describing you or your business will be a logical first step for going online for entrepreneurs and freelancers. You don't have to hire an expensive web design firm to create one for you. Look to do-it-yourself website hosting and design services like SiteKreator (sitekreator.com) or Synthasite (synthasite.com).

- **Publish a blog.** A blog can serve as an extended resume, as a display of your talents, or as a compendium of articles that might be useful to your customers. Search engines love blogs because they are frequently updated and often heavily connected with the rest of the web via links in and out. A blog can be a useful addition to a regular website or can serve as your home page.

- **Write articles for other websites.** You don't have to have your own website to get your ideas and name out on the web. Approach website and blog owners with your ideas for articles that fit their site. Many blog owners are regularly looking for guest posters to provide interesting content.

- **Become a talk radio show host by recording podcasts.** Now everyone can share their knowledge and opinions with the world. If you've never created a podcast before, don't worry, it's easy. Try a site like Odeo (odeo.com) that lets you record and publish podcasts without downloading any software onto your computer. Mac users can experiment with GarageBand, recording software that comes free with Mac OS X. You'll need a microphone of course—many laptops come equipped with them built-in.

- **Or look towards video stardom.** Make a video about your work with a digital videocam and publish it on YouTube (youtube.com).

LET YOUR REPUTATION ATTRACT CUSTOMERS TO YOU

If you're considering solo work, you might wonder how you go about attracting new customers. You don't have to make cold calls (or send cold emails). Instead, focus on raising your professional profile and attracting customers to you.

Social media consultant Stowe Boyd says on finding new clients, "I have a simple approach to marketing my services: I don't. Or, perhaps more accurately, I don't do any marketing other than blogging and attending conferences, which are the primary channels for potential clients. I leave the rest up to fate, the Tooth Fairy, and word of mouth." James Governor, founder of five-year-old industry analyst firm RedMonk echoes this, "You want a profile within a community that can look for opportunities for you."

Stowe and James suggest that you don't need to specifically look for customers. Instead, let your reputation find them for you. Focus on your reputation, on learning new things, and on connecting with people doing work that excites you. Then opportunities will come looking for you.

You can start building up your profile even before you leave full-time employment or as an adjunct to full-time employment. Start a blog and comment on other people's blogs, making sure to always put your blog's URL in your comment. When you say something intelligent, folks will follow the link back to your blog. Make sure your "Subscribe" link is prominent so people can continue to read what you have to say. Attend conferences that interest you, even if you're not sure how they fit in with your career plans. Speak at them, if you can—what a great way to show off what you know and how you communicate. Participate in online forums or IRC channels, sharing your expertise and building new knowledge and relationships at the same time.

Resist all urges to be sarcastic, know-it-all, or rude online. Answer questions as you would want them answered for you. If your reputation is negative, especially on sites you can't edit, it will take a long time to undo the damage. Be nice and show respect.

LET YOUR REPUTATION ATTRACT CUSTOMERS TO YOU (*continued*)

For developers, open source software efforts are an excellent way to learn new things, connect with like-minded people, and show your expertise. Designers can achieve similar professional visibility by producing and marketing free website templates or doing pro bono work for nonprofits. Consultants and writers will find that blogs are an ideal way of showing writing skills and insight. Professional service providers such as lawyers, accountants, and financial planners can share advice online in forums or on a blog.

One major benefit of the raise-your-profile-and-they-will-come approach is that working on your reputation and visibility is a whole lot more fun than cold-emailing potential customers or fighting with a bunch of other people for a PHP web development contract listed on Monster.com. Most people choose their work at least partly out of passion. Spending time writing about your work, talking about it, and learning about it is rewarding all by itself. How great that it also happens to be an effective way to find money-making opportunities too.

Of course there's more to turning your profile into actual income, including explicitly asking for work via proposals or more informal means, doing the work itself, and making sure you get paid once the work is done. See Chapter 9 for help with that.

Sell stuff online

Another way you can earn income and enhance your career online is by selling goods online. This can represent either an extension of your offline work or business or something altogether new. You'll need the following:

- **Something to sell.** A book you've written, something you've crafted, or goods you've found that you think other people would buy.
- **Web store.** You need a place online to promote and take orders for whatever you're selling. This might be your own website or an auction site like eBay. Of course, you may promote what you're selling all over the web and just direct people to your website for purchase.

- **Payment mechanism.** such as PayPal (paypal.com) or Google Checkout (checkout.google.com).
- **Fulfillment capability.** You don't have to store and ship goods yourself if you use outside fulfillment services or arrange for drop shipping, where the manufacturer ships goods to their ultimate destination for you. If you're selling informational goods like software or electronic documents, it's even easier: just provide them as downloads.
- **Customer support.** Whether it's by email or phone, you need to be ready, willing, and able to support your customers after you have their money. Then they may become repeat customers and could promote you by word of mouth.

For a really easy way to get started with e-commerce check out websites like GoodStorm (goodstorm.com) or Bravisa (bravisa.com). You select from their catalog of goods, set prices, and create a storefront, all using their online tools. You promote your store and then when people order from it, GoodStorm or Bravisa handles the payment and fulfillment logistics. It might be an easy way to experiment with selling stuff online.

Earn income from advertising

You can create your own ad-supported micropublishing company. It's easy to get started but not so easy to make significant money doing it. All you need to do is create a website—blogs are ideal because it's easy to keep them regularly updated—and plug in context-aware advertising from services like Google AdSense (google.com/adsense) or Yahoo! Publisher Network (publisher .yahoo.com).

One of the most accessible resources online for making money by putting advertising on your blog is Darren Rowse's ProBlogger (problogger.net). In addition to covering advertising-based income, he also discusses affiliate programs (for example, earning money by driving customers to Amazon where you get a commission on whatever they buy) and sponsorships.

New ways to make money online

Beyond the basic marketing, e-commerce, and advertising games online, there are all sorts of new ways to make money online. I've collected a range of ideas here so you can let your imagination roam.

Online professional marketplaces

No longer are you limited to looking for a permanent or contract job on old-style job sites like Monster or CareerBuilder. The new breed of freelancing and project-oriented sites let companies needing help describe their projects. Then freelancers and small businesses offer bids or ideas or proposals from which those buyers can choose. Check out Elance (elance.com), oDesk (odesk.com), and Design Outpost (designoutpost.com).

Be aware that many software developers and graphic designers who have tried such sites find the jobs too low-paying and the clients too demanding, so your mileage may vary. If you are a freelancer, however, you may be competing with those who offer their services on these sites, so it may be worth your time to understand them so you can craft your value proposition in response.

Sell photos on stock photography sites

If people regularly oooo and aaaaah over your Flickr pics, maybe you're destined for photographic greatness or maybe just for a few extra dollars. It's easier than ever to get your photos out in front of the public, which of course means a tremendous amount of competition, but also means it might be a convenient way for you to build up a secondary income stream. Where can you upload and market your photos? Try Fotolia (fotolia.com), Dreamstime (dreamstime.com), Shutterstock (shutterstock.com), iStockphoto.com (istockphoto.com), and Big Stock Photo (bigstockphoto.com).

Blog for pay

Despite the explosion of blogs, it's hard to find good writers who can turn around a solidly written post on an interesting topic quickly. How do you get noticed? Comment on and link to blogging network sites. Write blog posts that are polished and not overly personal (although showing some personality is a plus). Be aware that most blog jobs pay very little, if at all. You might be expected to write for a site in exchange for attention and reputation only.

If you blog for any length of time on a particular topic (parenting, mobile phones, or PCs, for example), you will likely be approached to do book or product reviews. You can get free stuff this way, but are you selling your soul? That's a decision you'll have to make for yourself, because no one agrees upon what ethical rules apply to bloggers. People agree even less on services like PayPerPost that pay you to write reviews on your blog. Check out disclosure rules closely and see whether such a gig would meet your own personal standards or not. Know that many people consider them unethical and that your reputation may be harmed if you choose this route.

Provide service and support for open source software

Just because the software is free doesn't mean you can't make money on it—just ask Red Hat, a well-known distributor of Linux that sports a market cap of more than four billion dollars. As a solo web worker, you might not want to jump in and compete with big companies offering Linux support, but how about offering support for web content management systems like WordPress or Drupal? After getting comfortable with your own installation, you can pretty easily jump into helping other people set them up and configure them. Also, consider providing enhancements for open source software, such as templates or plugins for WordPress.

Offer online life coaching

Who has time to go meet a personal coach at an office? And don't the new generation of web workers need to be met by their coaches in the same way that they work: via email, IM, and VoIP? You could, of course, go through some life coaching certification program, but on the web, reputation is more important than credentials. I bet Tony Robbins isn't certified as a life coach, and no one can argue with his success. For an example of someone building up their profile and business online as a coach, check out Pamela Slim of Ganas Consulting and the Escape from Cubicle Nation blog (escapefromcubiclenation.com).

Virtually assist other web workers

Freelancers and small businesses desperately need help running their businesses, but they're not about to hire a secretary to come sit in the family room and answer phone calls. As a virtual assistant, you might do anything from making travel reservations to handling expense reimbursements to paying bills to arranging for a dog sitter. And you do it all from your own home office, interacting with your clients online and by phone. You can make $20 and up an hour doing this sort of work, depending on your expertise. For information on working as a virtual assistant, check out the International Virtual Assistants Association website at www.ivaa.org.

Community moderator

Online communities devoted to an almost endless variety of topics need people to keep discussion lively and positive. For-profit websites often hire part-timers to work from home on forums and discussion boards, seeding new topics, stepping in if conversations deteriorate into animosity or name-calling, and ensuring new members are welcomed. You can build a name for yourself this way within a community of people interested in the same topic you are. For our profile of a community manager, see http://www.webworkerdaily.com/2007/05/17/web-worker-payoff-online-community-manager/.

And more

This is just a short selection of the many new ways of making money online. You may also want to consider entrepreneurship in virtual worlds like Second Life, search engine optimization consulting, t-shirt design via sites like Threadless (threadless.com), offering an online application or service, and more. Of course, we regularly cover these new options at Web Worker Daily. So check there for more ideas about how to make money online.

Employment vs. soloist work vs. other

One major shift many people contemplate making in their career is leaving traditional employment for freelancing or entrepreneurship. The web provides many opportunities and resources for those who want to escape the corporate climb.

If you're thinking about flying solo (there's another metaphor), consider how to make it work for you.

Not everyone needs six months' living expenses

You might need more than six months of living expenses; you might need less. If your spouse works full time and can carry the living expenses while you make a way for yourself, you can start almost any time. If, conversely, you are the sole provider for a family of five, you might need more than six month's salary in the bank.

You can start a side job before quitting your main job

It's more difficult to do it this way and may not give you a good idea of your real ability to make self-employment work. But if you're the cautious sort and have serious financial obligations, get some outside income going first and then make the leap. You might even be able to negotiate a part-time or contract arrangement with your current employer to give yourself time to get your side business off the ground.

Make a backup plan

You should know what you'll do if work and income doesn't come in like you hope. Could you return to work for your current employer, as an employee or a contractor? Could you get some temp work using your professional experience or doing general office work? Are you in a field that's in high demand, meaning you could easily get another job, even if not your ideal job? Make a realistic Plan B that you can put into action if necessary.

Just do it

If you're the risk-taking resilient sort, you may not need to make lengthy plans and preparations before going solo as a freelancer or other type of entrepreneur. Getting contract jobs or selling products is not that different from finding a full-time job—you need to convince someone that you have what they want and then you need to negotiate for what they're going to pay you. One of the nice things about employment is you don't have to do that too often. But remember that you have sold your skills to an employer at least once (that's how you have your job, right?) so you probably have the ability to sell your offerings to someone else. Quitting your job will get you motivated quickly, unless you're already independently wealthy.

Or don't

Going solo isn't right for everyone, and traditional employment offers many advantages such as comprehensive benefits, paid vacation and sick time, and an office outside your house. Plus, you can start an Internet business on the side and keep your day job. Just because you're an employee doesn't mean you can't be an entrepreneur too, but don't take advantage of your employer. Do your side work on your own time.

ONLINE HELP FOR WANNABE SOLOISTS

There are countless websites, blogs, and web applications aimed at free-lancers and small businesses. These are some of my favorites.

- **Escape from Cubicle Nation** at escapefromcubiclenation.com, from life coach Pamela Slim, shares ideas for how to take the leap.
- **Freshbooks** at freshbooks.com offers an online invoicing solution for small businesses. Their blog regularly addresses issues of interest to the self-employed.
- **Freelance Switch** at freelanceswitch.com provides up-to-the-minute advice and resources for freelancers of all types.
- **The Anti 9 to 5 Guide**, a website at anti9to5guide.com to go with a book of the same name, gives advice and profiles from women who've made the switch.
- **37Signals** at 37signals.com sells a range of online web services for small businesses including Basecamp project management and Highrise customer relationship management.
- **StartupNation** at startupnation.com has forums, articles, and even a small business public relations package.

And of course at Web Worker Daily we regularly offer tips and advice for the self-employed and the wannabe self-employed.

Flopping without folding

With every mistake we must surely be learning / Still my guitar gently weeps.

—The Beatles

You can fail or feel like you've failed in any kind of work; the web is no excep-tion to that rule. Taking an experimental attitude will help you understand failure as part of the process rather than something to avoid. But even if you accept that you're bound to flop sometimes, it still feels bad when it happens and you still need to clean up the mess.

How might you flop? Here are some I've either experienced myself or seen online:

- Writing an online article that receives heavy criticism.
- Starting a job with a big announcement to your online social network, then finding shortly thereafter that you're not suited to it.
- Launching an online web service that fails to win enough users to continue.
- Creating an online promotion or marketing effort that people label inappropriate or unethical.
- Making a decision about a community website that the community doesn't agree with.

Of course misjudgments, mistakes, flops, and failures happen all the time offline too. Knowing how to flop, then get up and keep going is a good skill for any kind of work.

Experimentation and failure

If you take an experimental approach to your career, failure is not only expected, it's a core part of the process. You experiment when you can't make a reliable prediction as to whether a certain project will work or not. Do the project, and see what happens. If it fails, you have learned something about what doesn't work. You can now adjust your plan based on what you've learned.

If you do choose an experimental approach (it's not right for every situation), keep in mind that you should plan for both success and failure. What does this mean? You could consider every new venture as a trial run. Don't get into long-term agreements before you've tested the waters unless you absolutely have to. If you're trying a new job, see if you can start as a contractor or structure it as a side job before getting rid of other commitments. Similarly, if you're hiring someone to help you out, hire him or her on a temporary evaluation basis before committing to a long-term full-time job.

You should still do some preliminary research and due diligence before taking on new projects, especially if other people have succeeded or failed in the area you're looking towards. Taking an experimental attitude doesn't mean being irresponsible. But don't get bogged down in research and planning when taking some small steps could give you useful feedback on your plans.

Coping strategies

You can't avoid failure, and if you do, that may mean you're not taking as many risks as you should with your work. When things go wrong, be resilient and ready to cope. That's far more important than trying too hard to avoid mistakes and failures in the first place.

Reach out beyond yourself

When a project goes wrong, you might feel like hiding out and nursing your pain in private. But social support can help you get through difficult times. Both your on and offline friends can provide perspective on what happened, reframing it for you and helping you see what to do next. They can share the times that they had similar difficulties and tell you how they got through it. They can make you laugh and forget your woes.

How do you let online contacts know what's going on without shaming yourself and without revealing private information about you or people you've worked with? You can share that something's gone wrong without telling all the details. You can limit the number of people you share it with, by sharing in relatively more private channels: instant messaging rather than a wide-open blog for instance.

Also, think about how you're helping other people by sharing your mistakes and failures. The web opens up a window on our very human work lives. You might provide inspiration or comfort to someone else who's going through similar trials. Also, you'll have a better chance of professional recovery because people will respect your candor and willingness to learn from your mistakes.

Re-narrate your story

Re-narrating and reframing your story in different terms can help you make sense of it in a way that's motivating and inspiring rather than depressing and deflating. Writing the story in the third person can help distance you from the emotional pain at the same time it helps you see the positive side. Putting your experience into the context of an archetypal story structure like the hero's journey allows you to take a broader view, one that finds meaning and power in difficulties.

REFACTOR YOUR CAREER

Refactoring your career means taking a critical eye to all your activities and figuring out how to reorganize and optimize them for satisfaction and success. The term comes from software development, where refactoring means revisit the structure of your software and rewriting for easier maintenance and improvement going forward.

When you refactor your career, you take a critical eye to each element of your work life: jobs, clients, activities, projects, and so forth. Then you consider what you should eliminate, what you should restructure, and what you might add to make it all work together better.

Examples of career refactoring might include:

- Eliminating any clients that hassle you more than you feel the income is worth.
- Adding more projects in an area you feel increased energy and possibility around.
- Discussing changing your responsibilities with your manager, if you want to focus more on certain tasks and less on others.
- Considering whether you need to change how you do your work, for example changing to part-time or telecommuting for better work-life balance.
- Spending more time on personal branding activities than you have been, or maybe spending less, depending on how many good opportunities are flowing your way.

Career refactoring is yet another metaphor for career management. You might find it useful if your career needs some rethinking, such as after you've suffered a setback or failure of some sort.

You can even go public with your reframed story, on a blog for example. Be careful, however, if you choose to do this, because your failure may involve other people and they might not be happy about having their story told to the world. Don't use the idea of re-narrating your story to justify publicly criticizing people you worked with.

Use active problem-solving

Don't just stay with the pain of failure: make a plan for dealing with it. Depending on what exactly happened, you'll need to prioritize different things. If you've lost your job and your family depends on you, you probably need to cut expenses and replace that income relatively quickly. If your startup has failed to get the funding you thought you'd get, you may need to restructure the company and make a new plan. If you just did something that makes you feel less than brilliant and less than competent, think how you can start to rebuild your confidence.

It's important to deal with your emotions, by re-narrating your story and by reaching out. But if you stop there, you're not really experimenting. You're wallowing. Get up, get out, get motivated. Make something else happen. It might fail too, but it gets easier over time to get up and get moving again after you fall. Each mistake teaches you something about what doesn't work, and helps you decide what might be a productive way to move forward.

Escape, avoid, quit

Though your mom might have told you that "quitters never prosper" there are times when the right response to a bad situation is just to quit. How do you know when that time comes? You don't. So follow your gut, talk to your mentors, and make a decision one way or the other. This is a topic that Web Worker Daily's sister site Found|Read has tackled; see, for example, Carleen Hawn's "Unconventional Wisdom: Quitting is Good for You" at `http://www` `.foundread.com/2007/08/15/unconventional-wisdom-quitting-is-good-for-you/`.

Sharing your work to share in success

> *When I give, I give myself.*
>
> —*Walt Whitman*

The social web works on the free sharing of information and ideas. Open source developers make their software and the instructions behind it available without a license fee. Bloggers share their opinions and analysis with anyone who happens to click by. Photographers share photos on free stock photo sites, with minimal restrictions on how you can use those photos in your own work. Foodies share reviews of restaurants and gourmet recipes. Travelers share their experiences of hotels. Web developers offer web applications without subscription fees. Experts from all fields offer advice and tips on forums and bulletin boards.

This sharing isn't just altruistic; good things will flow to you if you share online. In this section you'll see why, and then you'll see how to do it. As a bonus, I close the chapter with some other secrets web workers know about career success.

Why give your work away for free

There are many reasons to share your work freely. Most important, it's a way to show potential employers, clients, and partners your talents. As you saw earlier, sharing online builds your professional profile. Your professional profile can attract new opportunities to you; clients and employers and partners will come to you.

But there are other reasons to share your work. It gives you an easy way to get feedback. People who look at your work online won't hesitate to comment on it, if you give them the chance. This is both good and bad, because sometimes it's uncomfortable to have what you've done and what you think scrutinized regularly. It's useful, however, to understand what people think of your work.

You learn while you share. The best way to learn about something is to produce your own work in that area. Knowing that other people will evaluate and use what you offer puts additional pressure onto your work, making you work that much harder and make it that much better.

Sharing makes people familiar with your work and this may make them appreciate it more over time. Some parents follow a rule of thumb that kids need to be exposed to a new food 11 times before they'll like it. Similarly, exposing people to your work will, over time, make them more familiar with it and more open to what you're trying to achieve. Psychologists know this as the exposure effect.

And finally, giving your work away helps you build connections to other people. Sharing what's important to you helps you find other people with the same values. Then you and your contacts can mutually help each other succeed.

How to give your work away for free

If all you wanted to do was give your work away for free and you didn't care about ever profiting from it, that'd be easy. But you need to share in a way that benefits ultimately come back to you.

Give authentically

Give work that you believe in and that is consistent with your values in order to ensure that the people and opportunities that flow your way based on your sharing are ones that fit with what you want.

Try the "freemium" model

Many web applications of today use what they call the "freemium" model, where a free basic service is offered (often with advertising) that introduces users to the product and may convert them into paying customers. You can use the freemium model by sharing some work for free while charging for premium services or work. For example, if you're a writer, you can share blog articles freely, but charge for downloadable booklets in PDF format.

Explore Creative Commons licensing

Control how the work you share is used by other people. Creative Commons gives you fine-grained control over what kind of copying, modifying, and redistribution other people can do with your work. Read more at creativecommons.org.

Know your options are for sharing online

Pick the means that best suits your field and your particular situation. You can almost always share your work on your own blog or website, of course, but there are other alternatives that might get your work better exposure. See Table 8-2 for ideas to get you started.

Always read the terms of service of sites where you share your work. You wouldn't want to give away rights to your work without realizing it.

Table 8-2: Places to share online

Work	Suggested Tool	Examples
Writing, analysis, ideas, advice	Blogging	Blogger (blogger.com), WordPress.com (wordpress.com)
Photos	Photo sharing sites	Flickr (flickr.com), everystock-photo (everystockphoto.com), stock.xchng (www.sxc.hu)
Web design	Themes for blogging and content management systems, web design portfolio sites	WordPress theme viewer (themes.wordpress.net), Drupal themes (drupal.org/project/Themes), css Zen Garden (csszengarden.com)
Color schemes	Color palette sharing sites	Adobe Kuler (kuler.adobe.com)
PDF documents	Document sharing	Scribd (scribd.com)
Web application	Share as widget or application embedded in other platforms	Facebook applications (www.facebook.com), Google Gadgets (http://www.google.com/ig/directory?synd=open)
Videos	Video sharing	YouTube (youtube.com)

MORE SECRETS OF WEB WORKER CAREER SUCCESS

Giving your work away for free is one of the most important secrets of web worker success, but you'll need some other skills and methods too. You've seen a bunch of these ideas already, but it doesn't hurt to see them again and think how you might be able to use them:

- **Reach out beyond yourself.** People like to hang out with people like themselves (this is called *homophily*), but you might consider reaching outside your comfortable social sphere. Let's call that *heterophily* for love of the different. Sociological and management research indicates that reaching across social clusters—from the ones you feel most comfortable in into different ones—is key to innovation and productivity.

MORE SECRETS OF WEB WORKER CAREER SUCCESS (*continued*)

- **Use multi-channel communications.** Go beyond phone and email for communicating with colleagues and for creating new relationships. Effective web workers use instant messaging, text messaging, Twitter, blogging, wikis, VoIP, video conferencing, and web conferences.
- **Learn to write.** True, podcasting and online video are gaining adherents. Video conferencing should take off now that most PCs come with built-in cameras. But text still rules on the web, whether for email or blogging or wikis or instant messaging. Learn to write conversationally and casually, without rambling. Blog posts and other web writing shouldn't be as formal as printed memos, but they shouldn't be self-indulgent or filled with grammatical errors either.
- **Get your mind around search.** You need to learn to search effectively—using Google, in your email, other people's bookmarks, and so forth—but you also need to know how search engines work and have some understanding of basic search engine optimization concepts. You need to know how to find what you want and ensure people find you and your work too.
- **Experiment.** As a relatively new frontier for work, it's not always obvious what you should do to achieve your goals in web work. Don't hesitate to try something new, take some risks, then step back and see what happens. The web gives you a ton of feedback about how you're doing with your online work, whether in the form of emails from potential new customers or stats for your website. You can take what you've learned and experiment some more, proceeding step by step towards a successful and satisfying work life.
- **Question conventional wisdom.** Is surfing the web unproductive? Do you need to work long hours to show your commitment to work? Should you keep your personal life and activities hidden from colleagues? Maybe so; maybe not. While of course you're not going to want to toss out all the old rules just because they're old, you should be willing to reconsider what you thought was true.

MORE SECRETS OF WEB WORKER CAREER SUCCESS (*continued*)

- **Manage RSS feeds.** You need to be able to produce feeds for your own website or blog and you need to manage your consumption of them so that you get good information from the web without letting it overwhelm you. If you're a Google Reader user, check out Leo Babauta's tips on using it productively at `http://www.webworkerdaily.com/2007/08/15/15-ways-to-use-google-reader-productively/`.

- **Recognize and build on good ideas.** It's just as important as having your own good ideas. You're living in a wonderful soup of inspiration and innovation, but the person who thinks up something brilliant might not be the one who can successfully promote that idea or make it into a viable business. Human beings love to copy—and for good reason. It's the basis of our reproductive success and it's more efficient than each one of us trying to come up with good stuff on our own. But remember: if you do build on an idea, credit the original source any time you are public about it and respect copyright laws.

- **Show courage.** It's not always pleasant to leave comfortable old ways of working behind, to try new things in full view of the Internet, to experiment knowing you may fail a number of times before you succeed (and fail again after too). The web rewards bravery, so put yourself out there anyway.

Looking forward: Managing your money

No matter how you choose to use the web to make your career better, you'll still need to manage your money. The web doesn't change basic principles of money management, but it does make some things easier. Let's see how.

9 Manage Your Money

Y ou work for many reasons, not least of which is to earn a living. You need to manage whatever you earn as effectively as possible, so you can live the way you want. You may dream of working for yourself, of working in a different field that pays less than what you earn now, or of funding dreams like returning to school or taking a long-awaited vacation. Better money management might allow you to do those things.

The web helps you manage the money you earn and it can even change the way that you earn it, by making remote work, self-employment, and even employing others easier than before. Using the web, you might work from home instead of commuting to a far away office. You might work at your ideal job even though it's located far away (though unfortunately, far too few employers are open to remote hires). You might take a variety of small jobs with different employers or clients. You might start your own business online at the same time you cover your ongoing living expenses while receiving insurance coverage and other benefits with traditional employment. You might farm some personal or professional work out to virtual employees, because it's so easy to find and communicate with qualified people wherever they are.

These new ways of working could change how you manage your money, especially if you earn income from self-employment. While many web workers will be happy working for someone else for their entire careers, there are also those who'd like to work for themselves but hesitate because it seems complex and overwhelming. Self-employment changes money management drastically and so this chapter covers money management for the self-employed in detail, while still covering information relevant to those who earn income only as employees.

This chapter includes the following sections:

- **Your financial dream team.** Find the professional advisors, institutions, and online tools that will keep your financial life in order and help you achieve your financial dreams. Plus, learn how you can socially manage your money using the web.
- **Cashing in on web work.** Especially if you're self-employed, you need to keep your cash coming in so you can pay your bills. This section is mainly aimed at freelancers working hourly rates, but includes some ideas on bursty ways of generating income too.
- **Tax self-help for the self-employed.** If you are thinking about self-employment or already engaged in it, your tax situation is much more complex than the average employee's. Understand basic concepts like what expenses are deductible and how to handle estimated taxes.
- **Wealth, well being, and the web.** Will more money make you happier? Not necessarily. I look at the empirical research to see how you can spend your time and money most wisely. The web opens up new possibilities for making money and spending it, and for connecting socially—the real secret to well-being.

The two middle sections are mostly of use to those who are practicing or contemplating self-employment, but even if you're not, you might want to skim them to see how to manage earning money for yourself instead of as an employee.

Your financial dream team

To be perfectly honest, what I'm really thinking about are dollar signs.

—Tonya Harding

Whether you're an employee or entrepreneur, you need help managing your money. You'll find it from a variety of sources, from big financial institutions to small service providers to online tools and communities. You'll look to banks and brokerage firms, accountants, insurance agents, and attorneys. You'll also want to consider using both a professional financial advisor (ideally fee-based, not commission-compensated) and your online social network to keep you aimed in the right direction.

Banking and brokerage services

If you're comfortable working online, you might be happy with an online bank for checking and savings. While you don't usually get brick-and-mortar branches with an online bank, you may get higher yields, easy online access to your funds, and reimbursement of at least a portion of your ATM fees. HSBC Direct (hsbcdirect.com) and ING Direct (ingdirect.com) get good marks.

You can also consider consolidating your banking and brokerage at one online institution, like Charles Schwab (schwab.com) or E-Trade (etrade.com). Both of these offer you one-stop online shopping for everything from checking to savings to stock purchases to home mortgages. These two companies even offer branches in certain larger cities, for complex transactions or financial advice. As my financial life has gotten more complex, with a variety of retirement, custodial, and other accounts, I've found it eases financial management considerably to consolidate as much as possible at one place.

You'll probably want to enroll in the electronic bill pay that your bank offers. In order to keep control of the payment process, use your bank's bill pay system to set up electronic bills with those billers who offer it rather than signing up at individual sites like your cell phone provider or your electricity company. Ideally, you want all your bill pay to take place at one place in a way that's under your control. The fewer places you share your bank account information, the better.

Table 9-1 describes a few resources for managing your banking and investment needs online. This is just a sample of what's available as of fall 2007 to give you an idea of the range of advice and services you might find online.

Table 9-1: Online banking and investment resources

Site	URL	Description
Wesabe	wesabe.com	Online personal finance tool. Download financial transactions from your bank and credit card accounts, then tag and analyze your spending and income. Share goals with the community of Wesabe users.

continued

Table 9-1: Online banking and investment resources *(continued)*

Site	URL	Description
Mint	mint.com	Online personal finance tool similar to Wesabe. Automatically cleans and categorizes transactions. Suggests offers that might save you money, like lower-rate credit cards.
Expensr	expensr.com	Online personal finance like Wesabe and Mint. Includes ability to compare spending against what other people spend as well as forecasting tools.
NetBanker	netbanker.com	Blog covering online financial services including online banks, payment services, and mortgage lending.
Zecco	zecco.com	Stock trading community and brokerage that includes commission-free trades, blogs, forums, and market statistics.
Morningstar	morningstar.com	Mutual fund statistics and research. Premium reports available by subscription.
FOLIOfn	foliofn.com	Buy and sell entire portfolios of investments in a single transaction. Get the diversification of a mutual fund without the management fees.
Sharebuilder	sharebuilder.com	Provides automatic investment plan and purchase of partial shares of stocks.

DO YOU NEED TO RECONCILE YOUR CHECKING ACCOUNT? *Personal finance site Wesabe (wesabe.com) makes it easy to track your income and spending by getting regular updates from your bank. But it doesn't have a reconciliation feature! Why? Co-founder Marc Hedlund says that less than 1% of Wesabe users want to reconcile. If you download transactions from your bank every few days or so, you can catch any bank errors right then; no need to wait to reconcile against the statement. See Hedlund's rationale here:* https://www.wesabe.com/groups/3-make-wesabe-better/discussions/181-reconciling#comment_3167.

Accounting and tax expertise

The tax code has become so complicated that few people choose to tackle it all by themselves. At the very least, you'll want to use software like TurboTax to help. If your tax situation is at all complex, and it may get that way if you add some self-employment income to your W-2 earnings, you may want to find an accountant to help. A good accountant can advise you what business expenses are deductible, direct you to the best retirement savings options, and help you decide how much to have withheld from any regular paychecks you get or, alternatively, how much to pay every quarter in estimated taxes.

Just because you hire an accountant, however, doesn't mean you are immune from tax problems. Be sure to check over what your accountant does before sending it in; I've seen accountants make even basic errors. And find out up front whether your accountant is more aggressive or conservative in trying to save you money on taxes. You want to ensure that you two agree as to how aggressive a stance to take.

An accounting firm will use software to manage your taxes and any other services they do for you. You may or may not need specialized accounting software yourself. For basic freelance accounting, all you need to do is track your time, generate invoices, and record expenses. You can do this with office software like Microsoft Word for invoices and Excel for tracking time and expenses. If you want something designed specifically for financial management, you may be able to get away with personal finance software like Quicken on the desktop and avoid the pricier QuickBooks package that's designed for businesses unless you want to generate invoices, which Quicken won't do. You can also choose from a wide variety of online tools such as Less Accounting (lessaccounting.com), Simply Accounting (simplyaccounting.com), or QuickBooks Online (oe.quickbooks.com).

Insurance

Both employees and the self-employed need to carefully consider insurance needs. You need life, health, homeowner's or renters, disability, and possibly an umbrella liability policy. If you have your own business, explore whether you need business insurance such as errors and omissions coverage, which kicks in if a client charges you with inadequate attention to the professional standards in your field. A good insurance broker can help you find reasonably priced coverage, though you might want to talk to an independent financial advisor for an unbiased analysis of your insurance needs. Also, check with any professional associations or alumni groups you belong to for economical coverage.

Many people forget about the need for disability coverage in addition to life insurance. If you have kids, a spouse, or other people depending on you, you need to protect your income stream from accidents or ill health that could leave you unable to work. It's more likely that you'll become prematurely disabled than that you'll die, so make plans in case tragedy should strike.

If you want a rough estimate of what type and how much insurance you should have, check MSN Money's insurance planner at `http://moneycentral` `.msn.com/insure/welcome.asp`.

HEALTH INSURANCE

If you're contemplating striking out on your own, you might hesitate because of horror stories you've heard about the expense and difficulty of obtaining individual health insurance. But if you're relatively healthy, you might be surprised at how cheaply you can find it. Plus, many states have put laws on the books to help you find coverage even if you're not in good health, so don't rule out self-employment because of health issues without first checking into your options.

You have probably heard of COBRA, the Consolidated Omnibus Budget Reconciliation Act, which gives you the right to continued group health coverage for a period of time even if you leave your job. In the private sector, this only covers employers with 20 or more employees and the coverage can be quite expensive; however, it's a good option if you don't otherwise qualify for insurance.

The federal Health Insurance Portability and Accountability Act (HIPAA) also provides some health coverage guarantees in some cases. These limit exclusions for preexisting conditions and guarantee access to individual policies for people who qualify. To see if the HIPAA rules might help you obtain coverage or ensure that your health conditions are covered when you change jobs, see the FAQ at `http://www.dol.gov/ebsa/faqs/` `faq_consumer_hipaa.html`.

HEALTH INSURANCE (*continued*)

If you are healthy, you'll likely look to an individual policy that's "medically underwritten" meaning the health insurance company considers your health and your past use of health care in deciding whether to issue a policy. In contrast to medically underwritten individual coverage, group coverage through an employer often offers guaranteed coverage that doesn't depend on your health, although you may be subject to pre-existing condition exclusions for a period of time if you change jobs.

The Freelancer's Union (freelancersunion.org) now offers group health coverage for freelancers in New York, New Jersey, and Connecticut, so that may be an option if you live in one of those states. If you don't, you might check with any professional associations that you belong to.

If you are thinking of going solo but the thought of health care stops you, talk to a good health insurance broker in your area. They can help you understand what you might be eligible for and how much you might pay.

Legal advice

You may need to hire an attorney for a variety of reasons: for advice on creating a legal structure for a business, to write an estate plan and wills, or to review a contract of some sort or another. Be sure to hire an attorney who specializes in whatever tasks you need done. Just because Uncle Joe has his own legal practice doesn't mean he's the right person to create a partnership contract for you.

Attorneys can be very expensive, so before hiring one, make sure you understand exactly what they will bill you for, what increments of time they use to bill, and how much time they estimate your work might take. If you are concerned about going over budget, ask them to notify you as certain billing levels are reached.

You can search online for attorneys who understand new ways of doing business online; reading articles they've written or blog posts they've published can give you some insight into their expertise and approach.

For legal resources online, see Table 9-2.

Table 9-2: Online legal resources

Site	URL	Description
Nolo	nolo.com	Nolo Press's legal companion site offering legal advice, forms, and do-it-yourself kits.
LawGuru	lawguru.com	Free legal advice. Ask a question and receive answers from their network of over 5,000 attorneys.
FindLaw	findlaw.com	Lawyer locator and legal resource. Browse articles on many legal topics; search for lawyers in your area.
Martindale.com	martindale.com	Lawyer locator. Browse for attorneys in your area with the specialty you need.
Electronic Frontier Foundation	eff.org	Nonprofit defending digital rights; takes on some pro bono (that is, no fee) cases.

Financial planning

A fee-based financial planner can be a great investment in your financial future. In contrast to stock brokers or other financial planners who are compensated based on the investments you make, fee-only planners charge you either a set fee or hourly rate for considering your overall financial situation and making recommendations as to how to proceed.

A good planner will do the following:

- Gather data from all your records to come up with a snapshot of your current net worth.
- Help you determine what you're spending each month on fixed and variable expenses.
- Help you identify your future financial goals such as retirement and paying for children's education.
- Project your likely income and expenses into the future, identifying where you may fall short in terms of your goals and plans.
- Run a statistical simulation that gives you some idea of the likelihood that you will or will not have enough money to meet your goals.

- Identify areas where you can trim expenses or invest more wisely so as to improve your ongoing financial situation.
- Advise you as to specialized savings accounts such as for educational, health, and retirement expenses.
- Recommend investments and a portfolio allocation across asset types.
- Teach you why asset allocation can help you achieve good returns while minimizing risk.
- Use a power of attorney to actually implement portfolio recommendations to reflect the investment plan they propose for you.
- Analyze your insurance needs and make an unbiased recommendation as to what types and amounts of insurance you should have.

If you are considering leaving full-time employment for self-employment, it's especially important to consult a financial planner. They can help you see what kind of income you'll need to earn to meet ongoing expenses while saving for future goals, identify tax benefits available only to the self-employed, and give you more confidence in your ability to make it as a soloist.

SOCIAL MONEY MANAGEMENT

Though in the past finances have typically been kept private, the social web makes it possible for you to benefit from other people's money management expertise—and their missteps.

Here are some ways in which social web tools could make your money management better:

- **Net worth profiles.** NetworthIQ (networthiq.com) allows you to track the changes in your net worth and look at how other people's net worth is changing too. You can check by various attributes like geographic location, education, and so forth in order to see how you're doing relative to your peers.
- **Salary comparisons.** PayScale (payscale.com), Salary.com (salary.com), and other such sites will help you judge how your salary compares to others in similar fields and geographic regions.
- **Pricing guidelines.** If you run a service-based business, you can look at what other people are charging for similar services by checking their websites. You'll need to do some sleuthing on Google to find price lists relevant to your field and location.

SOCIAL MONEY MANAGEMENT *(continued)*

- **Joint editing and tagging of transaction information.** Money management site Wesabe (wesabe.com) lets you take advantage of other people's work in cleaning up and categorizing transactions.
- **Budget comparisons.** Tools like Expensr (expensr.com) allow you to compare your spending with the spending of people like yourself.
- **Sharing of financial goals and tips for reaching those goals.** Wesabe also lets you see what financial goals other people have and get tips from them on how to achieve your goals. Or use a more general social goal-setting site like Goalmigo (goalmigo.com) or 43 Things (43things.com).
- **Peer to peer micro-lending.** Sites like Prosper (prosper.com) and Lending Club (lendingclub.com) allow you to borrow money directly from other people rather than resorting to a bank loan or credit card. If you're flush with cash, you can lend money and make some interest.
- **Tracking IOUs.** Buxfer (buxfer.com) and BillMonk (billmonk.com) allow you to keep track of what other people owe you—or what you owe to them.
- **Investment intelligence.** Zecco (zecco.com) and Wikinvest (wikinvest.com) gather investment tips and information and analysis across many people.

Cashing in on web work

The two most beautiful words in the English language are 'check enclosed.'

—Dorothy Parker

You need to keep the cash flowing into your life, especially if you're self-employed. This section focuses mainly on freelance-type work, where you bill your time hourly, since that is such a common way for web workers to run a business.

In this section you'll read about:

- Setting your rates
- Invoicing customers
- Making a backup plan, for situations where the work doesn't flow in as planned
- Bursty ways of making money that get you away from the hourly grind

Setting your rates

You may have read formulas for calculating your hourly rate based on what you earned as an employee. Freelance Switch offers a calculator for taking into account your expenses, the amount of time you might bill, and how much profit you want to make (see `http://www.freelanceswitch.com/rates/`). While this approach can give you a good idea of what you need to make to see a certain income, it doesn't take into account the basic law of supply and demand. It calculates what you need rather than what you can get—and those are often two very different figures.

In a free market, prices for goods and services are set by the interaction of the supply of those goods or services with the demand for them. The more people who want your services, all other things equal, the more you'll make. And the fewer people who offer what you offer, the more you'll make.

Now that's in an idealized world. In actuality, what you can make is heavily dependent on factors like who you know and how well you negotiate. But you should recognize that the rates you can reasonably get in the marketplace might be far above or far below what that calculator computes.

So how do you figure out what's a reasonable rate to charge? Try this:

- Use a rate calculator like the one at Freelance Switch to gauge what you need to charge to turn a reasonable profit.
- Research rates and salaries on websites like Salary.com, Monster, and PayScale.
- Check with contacts doing similar work to see what kind of rates they charge. Note that many industry mailing lists forbid discussion of rates due to the possibility of being charged with price fixing.

- Assume you'll bill far fewer hours than you actually work. You will need to spend some time administering your business and marketing your services. You'll also spend a lot of time communicating and learning about your industry and the players in it. You want to leave room for vacations and illness. You may want to assume that fewer than half of your regular working hours will be billable over the long term.
- Try offering rates a bit higher than what you think. You can always negotiate down, but if you start out high, you have someplace to go.
- If a potential client balks and you really want the work, offer a discount off your standard rate. Then for later projects you can bring them up to the standard rate if you like.

Resist the temptation to under-price or give away services, thinking there will be dollars down the line. This isn't like participating in forums or blogging or other free sharing of your work. If you undersell yourself, it's very hard to get your true value later. If someone isn't willing to pay your rate, then they may turn out to be that high maintenance client you don't want anyway. Be prepared to walk away.

Also, you may want to try to get the client to give a figure first. If it's too low you can negotiate or turn it down, but sometimes the offer may be much higher than what you expected.

Don't hesitate to do "yield management" using your rates. Airlines price different seats at different prices depending on how well the flight is selling, what demand they expect in the future, and so forth. You can use higher rates for less desirable work (the higher pay will compensate you) and lower rates for more desirable projects. Over time as you gain more experience with different customers you'll get better at judging what rates get you the work you want.

And once you get the rate you think is fair given the market and your skills, be transparent and honest in your billings and dealings. Show clients exactly what they're paying for. Track your time carefully and bill only for the time you've spent on their work.

For more tips on setting and negotiating your rates, see Mike Gunderloy's Web Worker Daily post at http://www.webworkerdaily.com/2007/08/03/setting-your-hourly-rates/.

Invoicing customers

When I started my first contract job, my biggest worry was how I would bill my customers and get paid. It turns out that's one of the easiest tasks in freelancing. You've already negotiated the rates, tracked your hours (we have some tips on that later), and you've done the work. Now all you need to do is whip up an invoice in Google Docs and send it off.

It's even easier now, though, with web-based invoicing solutions. Take a look at FreshBooks (freshbooks.com), Simply Invoices (simplyinvoices.com), and Less Accounting (lessaccounting.com). Each of these offers a different set of features; one might have just what you need. Ask your client when you agree to a contract if they have any special requirements for their invoices (for example, an itemized list of the tasks you've completed). That way you can be sure to include it on your first invoice and avoid any delays in payment.

Send out your invoices right when you've done the work, on whatever schedule you've agreed to with the client. Some clients expect monthly invoices, so mark "invoice day" on your calendar and do it on that set day each month. Then track down the people who don't pay you. If you're self-employed, it's now your job to make sure you get paid on time. Consider making payments due 15 days after the invoice date so that you get paid faster and so that you can initiate collection sooner in case of delay. Not all clients will agree to this, especially larger companies that expect 30 or even 45 days to pay a bill.

Consider having a lawyer draw up "terms and conditions" that you attach to every proposal. It should cover issues like invoicing and late payments. You can use it to nudge delinquent clients. You can find sample terms and conditions on various websites. For example, Sessions Online School of Design offers a sample at `http://www.sessions.edu/career_center/design_tools/freelance_templates/index.asp`.

Your backup plan

Do what you love and what fits into your lifestyle, and the money may or may not follow. You never know what the economy might hold, so freelancers and employees alike need to make sure their financial plans are shored up.

Financial advisors might tell you to ensure you have three or six months income saved, but that may not be feasible for you and it might not suit your situation anyway.

SIX WAYS TO TRACK YOUR TIME

By Mike Gunderloy

Web workers do not live by tall Americanos alone. You need to eat too, and for many, that means billing clients for time spent on projects. But how do you keep track of that time? Here are half a dozen alternatives, each with their own pros and cons, for you to consider:

- **Don't track it at all.** At the end of the month, use your memory and your powers of deduction to figure out what you can get away with, and bill clients accordingly. Pros: No overhead or software expense for time-tracking. Cons: If clients figure out this is your system, they are likely to be crabby about it.
- **Pencil and paper.** Armed with a watch (or the timer on your cell phone) and any notebook from a dimestore special to a Moleskine or a Circa, you can simply write down the time as you work it. Pros: No need to boot up a computer to record time spent in meetings or phone calls, and you can feed the office supply habit that many of us have. Cons: Wasted time transcribing all those paper records to some computer format so that you can do your billing at the end of the month.
- **Spreadsheet.** Excel, Open Office, Google Docs & Spreadsheets—pretty much anyone can bang up a spreadsheet that takes hours times rate and then totals by client at the bottom. Pros: The least intrusive computer-based solution, and the easiest to "fudge" when you need to adjust hours so as to bill a client for more or less than actual hours worked. Cons: Ultimately, you'll spend so much time adding bells and whistles that it would have been cheaper to buy a dedicated application in the first place.
- **Accounting software.** If you're using something like QuickBooks or MYOB for your accounting, you can add on a payroll module to track time that should be billed to customers. Pros: Integration with customer billing, receivables, and taxes. It will make your accountant happy too. Cons: Likely to be the slowest solution, and you'll spend time learning accounting software that you'd rather use for something else.

SIX WAYS TO TRACK YOUR TIME (continued)

- **Time tracking application.** There are a ton of these on the market. Wikipedia has a page comparing some of the alternatives; FindApp has another. Look for one that has a stopwatch that you can use to track what you're doing as you do it, as well as export capabilities to your accounting or spreadsheet package. Pros: Single-purpose software is usually the best at what it does. Cons: Requires you to have the computer handy to track time, and most don't store their data in an open format.
- **Spy on yourself.** Use an application like TimeSnapper to automatically track what you're doing every time you turn your computer on. At the end of the day, use the automatic recording to figure out what's billable. Pros: Nothing to remember; it's like a flight recorder for your computer. Cons: Won't record non-computer billable time, and it can be depressing to discover just how much time you waste cruising the web and playing games.

I've known successful web workers who have used each of these systems, and I've used most of them myself. The real key to success with time-based billing probably lies not so much in a ruthless accounting for every minute as in your attitude: are you delivering value to your clients? If you are, they're far less likely to demand to see your detailed records.

Consider the alternatives you have in case your cash flow dries up:

- **Friends and family.** Cross-generational financial help is not just for twentysomethings. If you know your parents or siblings could help out with a loan if you got into trouble you don't need to worry quite so much about having that six months income in the bank. Of course, you'd want to have some solution in addition to counting on your loved ones, because you'll be paying them back, right?
- **Get high paying but less desirable work.** If my family ran into financial trouble, I'd start looking for a corporate job with benefits in software development management. Though I'd prefer to while away

the hours surfing the web for one exciting consulting job after another, if I really needed income I might be able to fall back to my previous career. What skills do you have that the market would pay for?

- **Find a side job.** Even while you're making a go of creating a business you can take on another job to smooth the income stream. You wouldn't want it to be so time-consuming that it meant you never got your business off the ground though.

- **Cut the caramel out of the budget.** Could you trade in your car for an economy model? Send the kids to public instead of private school? Rent a cheaper place? Drop the caramel macchiato habit?

- **Use a home equity line of credit.** If you own your own house and it has a substantial amount of equity, you can tap into that should financial disaster hit. Set up a home equity line of credit before you run into problems though. That way it will be there when you need it, at a time when you might not otherwise qualify.

- **Run up your credit card balance.** Given how high some credit card interest rates are, you don't want this to be your first pick. But especially if you know work (and cash) is coming soon, credit cards can be a convenient way to smooth short-term gaps in income. Get them paid off as soon as possible, though. Don't let credit card debt become a burden to you and those who depend on you.

- **Tap into non-retirement savings.** Many financial advisors recommend you have three or six months of living expenses in the bank. If you took their advice, then you should be able to deal with income swings pretty easily.

- **Steal from your retirement self.** For so many reasons, you should make this a last resort: the tax penalties, the robbing of your future self, and the precedent it sets. But if you are facing severe financial difficulties, plundering your IRA might be the way to go.

Bursty income possibilities

This section has focused on hourly freelance work, because so many self-employed web workers use such an approach for their income. But it's not the only way to make money and it can feel like a real treadmill if it's your only source of income. So consider ways in which you can make money without putting in hourly work.

CONTROL WEB SPENDING WITH A 30 DAY LIST

Spending a lot of time online means you're constantly tempted by the coolest new gadgets. Buying a new handbag or manbag is only a short click away. And wouldn't that cool multi-function printer/fax/copier/scanner make you more productive?

So what to do? Use a "30 day list." When you have the urge to buy something, write it onto your list of things you'd like to buy and record the date. After 30 days, if you still want to buy it, go ahead. Chances are you're on to some new yearning—and you can put that onto the 30 day list where it will likely prove to be just another passing fancy

Working by the hour is classically busy (versus bursty) work. For each hour you put in, you get more money. If you don't put in the time, you don't get the money.

What, then, are bursty ways of earning money? Let's look at three: stock options, product sales, and ad-supported websites.

Anyone who participated in the dotcom boom of the late nineties will tell you that stock options offer one source of bursty income. If you work with any companies that issue stock options, whether you're an employee or not, you may be able to convince them to give you some. You can't count on them for your future, but if they ever make money, it's like winning the lottery: a burst of money.

Selling goods online, whether intangible like software or electronic documents or tangible like products, can be another bursty way of making money. That's because the work you put in doesn't necessarily increase proportionately with sales; if your product takes off in popularity, you might sell additional units with very little work on your part. If you've made it so you don't have to do anything to sell one more item—for example your software is downloadable or someone else is handling fulfillment for your products—you can have bursts of income without putting in busy hours of work.

It's not easy, however, to market and sell goods of any kind so this is not a recipe for becoming rich with no work. It is, however, an entirely different model from hourly freelancing and one you may want to consider if you find the hourly grind to be too busy for you.

A third way to earn money in a bursty way is to build an advertising-supported website. If you do a good job of providing interesting content and building up your readership, you can earn more and more money with the same input of time. This is not an easy way to riches either, though, because it does take lots of work to create or find good content and to promote your site. In fact, you might find yourself very busy when you're searching for bursts of income. To learn about search engine optimization and other topics you'll need to know to make a go of advertising-supported publishing, visit WebmasterWorld at webmasterworld.com. But don't create spammy link farm sites thinking that's your ticket to riches. Your reputation is worth much more than whatever you'll earn that way.

Tax self-help for the self-employed

It's income tax time: gather up those receipts, get out those tax forms, sharpen up that pencil, and stab yourself in the aorta.

—Dave Barry

Even if you're not self-employed, you may start a little web-based business at some point just because it's so easy and fun. Or maybe you're contemplating freelance work. Either way, you should know some basic self-employment tax concepts: profit motive, deductible business expenses, estimated taxes, prior year safe harbor, independent contractor versus employee, and Schedule C. Those concepts are covered here, but only at a high level. Talk to your tax advisor about how they apply to your unique situation.

Profit motive

If you are not trying to make a profit, then it's not a business, it's a hobby, and you can't deduct your expenses from any other income you have. You need to show the IRS that you are serious about making a profit and not just trying to have fun. You can deduct expenses into eternity without showing a profit so long as you have good evidence that you've been trying to make money the whole time. One rule of thumb that's often used, however, is that you should earn a profit every three out of five years you're in business. That means you might be more likely to get audited if you fail to show a profit after three years in business.

How do you show intent to profit? In a number of ways, including marketing your services with a website or email newsletters, showing evidence of contacting potential clients via email (print the emails) or phone (keep a phone log), dedicating significant effort to your work (for example, by blogging regularly about the subject of your work), or best of all, actually profiting.

Deductible business expenses

Once you've demonstrated your profit motive (and continue to demonstrate it over time), you're eligible to deduct business expenses from your income on your taxes. That means you pay less tax. But what's deductible?

According to the IRS, "To be deductible, a business expense must be both ordinary and necessary. An ordinary expense is one that is common and accepted in your trade or business. A necessary expense is one that is helpful and appropriate for your trade or business. An expense does not have to be indispensable to be considered necessary."

The topic of deductible business expenses is huge. For more information, review the IRS guide on business expenses at http://www.irs.gov/businesses/small/article/0,,id=109807,00.html.

WHY YOU MAY NEED A SMALL BUSINESS CREDIT CARD

With the explosion of opportunities to make money online, even cubicle commandos might earn a little self-employment income. If you want to keep as much of that income as possible, you need to track the expenses that helped you acquire it. No, you can't deduct the cost of the expensive eye cream that made you look good for your blog's head shot. You can, however, deduct ordinary and necessary expenses which are aimed primarily at supporting your business and not your personal life.

Maybe you'll start by making a bit of money from advertising on your blog or by taking on occasional freelance work. Because the web has made it so convenient to raise your professional profile online, a little bit of work like that can lead over time to more and more outside work or even to full-time self employment. Meanwhile, you'll be so busy working that you won't want to hassle any more than you have to with managing and tracking your expenses. Enter the small business credit card.

WHY YOU MAY NEED A SMALL BUSINESS CREDIT CARD *(continued)*

A business credit card separate from your personal one will provide detailed reports of purchases you made during specific time periods, for example quarterly or yearly. This can be extremely helpful in organizing your deductions at tax time. You could create a Google Spreadsheet to maintain your own list of transactions, but why spend the time, if someone else will do it for you?

Even if you do use a business credit card, you must still retain your receipts: get a receipt for every printer cartridge, for each taxi ride you take while attending a conference, for your monthly web hosting cost, and for any other reasonable purchases you make in support of your self-employment earnings. If you use some of your equipment and supplies for both personal and business use, keep a log of that use for at least a month so you can prorate your deduction for that expense at tax time.

Just as in the personal credit card space, there are a seemingly infinite number of business credit cards. Take some time to choose carefully, and then make sure you use that card every time you buy something for your business. Also, remember to switch all your online accounts for business-related purchases such as web backups to using that card.

When it's time for you to report your income and expenses to the IRS, you'll be glad to have itemized lists of expenditures along with yet one more piece of evidence that you are not just a hobbyist in the new economy.

Estimated taxes

Life was easier when your employer bought your health insurance, paid half your social security obligation, and withheld taxes all year so that you stayed in the good graces of the IRS. Once you're in business for yourself you have to pay taxes as you go. The IRS is not about to give you a free loan until next April 15th rolls around.

If you expect to owe tax of $1,000 or more when you file your annual return, you likely need to pay estimated taxes four times a year. There is a loophole though—see the "prior year safe harbor" discussion coming up.

How do you compute your estimated taxes? IRS Publication 505, Tax Withholding and Estimated Tax gives you all the gory details (http://www.irs .gov/publications/p505/index.html). If you find that too daunting as a starting point, review the IRS summary page on estimated taxes at http://www.irs.gov/ businesses/small/article/0,,id=110413,00.html. Or do like I do, and hire an accountant to compute your estimated taxes. It's worth it if it lets you get back to moneymaking work.

Prior year safe harbor

If you're self-employed with a working spouse, you must understand this rule. It can get you out of having to pay estimated taxes—but you have to pay close attention.

If your total withholding—including your spouse's and any W-2 withholding you have (as in the case where you work as an employee in addition to your self employment)—meets or exceeds 100% of your previous year's total tax liability, you don't have to pay estimated taxes this year.

However, high-income earners be aware: if your adjusted gross income reaches a certain level ($150,000 or greater for tax year 2006), you will need to have at least 110% paid to the IRS via withholding or estimated tax payments in order to guarantee you don't pay interest or penalties on additional tax due.

Independent contractor or employee

Even though you think of yourself as self-employed, the IRS and one or more of your clients may not. According to the IRS, if a client controls both what you do and how you do it, then you are actually an employee, no matter what agreement you've struck with that client.

If you are an employee and have no other source of self-employment income, you can no longer file Schedule C and deduct business expenses. It also means that the company paying you must withhold taxes and pay a share of your social security taxes, among other things.

Make sure your clients only decide what you need to do, not how you do it, and you should be able to preserve your independent contractor status.

Schedule C

This IRS schedule associated with Form 1040 is where you report your business income and expenses. You will likely also need to file Schedule SE, the Self-Employment Tax schedule, which calculates your Medicare and social security tax liabilities.

You can read about these forms and download PDF versions from the IRS website. They're not too tricky—the trickiness comes earlier, with establishing your profit motive, keeping track of deductible business expenses, paying estimated taxes if necessary, and ensuring the IRS thinks you're a business owner rather than a de facto employee. If you get a handle on all of that, you're well on your way to managing your self-employment taxes.

Wealth, well being, and the web

> *What's money? A man is a success if he gets up in the morning and gets to bed at night and in between does what he wants to do.*
>
> —*Bob Dylan*

You might think more money would make you happier and it might, especially in the short run. But the relationship between money and happiness is not at all straightforward. Because it's so complicated, most people aren't very good at judging how to spend their money or time for maximum happiness.

Empirical research suggests that while in limited circumstances more money can make you happier, there are other factors that have a much greater effect on your psychological well being, most notably your social ties. The web makes it easier to get and stay connected with those you care about, whether you know them personally or professionally, so it can be a great source of nonmonetary wealth.

The relationship between money and happiness

Social scientists have been studying the relationship between money and happiness for at least a half-decade and philosophers have been tackling that question for eons. It's not all that easy to determine the relationship for many reasons.

For one, measuring happiness is difficult. You must rely on people's self-reports of their well-being. You can ask for a general report of happiness or you can measure it during the course of daily activities, but these two methods give different results. Also, it's hard to know if one person's "very happy" is the same as another's "very happy," so how do you reliably compare them? And what if you are looking at people surveyed during different eras or from different cultures? Can you really compare that?

Then relating reported happiness to income adds difficulty upon difficulty. Money and many other variables are intertwined with each other. For example, the more money you have, the more education you are likely to have, and more education could make you happier. The interlinked variables need to be teased apart.

Still, there are some empirical results that have been seen again and again. First, in a given place at a given time, there is a relationship between income and happiness: the more income you have, the happier you are likely to be. Paradoxically, however, once a certain subsistence-level income has been achieved, happiness over time seems to have stayed the same even as countries have become much wealthier and per capita income has increased greatly. This is known as the Easterlin paradox, for economist Richard Easterlin's classic 1974 paper identifying it.*

So what can you conclude about the relationship between money and happiness? It's probably fair to say the following**:

- **Relative income matters more than absolute.** How much money you have relative to people you compare yourself to (e.g., your neighbors) has a definite impact on your feelings of well being. Most people care more about being relatively wealthy than about the absolute amount of wealth and income they have.

---

*For a more updated version of Easterlin's research, see Richard Easterlin, "Will raising the incomes of all increase the happiness of all?" Journal of Economic Behavior and Organization, Vol. 27 (1995), available at http://www.paris-jourdan.ens.fr/forma/ape/wdocument/master/cours/ecpub2/Easterlin_JEB095.pdf.

**For an easy introduction to research about happiness, see David Futrelle, "Can Money Buy Happiness?" *Money Magazine* (July 18, 2006), available at http://money.cnn.com/magazines/moneymag/moneymag_archive/2006/08/01/8382225/index.htm.

- **Money is not as important as other factors in bringing about happiness.** Many factors other than money have more influence on your happiness. For example, having solid friendships and a strong marital relationship or other personal partnership will do more for your happiness than earning more money.
- **Your expectations rise with your income.** Some people call this the "hedonic treadmill." As you earn more money, you become accustomed to a higher standard of living. You can buy more things, but you adapt to having them. So while an increase in income initially gives you more satisfaction, over time you adapt to your higher standard of living as the default and you return to your previous level of happiness.
- **Most people aren't good at judging what will bring them lasting happiness.** When you decide how to spend your money, you may not take into account how you adapt to increases in income and to new aspects of your lifestyle. At the same time, you may underestimate how socializing or achieving deep engagement with your work might bring satisfaction. This leads some people to spend more time working so they can buy more things when they might be happier spending more time maintaining relationships.

Ways to be happier with the money you have

The more you can maximize the satisfaction you get out of the money you have, the less you will need to worry about a higher-paying job or more income streams or doing more hourly work.

Choose a comfortable pond

Most people care more about their financial situation relative to the people they compare themselves to rather than their absolute income. That means you can boost your satisfaction by either living in a place where you rank highly or, better yet, by refusing to play into the comparison game.

The web makes it easier than ever to choose a place to live that's far from where your work is. You don't have to live in a big coastal city with big average incomes to match. Theoretically, you can choose a place to live not based on its proximity to your job or your clients but rather because it's where you want to live—though not every field of work or employer will allow for that.

A bonus is that getting out of a place with high average income means a lower cost of living over all. If you choose to live in Kansas City instead of New York City, you may be able to afford a much nicer house.

Of course, if you thrive on the energy and activity of a world-class city, moving might not be the right choice. Even in that case you can find communities of people to work with online and to live with offline that don't focus on conspicuous consumption and showing off of high income.

Develop a supportive social network

When people report their happiness throughout the day, times spent socializing are among the happiest. Having friends and living within a community of people you care about has much more influence on your overall well being than having a high income or spending a lot of money.

Your online personal and professional networks can be a source of ongoing support and well being. So keep cultivating them, not just because they'll help you succeed better in your career, but also because you'll be happier that way.

A healthy marriage or other personal partnership will make you happier too. You can certainly be happy as a single, but if you are married or in a significant relationship, be sure to give it the time it needs. It'll give back to you.

Purchase experiences rather than stuff

Psychologist Leaf Van Boven of the University of Colorado at Boulder suggests that "experiences bring more joy than material goods because they are more open to positive reinterpretations, are a more meaningful part of one's identity and contribute more to successful social relationships."*

If you are choosing between a new car or a vacation to South America, that vacation to South America might give you more lasting pleasure. You'll get used to the car, but you can learn new things, stretch yourself, and create lasting memories with the trip.

---

*"Experiences Make People Happier Than Material Goods, Says CU Prof," (December 10, 2003), available at http://www.colorado.edu/news/releases/2003/465.html.

Think of your work life, too, as a series of experiences that you purchase with your time. You may choose a lesser paying job that provides you with more opportunities to learn and better memories than a higher paying one that's not as much fun or challenge. With the higher-paying job, you can buy more stuff, but since you get used to stuff anyway, why not focus on having the best possible experiences?

Achieve psychological flow as much as you can

When you get completely absorbed in a task so that time passes without your awareness, you've entered what psychologist Mikhail Csikszentmihalyi calls a state of flow. Being in flow is one of the most satisfying experiences in anyone's day, and it's worthwhile to pursue work and activities that bring it to you. Work that provides regular experience of flow and just enough income will probably bring you more day-to-day satisfaction than work that brings higher income but not so much flow. Yes, you can buy more stuff with more money—but remember the hedonic treadmill that means it's next to impossible to get ahead by increasing your income and buying more stuff.

Live within your income or even beneath it

Step off the hedonic treadmill by consciously choosing not to spend up to your income. Because you will tend to adjust over time to higher levels of spending, if you never take on the higher levels of spending you can be just as happy in the long run and stop the never-ending quest for more.

Working online presents a special challenge because you not only come across all sorts of cool gadgets and software on a regular basis; you can buy them immediately with a few clicks. Use the 30-day list trick described earlier to curtail impulse shopping online.

Express your gratitude on a regular basis

Consciously cultivating and expressing gratitude can make you more satisfied with your life. It focuses you on what you do have rather than on what you're missing. This can be the best antidote of all to comparing your own financial situation to other people's, because it turns your attention onto your own blessings rather than noting what other people have that you don't.

Take time each day to remind yourself of what you're grateful for: your friends and family, your online social network, your work, or whatever it is that makes you feel thankful this moment.

Looking forward: Finding balance

You've read a great deal about finding success and satisfaction in your work life, but what about the rest of your life? You surely have friends and family you want to spend time with, hobbies you want to pursue, vacations you want to take, and goals outside of work you'd like to achieve.

Let's turn now to seeing how your work fits into the rest of your life, and how web working tools and principles can help you find the right mix of business and leisure.

10 Blend Your Work and Your Personal Life

The web makes work-life balance both harder and easier. It makes it harder because you can stay connected to your work no matter where you are, who you're with, or what time it is. But it makes work-life balance easier for those same reasons. You don't have to work nine to five in an office, unable to meet the refrigerator repairman, attend your daughter's field trip, or take a nap after lunch. Even if you do work in an office, you can stay in touch with your friends and family throughout the workday with instant messaging or on social networks like Facebook or Twitter.

In this chapter, you'll read about how to find the mix of work and personal life that suits you:

- **The work-life smoothie.** With the web, work and nonwork intertwine and connect more than before. You may blend all aspects of your life into a flavorful smoothie rather than balancing large isolated chunks. But this blended lifestyle makes boundary-setting all the more important—and difficult too.
- **When life gets lumpy.** Great satisfaction and success sometimes requires imbalance and excess, not balance and moderation. Consider how to balance your life across months and years rather than hours and days. Know that sometimes you'll be too busy while other times your work life will go through periods of quietness, preparing for a burst of activity later on.
- **Your web of connection and support.** You will feel most satisfied when you create and care for important relationships in your life,

whether they are personal or professional. Use web tools to stay in close contact.

- **Work-life medicine: flow and mindfulness**. Becoming expert in finding flow and mindfulness through your on and offline activities can treat whatever work-life ailment you have, from work addiction to boredom.

With web work, you define your work-life balance and blend individually and authentically. Ultimately, you are the one who decides and creates the right mix of work and life for yourself.

Before you read on about blending and balancing, think about what symptoms might indicate a less than ideal mix of work and personal activities. Workaholism suggests you're too engaged with your work, to the detriment of your personal relationships. Burnout happens when you've suffered too much stress for too long, leaving you unable to meet your professional responsibilities. Frustration might occur when you can't make your way through obstacles that keep you from meeting your personal or professional goals. And malaise can lead to procrastination and spending too little time on work or personal projects that might fulfill you.

The work-life smoothie

I feel as well a growing distrust of spending too much of one's life deifying work. Finding that running balance among ambition, solitude, stimulation, adventure—how to do this?

—*Frances Mayes*

In Chapter 8, you read about the different metaphors that you can use to frame your career planning and management. "Work-life balance" is the most common metaphor used to frame a good mix of work and personal activities, but it's not the only way to think about it.

Web work can give you a work-life blend rather than a balance. A blend fluidly mixes just the right amount of each activity, ensuring they complement and support each other whereas a balance hints at setting your isolated activities against each other. But a blend has disadvantages. A blend of your professional and personal activities can leave you unable to find the place where work stops, and that can harm personal relationships or lead to burnout or both. So you need to know how to put boundaries in place when work and personal life connect in so many ways.

Metaphors for work-life mix

Just like with career management, the process of deciding how to allocate your time to work and personal activities of various types can be understood better through metaphor. "Work-life balance" is such a common phrase that you might not even think of it as a metaphor, but it is, because balancing means a kind of weighing of separate, isolated elements that only add and subtract from each other, never complementing or multiplying one another.

You can think of other metaphors for allocating your time and energy too. For example, you can think of it as the juggle, keeping many balls in the air. Or you can imagine it as a tapestry: weaving activities together so that they complement each other, creating a whole out of parts.

Today's web brings us into connection with each other, and that's the source of its power. So it's useful to manage your work within the greater context of your life by thinking of its interconnectedness.

When my husband worked for Boeing, the huge aerospace company, he attended a human resources session where they proposed a work-life blend instead of a work-life balance. I rebelled against that, wondering, "Should my life be pureed into a soupy mess?" But since then, I've started using this metaphor in a different way, to think of making a very flavorful and smooth mixture of my work and my life: a work-life smoothie.

Blending work and personal life

Balancing your work with your personal life suggests that work and personal life are separate and that they have to be set off against each other. Blending your work means you mix the work with the personal, ideally finding a lifestyle in which they complement each other. How do you do that? Here are a few ideas.

Don't isolate work and personal activities from one another

You can take a personal phone call or a leisurely nap during the workday if that makes you feel good. That's not just about feeling better, either; it can help you work better too. A warm shower in the middle of the day could get you past a creative block. A hard run could eliminate some stress and worry. A personal phone call could make you feel supported and connected. Take advantage of the smooth mix that web work allows.

Some home-based workers like to draw strict boundaries between work time and personal time—and that may be the sort of lifestyle you need. Many workers, however, myself included, prefer a more flexible mix that adjusts based on what's happening at work and home. I don't put strict time limits on when I work or when I do personal stuff; I choose daily and hourly depending on deadlines and what's happening outside my work. Fortunately, the connectedness of the web allows for just such a flexible mix.

Mix personal passions into your work

Your work may be able to help you achieve your personal goals and explore your personal interests. For example, if you want to travel to as many countries as you can, you might be better off trying to get a job that supports that—and mixing it right into your work—rather than trying to balance leisure travel with corporate office work. If you want to be a better parent, maybe you can find work related to child development or family success. Whatever your personal interests and responsibilities, you can probably find a way to bring them into your work.

You could look at work as strictly for income purposes and not for fulfilling personal dreams. Most people, however, will spend a good deal of their time working, so it can make good sense to get both money and personal satisfaction from it.

Mash up different kinds of work so they taste good together

If you work in more than one field, see how you can arrange them to complement each other. My editor for this book is studying nutrition science; perhaps some day she'll edit articles or books on that subject. I'm not just a writer; I also dabble in web design and development. Blogging gives me a platform to hack up my own website and then write on it too. In both cases, we can combine multiple interests and skill sets into one project.

Another way of mixing different threads of your work life is to choose separate businesses or jobs that taste better together. A child care provider who sells child safety goods, an interior designer who writes freelance articles about feng shui, a software developer who provides life coaching for geeks: these are all examples of how you can better blend aspects of your life together so that they add up to more than the sum of their parts.

BLENDING KIDS AND WORK IN THE HOME

Working from home can make it a lot easier to balance parenting and career. But blending kids and work in the same place brings its own set of challenges. Most people can't get any work done with kids in the house unless they have arranged formal child care. So if you're about to have a baby and you are thinking of working while the baby sleeps, you might want to make a backup plan in case the baby doesn't sleep enough for you to get work done.

If you have a door on your office, let your kids know that when the door is shut, they shouldn't disturb you. When you're just browsing the web or straightening your desk, you can open the door and let the kids come in. If they're younger, have a basket of crayons and coloring books ready so they can work quietly while you do the same.

Introduce older children to the social web, if you feel comfortable doing so. The more your kids understand what you do, the more respect they'll give to you when you're busy with it. Elementary schoolers enjoy Club Penguin (clubpenguin.com) while teenagers might like to try MySpace (myspace.com). If your child shows an interest in art or photography or writing, investigate how they might share their work online in a privacy-controlled setting like Vox (vox.com) or Flickr (flickr.com). Technically oriented kids might like to develop their own website using HTML.

For more ideas about managing kids and the home office, see Mike Gunderloy's Web Worker Daily article on that topic at http://www .webworkerdaily.com/2007/01/18/how-to-manage-kids-in-the-home-office/. Mike's a father of four home-schooled children who works from home, so he has ample experience. Also, see Leo Babauta's tips on the same topic at http://www.webworkerdaily.com/2007/08/03/10-tips-on-doing-productive-web-work-with-kids-in-the-house/. Leo is a father of six!

Use connected productivity

With connected productivity, you intermix social contact with your workday instead of isolating yourself in busyness. You will have regular projects where you do need to isolate yourself, but you don't have to make that your default approach. With blending, you stir social and professional communication into your hour-by-hour work. At first you might find this distracting, but it's something you can train yourself to do more effectively over time—and its benefit lies in keeping you regularly connected. That's psychologically satisfying and will promote your career too.

Share your personal life online

While there are limits to how much of yourself you should share online, being open about yourself, your life, and your work can make it easier to build an authentic and connected career. Show yourself as a real person online and you'll be more likely to make genuine connections, find authentic work, and experience real satisfaction with your web work and your web life.

Feel gratitude for your work-life blend

Cultivating gratitude helps you appreciate the good things in your life while distracting you from comparing yourself with other people. The ability to mix work and life smoothly is a huge benefit of the web's connectedness, and one you might start to take for granted after a while of using it. So remind yourself daily how lucky you are.

Putting boundaries between you and work

The work-life blend metaphor has as many drawbacks as benefits, as any web worker who's ever checked her Blackberry at the dinner table knows. The fact is that you do need boundaries sometimes; you do need to firewall your attention for big solo projects; you do need to focus on your friends and family regularly without thinking of work. And so, in addition to practicing interconnected work-life blend, you also need to draw some lines between your professional life and all the rest.

Especially if you arrange a work at home situation you may find it hard to know where your work stops and your personal life begins. You can decide to work only certain hours of the day—for example, set a work cutoff time of 6 PM every night and shut down the computer at that point. This isn't always feasible, especially if you work on a team with people in different time zones. Both your family and your colleagues may need to accept some compromise.

You can also use location to define work and non-work. If you're in your home office, you're working. If you're outside it, you're not.

If you're like me, you might find your work so engrossing that time or location boundaries don't keep work and work thoughts from seeping into all parts of your life. If this describes you, you may want to choose some non-work activities that are so compelling that they pull your focus away and give your mind the rest it needs. For example, in my free time I enjoy painting and cooking, two activities that are so different from writing and web work that they redirect my attention. I can also do them with my children, which are of course a priority in my personal life. For more about finding deeply engaging nonwork activities, see the section on finding flow and mindfulness later in this chapter.

For more ideas on how you can transition between work and home, see Sabra Aaron's Web Worker Daily article "When Worlds Collide: Transitioning Between Work and Home" at `http://www.webworkerdaily.com/2007/03/23/when-worlds-collide-transitioning-between-work-and-home/`.

DO YOU NEED TO GET OUT OF THE HOUSE?

As I mentioned in Chapter 1, home-based work just doesn't suit some people. Despite its many benefits, it has serious disadvantages too. It can feel isolated. You might get distracted by household chores like laundry, cooking, or cleaning. If you have kids or a roommate, they might interrupt and disturb you. So what do you do? Maybe you need to get out of the house:

- **Go to a wifi café.** Sites like Hotspotr (hotspotr.com) can help you find free Internet access nearby with the beverage of your choice.
- **Lease an office.** It could boost your moneymaking capacity enough that it pays for itself.
- **Look into coworking.** Bigger cities like San Francisco and L.A. offer cooperative workspaces. Search Google with "coworking <*your city name*>" to see if there's one near you.
- **Return to the cubicle.** If you're an employee who transitioned to telecommuting, you might be able to have your cubicle back. It doesn't have to be all or nothing—you may be able to work out of your cubicle a day or two a week for a change of pace.

Despite its benefits, working from home isn't right for everyone. If it doesn't suit you, find an alternative.

Finding balance with your blend

Just like you'll work in busy and bursty modes at different times, you'll sometimes blend your work with your personal life smoothly and other times draw thick boundaries between the two kinds of activities then weigh them against each other. In the remainder of this chapter, you'll read about blending and balancing not as two totally separate activities or approaches but as a way of capturing your ongoing mixing of work with the rest of your life.

When life gets lumpy

Moderation is a fatal thing. Nothing succeeds like excess.

—*Oscar Wilde*

Your life isn't always going to feel smoothly blended or nicely balanced; sometimes it will feel decidedly lumpy. Or it might look lumpy to other people: what feels blended and flavorful to you might not suit someone else. Fortunately, the web makes it easier to define your own professional and personal way, whether that means balancing over years instead of over days and weeks or accepting imbalance and crazy passion and the lumps that come with those as part of your personality.

Even if you do want to maintain a relatively even work-life balance most of the time, you might find that some times you are insanely busy and other times your work life seems curiously inactive. Understand that you may have fruitless times in between your major efforts and your bursts of progress. You can't necessarily hurry through the slow times.

You may also suffer burnout at times, where you feel depressed and irritable after too much stress over too long a period renders you unable to work productively. Unfortunately, the web might make burnout more likely because of the ultraconnectedness it brings.

Define your own balance

Who decides how much work balances against how much personal? You do. There's no objective scale—although some people might tell you there is. There will always be those who question your decisions. Mothers with kids face this most obviously. People who favor staying at home might think that any amount of work when your kids are small is imbalanced. Proponents of staying in the workforce would say the opposite.

So decide for yourself. Just because the standard workweek is 40 hours doesn't mean you need to work exactly that much. Maybe you have so many outside activities that you need to work far less. Or maybe you're immersed in such an exciting and important project that you work far more than that. Either way can represent a balance to you.

Also, your life doesn't need to be balanced across days and weeks as much as across months and years. There are certain things in your life that will require imbalance and passion and excess. If you launch a startup, you will likely give it your all for months or years. When you have a baby, it can be all consuming. If you're writing a book, it can feel like it's taking over your life.

The slow times

Just like there will be times when you give your all to a personal or professional project, there will be times when your work or aspects of your life seem inert and unchanging. In his book *Transitions: Making Sense of Life's Changes*, William Bridges calls this the neutral zone. It's the time between endings and beginnings; in web work, it's the time between bursts. You feel detached, disoriented, and disengaged. Bridges suggests that you can't hurry through these gaps, because growth and development and rethinking is happening underneath the surface in your subconscious.

The idea of work-life balance doesn't take into account the ebbs and flows of a career over a long period of time, but you should. If you get unexpectedly laid off or if your startup doesn't succeed like you had hoped or if you just suffer severe burnout in work that used to fill you up, you may need a time of regrouping and rethinking. This kind of imbalance is just as useful as the kind where you throw all your energy and passion towards a huge endeavor.

When you hit a slow time, be gentle with yourself. You might want to rush through it, but that's not always possible. Accept it as an inevitable and important season of your work life.

Are you doing too much?

Whether you're blending, balancing, or juggling, you can only accomplish so much. If you find yourself increasingly stressed, if work seeps into every corner of your life including times you should be sleeping or enjoying your family and friends, if you can't rest for even a moment, perhaps you are trying to do too much. Web workers may be especially prone to taking on too much, as the explosion of possibilities for making money and connections online makes it hard to draw the line. If you're self-employed, you might feel you need to work as much as you can in order to maximize your income. If you work out of your home, you may accept too many personal chores and community volunteer projects, since you seem to be so available for such tasks.

How do you know when enough work becomes too much work? You don't want to tip over into burnout, so you need to figure that out before you get fried.

COPING WITH BURNOUT

Even if you love your work, there will be times when it no longer fills you with passion and energy. You feel emotionally exhausted and cynical. Your health suffers as stress mounts. You wonder whether you have the resources, internal or external, to meet your responsibilities.

Web workers may be especially prone to burnout in a hyperconnected world. That damn laptop's always around, waiting with email at the ready.

What do you do if you're close to burnout or already there? You could leave your job for another—and that might be exactly what you need to do—but that's not always feasible or sensible. Before taking that drastic step, try these things first:

- **Find a new project.** Especially if you work in a team of substantial size, there's usually room for individual workers to move around to different tasks or projects. If you ask for changes too regularly and never finish any of the projects you're assigned, this turns into a way of shirking rather than rejuvenating. But sometimes, it's the ideal way of dealing with burnout without setting bridges or income on fire.

COPING WITH BURNOUT (*continued*)

- **Offload some responsibilities.** You might like certain parts of your job just fine. Talk to the person in charge about whether you might be able to offload the tasks that are burdensome in favor of focusing on what satisfies you. Most jobs do involve some tasks you don't like to do, but if the balance has shifted so much towards unpleasantness that you are facing burnout, you need to make a change.

- **Reach out of yourself.** When you start to burn out, you may push people away with your grumpiness, but connecting with other people can be just what you need to change your thinking around. If you feel comfortable with it, share your exhaustion and pessimism online with your friends. Instead of annoying people by using IM as your personal therapy provider, broadcast your angst on Twitter or Facebook or Jaiku. Then the people with some free emotional cycles can come to your aid. Or maybe venting stress was all you needed.

- **Hibernate.** Especially if you have a bursty sort of temperament, you may go through periods of massive achievement and accomplishment followed by sloth and torpor. If your job allows it, take it easy while you recover from big efforts—don't put too much pressure on yourself. Your boss will put up with your lulls if you produce bursts of results during your energetic times.

- **Start a side job or project.** What, work more? Yes. Sometimes enthusiasm for a second project can rekindle your energy for your other work. The web offers all sorts of ways to experiment with new ways of making money. Maybe you need a whole portfolio of jobs, not just one. Maybe you have a personal promotional project you could work on: changing your blog design, starting a new one, or putting ads on it to see what happens. Maybe there's a software package or web application you've been meaning to try.

- **Take a sabbatical.** If you have the financial wherewithal, take some paid or unpaid time off. Don't think of it as a vacation. Use it to renew your zest for work. Take a class or volunteer for a cause you care about or teach yourself something new. Maybe you'll come back refreshed; maybe you'll decide you're ready to quit that job and find something new.

Your web of connection and support

Only connect!

—*E.M. Forster*

What would make you most satisfied? More money? You may be better off focusing on increasing your social bank account rather than your financial one. Fortunately, the web gives you many ways to build and maintain both professional and personal relationships—and this is key to creating a happy work-life blend.

Why you need close social relationships

There's ample research evidence that having close social relationships makes you happier and healthier. Social connectedness is associated with increased autonomy, lowered stress hormones, and a stronger immune system. Assuming you have enough money to house, clothe, and feed yourself and your family, social connectedness is likely more important to your overall happiness than your material wealth.*

Part of achieving the right mix of work and nonwork activities involves finding the social support network, both professional and otherwise, that you need to be happy. But do online interactions and relationships count? Do they contribute to increased feelings of well being and decreased stress? Yes, especially if they complement your offline relationships and don't substitute for them.

Although face-to-face interactions may be the ideal way to create and deepen relationships, they're not always possible. You can build strong relationships without meeting people in person, with the right tools. Email alone probably isn't good enough, but by using social networking, instant messaging, phone calls, and text messaging, you can build genuine human relationships.

*Ed Diener and Shigero Oishi, "The Nonobvious Social Psychology of Happiness," Invited Paper, *Psychological Inquiry*, (draft October 27, 2004), available at http://www.psych.uiuc.edu/~ediener/hottopic/nonobvious.htm.

INTERNET ADDICTION: DOES IT EXIST?

The bible of psychiatric diagnosis, the DSM-IV, doesn't include a category for Internet addiction. And why should it? People don't get addicted to the Internet itself but rather to the activities they can engage in online—gambling, viewing pornography, and playing video games, for example.

The Internet, however, does have some characteristics different from so-called real life that might make it a better delivery system for addictive activities. Online, you may feel less inhibited and so you might engage in activities you wouldn't otherwise do. Plus the potentially addictive activities are much easier to get to than ever before. Less inhibition and more availability add up to a risky situation.

Excessive use of the Internet can cause problems in your life. You can neglect your family and friends, your health, and your work if you get too caught up in what's available on the web. Whether it can be classified as a psychiatric disorder or not is somewhat beside the point. If you've gone over the edge, get some help from a counselor or an addiction group.

Making online relationships real

If you want a blend that makes you happy, emphasize relationship-building activities over wealth-building ones. As you saw in Chapter 9, you will adapt over time to the things that you buy. Your social connectedness, though, keeps giving you good feelings and good health. And, as a bonus, a good personal and professional network makes it easier to make money later on.

Some people make the mistake of building relationships, whether on or offline, only so as to benefit professionally or financially. Yet people who focus more on material rewards than social ones are not as happy as those who look to connect mainly for the pleasure of connection. You could easily put your life off kilter if you focus on making money to the detriment of your relationships.

Here are some ways you can deepen your online relationships and make them more satisfying:

- **Use instant messaging where possible instead of email.** Email isn't very good at building intimacy. Instant messaging is both more immediate and more human, so give it a try if you need to ask your colleague a quick question or if you just want to say hi when you see someone come online in the morning.

- **Try social networking websites to show yourself as a three-dimensional human and to see other people in the same way.** Facebook, for example, can show your contacts what movies and books you like, what you're up to on the weekend, and where you've traveled.

- **Comment on people's blog posts with an aim towards social connection rather than being right.** Even if you disagree with what someone wrote, there's probably a way to recognize their ideas and achievement in a way that either starts or continues a relationship.

- **Think about connection over profiting.** When you meet someone new, take your mind away from how they can benefit you or your career or your startup. Instead, try to find a way to connect with them on a human level. Perhaps this means exploring your common interests or complimenting them on something you like about their work or just saying hello when you're inspired.

- **Know that negative interactions affect people far more than positive.** The "Gottman ratio," named for the marital researcher who discovered it, suggests that for each negative interaction (for example, a criticism), a couple needs five or six positive interactions to get back to neutral. If you criticize someone or otherwise treat them harshly, you will have to balance that with multiple positive interactions in order to return the relationship back to positive territory.

The relationships you build online, like the ones you create offline, enrich you just by the human connection they offer. Mutual partnerships and benefit could follow, but that's not what you should focus on.

Use the web for better personal relationships

At the same time that your new connectedness makes it possible for work to get into every corner of your life, it also makes it possible to bring your personal relationships and interactions into your workday. Using web tools, you can communicate with your partner or spouse throughout the day. You can easily make plans to meet up with friends after work. You can even share the work you do with your friends and family, allowing them a look into your professional activities.

MULTIPLY THE POSITIVE *If you have a big blowup with your spouse or room-mate right before work, you can fix it up throughout the day with instant messaging or text messages. Because people weigh negative interactions more heavily than positive ones (perhaps by as much as five or six to one, according to the Gottman ratio), you'll have to make up for that fight with multiple positive interactions during the day.*

Table 10-1 suggests some ways you can use web tools to keep close to the people that matter to you.

Table 10-1: Web tools for personal relationships

Tool	What it's good for
Blogging	Telling your friends and family what you're working on. Letting them comment on and compliment your work. Giving them an appreciation for your work. Inspiring them to try sharing their own work online. If you're just starting out, you may want to make your blog available only to friends and close family at first.
Instant messaging	Staying in touch throughout the day. Quick back-and-forths about household management. Venting about work-related stress.
Text messaging	Sending messages of intimacy or friendship. Short updates about daily plans or meeting for lunch.
Video chat	Feeling close even while far away, for example when you're on a business trip and it's time for the kids to go to sleep.
Voice over IP	Cheap or free long-distance calls. Great for staying in touch during overseas trips. Multi-person calls allow you to connect many to many, not just one to one.
Shared calendars and to do lists	Family and household planning.
Microblogging, status updaters, IM presence	Let your friends and family know what you're up to throughout the day. Seeing what they're doing.
Social networking	Learning new things about your friends and family. Staying in touch. Deepening relationships. Finding new friends.

Work-life medicine: Flow and mindfulness

Do not dwell in the past, do not dream of the future, concentrate the mind on the present moment.

—*The Buddha*

Flow and mindfulness are two related psychological concepts that you can use to find a better blend and balance of work and personal life, whether you're web working or not.

- **Flow**, a concept developed by psychologist Mihaly Csikszentmihalyi, is a psychological sense of effortless engagement with whatever task you're working on. It arises with tasks that are active rather than passive, goal-oriented, and just challenging enough to keep you engaged without frustrating you.
- **Mindfulness** is a psychological sense of focus and attention to the present moment, no matter what you're doing. Flow produces mindfulness, but many activities don't have the characteristics that would produce flow. You can train yourself to bring mindfulness to any activity: watching a sunset, caring for children, taking a walk, eating dinner, or writing a book, for example.

The regular experience of flow and the practice of mindfulness can act as fix-it pills for many types of work-life imbalance. Achieving flow and being mindful regularly can help you overcome workaholism by showing you how to tap into challenge and enjoyment outside of work. They can help you overcome burnout by reconnecting you with the joy of work. And they can help you combat overwhelm by getting you out of worries about the future and back into present-moment productivity.

Understanding and achieving flow

Csikszentmihalyi's research suggests that achieving flow is one of the most satisfying and rewarding experiences of everyday life. If you regularly achieve flow during work, it can be so compelling that you neglect your personal life. Conversely, if you have trouble reaching flow during work you might find yourself spending too little time and attention working.

Some web workers find so much flow online that it's hard to tear themselves away from the screen. Online work is challenging and provides ample feedback—and so it's a good environment for producing flow. That can lead to workaholism.

Learning to achieve flow in both your work and your personal life can help you achieve a better balance of work and non-work activities. If you understand how to bring a feeling of flow into everything you do, you can meet the needs of your job, of your family and friends, and of your personal purpose while feeling engaged and satisfied.

How can you bring more flow into your daily activities, whether you do them for work or for personal reasons? Let's look at some ways.

Choose active over passive activities

To feel a sense of flow, you need to respond to some external demands for performance and achievement. Watching YouTube videos is unlikely to get you into flow, unless you're viewing them with some goal in mind, like perhaps figuring out what to put in your own video. Reading blogs and commenting on them will bring you into flow faster than just reading RSS feeds without responding.

In your personal life, hobbies and sports are more likely to bring you a sense of flow than simply watching TV. A computer game that makes demands on you will likewise bring you closer to flow than passively web surfing with no destination in mind.

Act with purpose

Web surfing with no task in your mind probably won't get you into flow. Web surfing in order to write a blog post may. Structure your activities with a short-term achievement in mind.

You can build in minor achievements too: promise yourself you will comment on five blog posts during your surfing or save three links or find one new person to connect with during a surfing session.

Match challenges to your skills

Activities that challenge you just slightly beyond your current abilities are the best for inducing flow. If a particular project seems too difficult, you may get frustrated. If it's too easy, you may get bored.

So break a too-big project into manageable chunks. For example, if you've decided to create a website for your business but you've never made one before, start with the basics. Investigate how to register a domain name first. Read all you can on it. Write a little tutorial on it even. You don't have to do things fast when you're learning.

Structure your activities to get feedback

When you were in school, you received test scores and grades that told you how you were doing. If you work in a typical employment situation, maybe you get a once or twice-yearly performance review. If you work for yourself, you might feel like you're doing without feedback for long periods of time. But you can use the web to get feedback. Share your work online and you'll get more feedback than you ever imagined.

The immediacy of the web is part of its power. You don't have to wait for print publishing to share your ideas. You don't have to get your artwork displayed in a gallery. You don't have to convince a big company to use your web design.

Bring care and attentiveness to whatever you do

Even easy tasks can be made engaging. Find challenge in a boring task by seeing how you can learn something new from it or do it better than you've ever done it before.

Don't be content with the level of achievement you have in a particular area; you can always improve, and aiming a bit higher than your current skills is a good way to bring yourself into flow.

For example, if you're a writer, read some tips on writing before you tackle your next blog post. If you're a web designer, subscribe to blogs about how to create websites that are both accessible and beautiful. If you're in customer support, try to maintain pleasantness and sincerity even when customers become irate.

I had a mailman once who learned the names of every dog that lived in the neighborhood. He carried huge doggie treats with him so he could give them to the dogs that he met. At holiday time, he made a tree ornament for each family that had a picture of the dog. I think he felt some flow and mindfulness when he did his mail route, and I know he brought a lot of joy to the people and dogs in our neighborhood.

Mindfulness: Engaging with the present moment

Mindfulness and flow are much the same thing: attention to the present moment. The difference is that flow is generally something handed to you under the right circumstances (clear goals, immediate feedback, challenge matched to skill, active engagement) while mindfulness is something you can train yourself to achieve in any situation.

What is mindfulness?

When you are mindful, you fully attend to the present moment. Distracting thoughts might come into your mind, but you don't dwell on them. Snap judgments might occur to you, but you discard them in favor of experiencing your present situation in its every detail rather than assuming you know what's going on and how exactly you should respond. Multiple things might happen at once, but you handle them without becoming flustered.

When you achieve flow, mindfulness comes along with it. But many things you do—paying bills, sitting on dull conference calls, cleaning the bathroom—don't naturally produce flow. For those times, you can cultivate mindfulness.

Mindfulness and web work

One key to web working productivity is being able to stay connected—via instant messaging, email, social networking, and so forth—while still getting your work done. In Chapter 3, you learned about how you can train yourself to use social productivity. You can stay connected and be productive at the same time.

But social productivity makes it all the more important to be able to focus and attend to the present moment, even when you switch back and forth between different things. Because web work gives you the best results when you stay connected rather than putting up barriers between you and your colleagues, you need to be able to pay attention better than ever before.

Think about being interrupted by a colleague with an urgent question when you're in the middle of a big project. If you've trained yourself to be mindful, you will be able to turn your whole attention onto your interaction with your coworker, without letting thoughts of your project distract you. Then, when you finish interacting with your coworker, you can return to your project and again redirect your focus.

Mindfulness is also helpful for web work because web work is not business as usual. It's a new and rapidly changing environment in many ways. You need to stay flexible and fluid in your dealings with it rather than relying on habitual reactions or snap judgments. You can do this if you stay aware of what's happening in the present moment and don't let your biases or beliefs keep you from trying new things or meeting new people.

MINDFULNESS PRACTICE

The psychology of flow focuses on how you can arrange your environment and activities to promote a sense of engagement and attentiveness. You can also train yourself to be more mindful and attentive, no matter what's happening. Meditation is the practice of this.

You can sit or lie down, whichever is more comfortable. If you sit, you don't have to contort your legs into strange positions. You can sit on a chair or cushion, if you like. Some people fall asleep when lying down—so if that happens to you, sit up instead.

Set a timer for five minutes or more or less depending on you. Open or close your eyes. Now you're ready to practice:

- **Pay attention to your breath coming in and out.** Don't change your breath to make it deeper or noisier. Just feel it coming in and out through your nostrils. Feel the gentle rise and fall of your chest.
- **As thoughts or feelings come into your head, label them silently:** "thinking" or "worrying" or "discomfort" or "remembering." Then let them go.
- **Bring your mind gently back to your breath after each thought or feeling arises.**
- **If you discover your mind has wandered, bring it gently back to your breath.**
- **If you feel so uncomfortable that you want to adjust positions, first just label the feeling** ("leg hurting" or "wanting to shift"). Sit or lie with the feeling to see if it goes away.
- **You can adjust positions, but do it with mindfulness.** Feel the sense of your limbs shifting. Feel the sense of relief that comes from adjusting. Label any feelings and thoughts you have while moving.
- **Keep returning again and again and again to your breath.** This ability to return to present moment focus on the breath is what you are training your mind to do.

Flow and mindfulness for work-life balance

The better you get at achieving flow and mindfulness in all aspects of your life, the easier it will be to balance your work with demands you face outside of work. Table 10-2 describes how finding flow and mindfulness works to blend and balance your life.

Table 10-2: How flow and mindfulness can help

Symptom	When it might happen	How they can help
Workaholism	Your friends and family think you work too much and are too connected. You agree, but your work is so exciting you can't stop thinking about it or engaging with it. Personal life seems comparatively unrewarding.	Find flow activities you can engage in with your friends and family. For example, do crafts with your kids or go hiking with your spouse.
Burnout	You have been working too hard with too many demands for too long. You no longer love what you do and can't find any energy for it.	Re-engage with your work by approaching it mindfully.
Overwhelmed	Even when you still feel engaged with your work, you might feel overwhelmed by demands.	Use present-moment attention to focus on what you're doing at each moment instead of on all that you must do in the future.
Frustration	You lack a sense of achievement and progress. You feel like you're not getting anywhere.	Use flow activities and present moment attention to see daily progress instead of focusing on grander achievements.
Malaise	You feel generally bored and unmotivated. You spend too much time doing personal tasks during the workday because you're bored by your work. Maybe you're not burned out, but you're not fired up either.	Treat mundane tasks with careful attention. See how you can do an excellent job. Arrange the tasks you have so that they are likely to produce flow.

Looking forward: The future of web work

Now you've seen how your Internet connection hooks you into a rewarding and very human network of work possibilities. What does the future hold for our work life? Let's take a look in the next chapter.

11 The Future of Web Work

I f you've read this far, you know what it means to be a web worker. You know that web working means more than using online tools for better productivity and effectiveness; web working means using online tools to connect with a world of people and possibility online. Web working revolutionizes work socially, using technological advances.

Web working means you can work where you want: at your house, in a wifi café, or in an office. Web working means you can work when you want, because you can almost always find an Internet connection with access to colleagues, to information, and to the work you need to do. Web working means you can work with whom you want, even if they live far away. And ideally, web working means you work at what you want, because the broad possibilities online make it easier than before to find just the right niche for yourself.

The easy answer to the question "What is the future of web work?" is "More of the same." More companies will see the benefits in freeing their workforce from facetime requirements. More people will experiment with self-employment, either as their sole source of income or as an adjunct to traditional employment. More places, including airplanes, will provide Internet access. And more connections will be made, through social networking platforms, blogging, online chat, and so forth.

In this chapter I'll tell you about three trends that I believe could have major impact on the web workforce. Then I'll leave you with my wishes for your own web working future.

Trends to watch

The future is already here—it's just unevenly distributed.

William Gibson

In Chapter 1, I outlined trends underpinning the web working revolution. These included the rise of the people web, the move towards bursty work styles, a new appreciation for open thinking, and the use of web-based software alongside desktop applications.

There are many trends that will influence the future of web work but I find these three particularly important and interesting:

- **The entry of the MySpace generation into the workforce**, with their preference for ultraconnectedness via social networking platforms, text messaging, and instant messaging.
- **Global economic uncertainty** due to the housing market decline in the U.S. and credit tightening everywhere.
- **Increasing discomfort with Google's power**, with its vast knowledge of individuals' actions online and with its market power that might be abused.

The MySpace generation arrives

Adults in their twenties—sometimes known as Millennials and other times as Generation Y—have entered the workforce and have already begun to change it. Having grown up during a time of affluence and indulgence, they expect companies to bend to what they want and how they want to act rather than the other way around. Their appearance on the workforce scene, along with those who come after them (sometimes known as Generation Z), will hasten the move to bursty styles of work that allow them the autonomy they're used to.

Generation Y and those after them expect to be able to connect to other people with new technologies like MySpace and text messaging. Corporate employers will have a hard time limiting use of social software during the workday. But should employers limit it? As you've seen, staying connected during the workday to both personal and professional contacts can mean a more satisfying and sustainable work life. Although it could be abused, it can also lead to an engaged and effective workforce.

Younger generations practice social group-oriented productivity much more frequently than their older counterparts. They are less likely to use email and more likely to use instant messaging or text messaging. Over time, email use will likely decrease while more synchronous or semi-synchronous communications methods take over.

At the same time that the MySpace generation arrives on the work scene, middle-aged people such as the baby boomers are discovering social networking and other possibilities for connecting online. Facebook already has plenty of middle-aged members, and a number of social networks aimed at those aged forty plus have launched, including Eons (eons.com) and TeeBeeDee (tbd.com). Older generations are learning to text message and instant message and finding that those tools can keep them in touch across geography and generations.

Economic uncertainty

The future of web work, or any work at all, isn't a bed of disease-free roses. As I'm writing this chapter in late summer of 2007, the economic situation in the U.S. and around the world is deteriorating. The housing boom of the past few years is ending, with repercussions felt throughout the financial system. Wall Street bet big on questionable home loans transformed into complex investments with more risk than people knew. Now that increasing housing prices no longer give homeowners in trouble an easy way out of a burdensome mortgage, foreclosures are rising, and those home loan investments have turned sour, with billions of dollars at risk.

The residential real estate market has been a driver of growth for our economy over the past few years and the fallout from its problems won't be limited to homebuilders and home sellers. Different parts of the economy are linked in ways that make us vulnerable to a worldwide recession. The online economy won't escape harm. For example, a large portion of online advertising comes from home mortgage companies and other financial services firms who were riding the housing wave. A pullback in advertising spending could hurt many websites and web applications dependent on advertising for their revenue.

Economic troubles could very well affect the workforce too, leading companies to layoff employees and decreasing the availability of consulting jobs for freelancers. Taking a mashup approach to your career—mixing a variety of income streams and professions—can insulate you from the risk by allowing you to increase work in one area when another area falters.

Discomfort with Google's power

Search Google on the phrase "Who's afraid of Google?" and you'll find articles from the likes of *Wired*, *The Economist*, and *BusinessWeek* as well as many blog posts commenting on that topic. Google knows so much about its users and has become so powerful in the online economy that people worry whether it might use its strength for ill instead of good.

Google knows ever more about you as you use its search and other tools in your daily life. Google's informal company motto is "Don't be evil," but that doesn't seem quite enough when they store so much information about individuals' online activities. Google needs to be better than "not evil." Google needs to be responsible and good and careful.

In the summer of 2007, human rights group Privacy International rated Google as "hostile" to privacy. Google does take some steps to anonymize search logs and terminate cookies that track user behavior after a period of time. But the time periods they use (18 months for search logs and 2 years for cookies) don't limit their knowledge of your activities much. What if an employee with foul designs takes advantage of that data? How much are you willing to give up privacy in return for the benefits of Google's various web tools?

And Google's approach to privacy is not the only thing to worry about; its increasing marketplace power could also be misused. With its billions in cash flowing from advertising revenue, Google can bring us many good and useful tools, from its powerful search engine to its game-changing email Gmail to its online office suite and full-text indexing of books. But in so doing, it might control markets in a way that doesn't benefit consumers. Just like Microsoft misused its monopoly power to control the browser marketplace, Gmail could do the same in the area of search.

At Web Worker Daily, we're fans of Google's tools and its willingness to try new things. But this enthusiasm is tempered by wariness over privacy and competition.

Wishes for your future as a web worker

If I were to wish for anything, I should not wish for wealth and power, but for the passionate sense of potential—for the eye which, ever young and ardent, sees the possible. Pleasure disappoints; possibility never.

Soren Kierkegaard

I hope I've inspired you to figure out how connecting online can make your work life more satisfying and successful. No matter what your profession or vocation, no matter what your goals, you can almost certainly find a way to use the web profitably.

I wish for you to:

- **Find authentic work** that supports you financially and psychologically. Explore the possibilities online and off, then use the web to connect to partners, customers, and employers who might enrich your work life while you enrich theirs.
- **Prioritize connecting with people**, whether for professional or personal purposes. Your social connections and activities will bring you satisfaction and success like nothing else. Making money and achieving highly efficient productivity are not as important as human relating.
- **Remember that more money may not be the key to happiness.** Over time, you may adjust to higher levels of income and standards of living, settling back into a base level of happiness. Make sensible financial decisions, but don't let monetary payoff rule your life.
- **Look at failure and mistakes as learning and growing experiences.** If you take risks, you will fail some of the time, especially in ambiguous and uncertain situations like you may find in web work.
- **Share your work online**, to the extent that you feel comfortable doing so. By opening up your work online, you can attract new opportunities and connect with likeminded people. You can raise your professional profile. You can get fast feedback on your progress and your approach.

- **Be a role model for others.** By chronicling your successes and your failures online, you show other people the paths to take and those to avoid. You help them gain confidence vicariously through you, even as you make sense of your experiences for yourself. The abundance of web work is based on open thinking—and that includes telling your story, so that others can learn through you.

- **Reach out from all facets of yourself.** The number of contacts you have is less important than the links you create across groups, because cross-group links provide the best chance for innovation and growth. Connect to people on all the dimensions of your being—geographically, by hobbies, by profession, religious and political beliefs, and demographics, for example. This will make you more creative and effective by giving you access to different frameworks of ideas, different ways of doing things, and different sets of opportunities.

- **Find a balance between busy and bursty that works for you.** I hope your employer, if you have one, will allow you to work burstily when and where you want, to the extent that it fits with their business structure and goals. And I hope you can find the busy motivation and work habits that allow you to produce results when you need to.

- **Enjoy the interdependence of the connected age.** Any time you achieve anything, you build on the work of others and you create more value through interacting with others. When you find advice, software, ideas, images and other resources online, reflect on how you stand on others' shoulders to accomplish your goals and give back to the communities in which you live and work. And give generous credit to those whose work you build upon.

- **Experience a sense of possibility and opportunity each day.** Especially when you're down or unmotivated, remind yourself that there's always someone on the other side of the Internet, ready to connect and work together. Use all the tools you've learned about here—blogging, social networking, instant messaging, wikis, and so forth—to find and explore possibilities.

Join us at Web Worker Daily

Along with our team of web working writers, Judi and I will continue the mission of "rebooting the workforce" and continue the conversation about how the web changes work. On the website, you'll find practical tips and resources every day as well as a broad community of commenters with their own advice to share. I hope you'll join us there regularly so we can create the future of web work together.

Index

accountant/accounting
  and online business, 233
  software for, 242
action, and productivity, 63
addiction
  Internet addiction, 269
  and social web, 11
add-ons
  for browsers, 52–54, 125
  for email, 98
ad hoc relationships, and burst work, 19
Adium, 15, 143–144, 182
Adobe Acrobat Connect, 158
Adobe Kuler, 226
advanced presence management, 40
advertising, on blogs/web sites, income from, 214,
      245–246
affiliate programs, 214
Agile Software Development, productivity
      principles, 73, 75
AIM, 15, 144
AirSet, 65
AirTrafficControl, 180
Anti 9 to 5 Guide, 219
Ask MetaFilter, 129
attention span, firewall versus social mode
      approach, 85
authenticity
  authentic goals, 75–77
  web as aid to, 78
  and web workers, 10–11, 78, 164
availability system, 39–40

Backpack, 94
banking, online, sources for, 231–232
Basecamp, 64, 157
Bebo, 15
BigContacts, 65, 165
Big Stock Photo, 215
Blackberries, 45, 66, 184
Blackberry operating system, 185
BlinkList, 150
blog(s)/blogging
  advertising income from, 214, 245–246
  blog for pay, 215–216

blogrolls, 126
bookmarks, publishing to, 135
  for knowledge management, 150
  microblogging, 16, 40, 147–148, 271
  mission statement on, 209
  as online resume, 211
  open source, 28
  as open thinking tool, 28
  at personal domain, 206
  and personal relationship-building, 270, 271
  platforms for, 16, 74
  as reputation builder, 212
  tag lines, 209
Blogger, 16
Bloglines, 30, 116, 126
BlueDot, 150
Bluetooth device, 49, 180, 186
bookmarks, 121–124
  and browsing workflow, 123
  publishing to blogs, 135
  tagging, tips for, 124
  See also social bookmarking
brainstorming tools, 157
branding, personal, elements of, 208–210
Bravisa, 214
broadband over powerline (BPL), 47
brokerage, 169
browsers, 50–54
  customizing, 52–53
  most popular, 51
  security, 52
  of smart phones, 184–185
  tabbed browsing, 52
  web surfing, fine-tuning for, 121
burnout
  coping with, 266–267
  flow/mindfulness as aid, 277
burst work, 16–21
  characteristics of, 17–21
  and productivity, 71–73
  web versus knowledge work, 4, 17–18
  and workstreaming, 18
business cards
  online ordering, 191
  use of, 195

business models, web versus knowledge work, 5
busy work, 4

cable Internet connection, 47
calendaring
    with GMail, 97
    text messaging input, 187
    time zone support, 153
    tools for, 30, 65, 67
    See also scheduling
camera
    in headset, 49–50
    as travel accessory, 177
Camino, 51
Campfire, 40, 146
career(s), 197–228
    advertising, income from, 214, 245–246
    blog for pay, 215–216
    bursty work solutions, 245–246
    community managers, 217
    failure/coping methods, 220–223
    financial aspects. *See* money management
    freelance work, information sources, 215, 219
    identity online, protecting, 207
    legal advice, 235–236
    life coach, 216
    marketing, 210–213
    metaphors related to, 199–204
    new, transitioning to, 217–218
    online presence, building, 205–206
    online presence, rewards of, 21–23
    open source support service, 216
    personal branding, 208–210
    photos, selling online, 215
    refactoring, 222
    reputation-building, 212–213
    selling online, 213–214, 245
    sharing work for free, 223–226
    slash careers, 201–202
    success, tips for, 226–228
    virtual assistants, 216
    Web Worker Daily as resource, 217, 223
CareerBuilder, 215
Cascading Style Sheets (CSS), 25
Charles Schwab, 231
chat rooms, 146–147
    chat services, 146
    in/out, 40
Clipmarks, 123
Club Penguin, 261
clustering, 166, 168
coffee houses, as workspace, 36
Coghead, 56, 157
collaboration
    communication methods, 142–151
    conference calls, 157–161
    contact management, 164–165
    desktop sharing, 41
    networks, 166–171
    scheduling, 151–154

social factors, 162–164
    tools for, 156–157
    virtual teamwork, 155–156
    web-based tools, 156–157
color schemes, sharing, 226
communication, 142–151
    blogs/blogging, 150
    chat rooms, 146–147
    firewall versus social mode approach, 84
    functions of, 142
    instant messaging (IM), 143–146
    phatic communications, 142–143
    phone-based, 147
    preferences of others, learning about, 163
    RSS feeds, 148–149
    social bookmarking, 150
    social/professional networking, 149–150
    status updaters, 147–148
    video chat, 147
    videoconferencing, 147
    and virtual team, 156
    wikis, 150
community managers, 217
computer equipment, 43–46
    displays, 46
    long-term solutions, 43–44
    operating system options, 44–45
conference(s), 192–196
    cost-cutting, 192–193
    Internet connection, 194–195
    post-conference tips, 195–196
    preparing for, 193–194
conference calls, 157–161
    closing call, 161
    dial-in, 158–159
    headset for, 158
    with instant messaging, 146, 160–161
    instant messaging (IM) with
    mute, use of, 160
    online services for, 158
    preparing for call, 158
    presentation sharing tools, 158
    recording call, 159
    rescheduling, 159
    turn-taking, 161
conference space, 41
Contactify, 102
contact management, 164–165
    GMail, 98
    tasks in, 164–165
    tools for, 165
content management systems, 28
cookies, management of, 54
Copy Max, 191
corporate web, 8
coworking, 37, 236
Creative Commons, 26, 225
creativity
    mindful, 88
    web versus knowledge work, 6
credit cards
    short-term use, 244
    tracking expenses with, 247–248

cross-pollination, 169
cubicles, 34, 36, 40
customer relationship management (CRM), 68
customer support, 214
CustomScoop, 129

DabbleDB, 56, 157
deductible expenses, 247
del.icio.us, 14, 16, 26–27, 122, 150
Design Outpost, 215
desktop information managers, 125
desktop sharing, 41
desktop software
  benefits of, 30–31
  webware equivalents, 29–30
DevonThink, 125
dial-in, conference calls, 158–159
Digg, 115, 122–123
dilution, 167, 170
disability insurance, 234
displays, size/configuration for, 46
docking station, 46
document creation
  content, features of, 55
  online document editing, 156
  simple versus desktop, 55–56
Dodgeball, 147
domain name
  private registration of, 207
  setting up, 206
Doodle, 154
Doppir, 189
Dreamstime, 215
Drupal, 28, 216, 226
DSL Internet connection, 47
dual booting, 44

Easterlin paradox, 251
eBags, 176
e-commerce
  creating store, 213–214, 245
  web resources for, 214
eFax, 57, 126
Elance, 215
Electronic Frontier Foundation, 236
email, 91–112
  add-ons, 96, 98
  advantages of, 92, 150–151
  alternatives to, 101, 103, 108, 111. See also
    communication
  basic assumptions about, 104–105
  and burst work, 19
  contact management, 165
  disadvantages to, 93–94, 100–102
  discarding, steps in, 108–111
  empty inbox, approach to, 104, 107–108
  etiquette, 105–106
  filing versus piling, 99
  GMail, benefits of, 97–98
  immunity to, 100
  limitations, solutions to, 94–95

multitasking approach to, 82
  as obsolete, 99, 281
  one-touch model, 92–93
  security, 181–182
  smart phones, 183–185
  software for, 15, 29
  spam, avoiding, 102
  via text message feature, 187
  web-based resources for, 98
emulation, operating systems, 45
encryption
  hot spots, 181
  web sites, 181
Eons, 281
ergonomics, workspace tips, 42
Escape from Cubicle Nation, 216, 219
estimated taxes, 248–249
etiquette, email, 105–106
E-Trade, 231
EVDO cellular broadband, 47–48
EverNote, 125
Evolution, 15
exercise, taking breaks, 42
Expensr, 232, 238

Facebook, 14, 15, 65, 68, 74, 149–150, 165, 226
face to face meetings, 188–192
Farecast, 189
Fauxto, 29
fax
  digitizing information with, 126
  machines, 57
  online services for, 57
FaxZero, 57
FeedDemon, 116
Fiber to the home (FTTH), 47
15 Second Pitch, 207
file transfer protocol, 53
financial planning. See money management
FindApp, 243
FindLaw, 236
firewall, configuring for hot spots, 182
firewall mode productivity, 83–85
flamers, 12–13
Flickr, 14, 191, 226, 261
FlightAware, 189
flow, 272–274
  achieving, tips for, 273–274
  defined, 272
  therapeutic value of, 277
FOLIOfn, 232
Forbes wifi guide, 180
43 Folders, 64
43 Things, 238
Fotolia, 215
Found/Read, 223
4INFO wifi guide, 180, 187
FreeConference.com, 158
Freelancer's Union, 235
Freelance Switch, 219, 239
freelance work

information sources, 215, 219
virtual assistants, 216
See also careers; money management; taxation
FreshBooks, 219, 241
fulfillment services, 214

GarageBand, 211
Generation Y, 280–281
getAbstract, 128
Gizmo, 158
Glance, 158
Gliffy, 29, 56
Gmail, 15, 29, 65
    benefits of, 97–98, 102
    mobile phone optimized, 185
    security, 181
Goalmigo, 238
goals
    authentic, 75–77
    online connections, sharing with, 78–79
    and self-efficacy, 77
    tracking, 66
Goggle Docs, 156
Goggle Talk, 144
GoodStorm, 214
Google
    privacy issue, 282
    search, operation of, 117–118
Google AdSense, 74, 214
Google Apps, 29, 56
Google Calendar, 30, 65, 67, 97, 154, 187
Google Co-Op Search, 121
Google Docs & Spreadsheets, 242
Google Gadgets, 226
Google Mobile SMS search, 187
Google News, 129
Google Reader, 30, 116, 126, 228
GoPlan, 157
GoToMeeting, 158
Gottman ratio, 270
GrandCentral.com, 43
GTalk, 15
Gubb, 64, 187

happiness and money, 250–254
HassleMe, 65
headsets, 49–50
    for conference calls, 158
    smart phones, 186
    as travel accessory, 177
    with videocams, 49–50, 147
health insurance, 234–235
    group coverage, source for, 235
hero's journey, career as, 202–204
Highrise, 65, 68, 165
home office, 36
homophily, 166–167, 226
Hotmail, 15, 29
Hotspotr directory, 180, 263
hot spots, 179–182
    finding hot spots, 180, 263

security measures, 181–182
smart phone access, 186
wifi access subscription, 48–49, 179
wifi detectors, 180
wireless connection methods, 48–49
Hypertext Markup Language (HTML), 25

iCal, 153
illustration, software for, 29, 56
independent contractors versus employees, 249
information technology, web versus knowledge
    work, 5
innovation through cross-pollination, 167, 169
instant messaging (IM), 143–146
    and burst work, 19
    conference calls with, 146, 160–161
    versus email, 101
    IM aggregators, 143–144
    and personal relationship-building, 269–270, 271
    presence indicators, 40
    pros/cons of, 144
    security, 182
    software for, 15
    tips for use, 145–146
insurance, 233–235
    disability, 234
    health, 234–235
Internet addiction, 269
Internet connection, 46–49
    broadband over powerline (BPL), 47
    cellular 3G/EVDo, 47–48, 180
    at conferences, 194–195
    fiber to the home (FTTH), 47
    municipal wireless, 48
    satellite, 46–47
    wifi hotspot access, 48–49
    WiMAX, 48
Internet Explorer (IE), 51–52
Internet Relay Chat (IRC). *See* chat rooms
Internet tablet, 45
interruptions, approaches to, 84
intrinsic rewards, 88–89
investment services, online, sources for, 231–232
invoicing, Web-based invoicing, 219, 241
iotum.com, 40
iPhone, 66, 184
iStockphoto, 215

Jabber, 144
Jaiku, 16, 40, 147
JiWire wifi directory, 180

kaleidoscope, career metaphor, 202, 204
Kayak, 189
keyboard, ergonomic tips, 42
keyword searches, 121
Kmail, 15
knowledge management, methods for, 150
knowledge work
    multitasking for, 81–82
    versus web work, 2–6

Kolobags, 176
Konqueror, 51

LAMP stack, 28
laptops
  alternatives to, 45, 186
  bags for, 174–176
  versus desktop system, 43–44
  stands for, 46
  travel accessories, 177
Last.fm, 70
LawGuru, 236
legal advice, 235–236
  and invoicing, 241
  online, sources for, 236
Lending Club, 238
Less Accounting, 233, 241
life coach, online business, 216
Lifehacker, 64
lifestreaming, 148
LinkedIn, 14, 15, 65, 68, 74, 149–150, 165
Linux
  mobile OS, 186
  and open source
LiveOffice, 158
loans, micro-lending, 238
lurking, pros of, 14
Lynx, 51

Ma.gnolia, 150
Mail.app, 15
  spam filtering, 102
Mailinator, 102
Makik, Om, 2
mantra, 209
marketing, online businesses, 210–213
Martindale, 236
mashup, 84
Maxthon, 51
MediaWiki, 150
Me.dium, 115
meetings
  conference calls, 157–161
  conference space, 41
  face-to-face, 188–192
  scheduling, 151–154
  videoconferencing, 147, 227
meme trackers, 117
memex, building, 125–127
metaphors
  career-related, 199–204
  work-life mix, 259
microblogging, 271
  platforms for, 16, 147
  pros/cons of, 147–148
Microsoft Office, alternatives to, 56
Microsoft Office Live Meeting, 158
Microsoft Outlook, 15
  spam filtering, 102
mindfulness, 274–277
  achieving, tips for, 275–276

defined, 272
  therapeutic value of, 277
mind mapping, 157
MindMeister, 157
Mint, 232
mission statement builder, 209
mobile phones, 183–187
  cellular broadband, 180
  feature phones, 183
  GMail, 98
  locked/unlocked, 184
  smart phones, 45, 183–186
  text messaging, 186–187
money, earning
  attention online, 21–23
  and happiness, 250–254
  multiplier effect and web, 22
  See also careers; money management
money management, 229–255
  accounting, 233
  backup money reserves, 241, 243–244
  banking/investment services, 231–232
  financial planning, 236–237
  insurance needs, 233–235
  invoicing customers, 241
  legal advice, 235–236
  overspending online, avoiding, 245
  rates, setting, 239–240
  social money management tools, 237–238
  stock options, 245
  taxation, 246–250
Monster.com, 213, 215, 239
Moo minicards, 191
Morningstar, 232
mouse, ergonomic tips, 42
MoveableTypeySpace, 16
Mozilla Firefox, 51–52
  add-ons, 53–54, 125
  benefits of use, 51–52
  with GMail, 97
  keyword searches, 121
MSN Messenger, 15
MSN Money, 234
multi-dimensional identities, 168
multitasking, 80–82
  for knowledge work, 81–82
  and productivity, 80–81
  technology for, 82
municipal wireless, 48
music, productivity-boosting, 70–71
Musicovery, 70
mute, conference calls, 160
MyFax, 57
MYOB, 242
MySpace, 15, 149–150, 261
MyStrands, 70

neo-Bedouin, 35, 176
NetBanker, 232
NetNewsWire, 116
NetStumbler, 180

network(s), 166–171
  best use of, 171
  brokerage, 169
  clustering, 166, 168
  cross-pollination, 167, 169
  dilution, 167, 170
  homophily, 166–167
  multi-dimensional identities, 166, 168
  small worlds, 166, 168–169
  social problem-solving, 167, 170
  stagnation, 167, 169
  weak ties, 167, 170
networking services, sites for, 15
NetworthIQ, 237
Neuberg, Brad, 37
news readers, software for, 30
Nolo, 236
Norton Internet Security, 182
notebooks, online, 117, 123
note-taking, tools for, 64

Odeo, 211
oDesk, 215
office suite, software for, 29
Olsen, Greg, 35
OneNote, 125
one-touch model, email, 92–93
online mind concept, 131–134
OpenID, 10
OpenOffice.org, 56
open source, 24–28
  blogging, 28
  browsers, 50–51
  common uses of, 24–25
  defined, 25
  LAMP stack, 28
  support service online business, 216
  value gained from, 25–26
open standards, web-related standards, 25
open thinking
  guidelines for, 27–28
  and open source, 24
Opera, 51
Opera Mini, 185
operating systems
  emulation, 45
  smart phones, 185
  virtualization, 45
organic productivity, 61–62, 75–76
  career decisions, 199–201, 204
orienteering, 118–120
Orkut, 15
OvernightPrints, 191

Palm Centro, 184
Palm operating system, 185
Pandora, 70
panes, browsers, 53
Parallels Desktop, 44
parenting, kids/home office mix, 261
PayPal, 214

PayPerPost, 215
PayScale, 237, 239
PBWiki, 127
PDF format, 226
  digitizing information with, 126
PearPC, 45
people web
  authenticity as ideal, 10–11
  elements of, 9
  joining, steps in, 14
  See also social web
personal digital assistants (PDAs), 45, 66
personal information management software, 66
personal life-work balance, 257–278
  boundaries, setting, 262–263
  flow/mindfulness, 272–277
  getting out, solutions to, 263
  metaphors for, 259
  parenting, 261
  slow periods, 265
  stress/burnout, 266–267
  tips for, 259–262
  See also social relationships
personal relationship management (PRM), 65, 68
phatic communications, 142–143
photographs
  marketing/selling photos, 215
  photo editing software, 29, 56
  photo sharing, 14, 226
  stock, web sites for, 215
Picnik, 29, 56
Pidgin, 143, 182
pitching company, pitch tool, 207
Planypus, 154
Plaxo, 65, 165
Plazes, 189
podcasts, talk radio show hosting, 211
Pownce, 147
Preezo, 56
presence indicators and instant messaging (IM)
presentation software, web applications, 56, 157
printers, 57
privacy
  Google issue, 282
  identity online, protecting, 207
  negative material on web, hiding, 207
PRNewsWire, 128
problem-solving
  active, 223
  social, 167, 170
ProBlogger, 214
productivity
  Agile principles, 73, 75
  and burst work, 71–73
  firewall mode productivity, 83–85
  and flow/mindfulness, 272–277
  goals, authentic, 75–77
  goals/projects, tracking, 66
  and life-work balance, 262
  multitasking, 80–82
  music for, 70–71
  organic productivity, 61–62, 75–76

productivity (*continued*)
projects, rejecting, 86–90
and regular work, 68–69
and self-efficacy, 77, 79
social mode productivity, 83–85
and taking action, 63
task management, flexibility in, 73
and text messaging, 187
tips, online resources for, 64
and workspace, 79
productivity tools
calendars, 67
personal relationship management (PRM), 68
reminder systems, 67
to-do lists, 66–67
project management tools, 64, 157
project tracking, tools for, 64
prospective search, 130–131
Prosper, 238
pseudonyms, best use of, 14
PubMed Central, 129

Questia, 128
QuickBooks Online, 233
Quicken/QuickBooks, 233, 242

radio shows, podcast hosting, 211
rates, setting, 239–240
recording software, 211
Red Hat, 216
Remember the Milk, 30, 64, 94, 187
reminder systems, tools for, 65, 67
RemindMe, 65
Renkoo, 154
retirement plans, borrowing from, 244
rewards, intrinsic, 88–89
Rollyo, 121
RSS feeds
as communication tool, 148–149
management of, 228
operation of, 116
RSS feed reader, 116, 127–128

Safari, 51
Salary.com, 237, 239
satellite Internet connection, 46–47
scanners, 57
Schedule C, 250
scheduling, 151–154
calendar sharing, 153–154
conference calls, 159
free/busy calendar, publishing, 154
time zone issues, 152–153
web-based tools, 154
wiki for, 154
Scribd, 129
scripts, browser add-ons, 54
search engines, 117–118
Googleability of name, 206
operation of, 117–118
prospective search, 130–131
specialized, 117, 118
SeatGuru, 189
Second Life, 217
secure sockets layer (SSL), 181–182
security
email, 181–182
encrypted web sites, 181
Firefox versus Internet Explorer, 52
hot spots, 181–182
instant messaging (IM), 182
virtual private networks (VPNs), 182
self-efficacy, and goal achievement, 77
self-employment. *See* careers; freelance work
semantic search engines, 118
semi-synchronous writing, 144
Sharebuilder, 232
sharing work, 223–226
web resources for, 225–226
shoulds, avoiding, 87
Shutterstock, 215
sidebars, browser add-ons, 54
Simply Accounting, 233
Sir Speedy, 191
SiteKreator, 211
six degrees of separation, 168–169
Skype, 158
slash careers, 201–202
SlideShare, 157
small worlds, 166, 168–169
smart phones, 45, 66
choosing phone, 185–186
email/browsing, 184–185
operating systems, 185–186
types/features of, 183–184
wifi access, 186
Smugmug, 16
social bookmarking, 14
elements of, 26–27
for knowledge management, 150
services for, 16, 116, 122–123, 150
social cognition, and productivity, 83
social mode productivity, 83–85
social problem-solving, 167, 170
social relationships
importance of, 268
online relationships, enhancing, 269–270
web tools for connecting, 270–271
social web
baby boomer sites, 281
criticisms of, 11–13
human level communication, 162–164
joining, steps in, 14
money management tools, 237–238
and personal relationship-building, 270
as pre-meeting tool, 190
professional use, resources for, 150
software/activities for, 15–16, 149
SomaFM, 70
spam, avoiding, 102
SpamBayes, 102
SpamCop, 102

Spamex, 102
spamgourmet, 102
SpamSieve, 102
spreadsheets
  time management tool, 242
  web applications, 56, 157
stagnation, networks, 167, 169
StartupNation, 219
status updaters, 147–148
  See also microblogging
stikkit, 64
stock options, 245
stress
  burnout, coping with, 266–267
  flow/mindfulness as aid, 277
StumbleUpon, 16, 115, 122
surfing. *See* web surfing
Symbian, 185
Synthasite, 211

tabbed browsing, 52
tablet PC, 45
Ta-da list, 30
tagging, bookmarks, 124
taxation, 246–250
  business credit card, tracking expenses with,
    247–248
  deductible expenses, 247
  estimated taxes, 248–249
  independent contractors versus employees, 249
  prior year safe harbor rule, 249
  Schedule C, 250
teamwork, virtual teamwork, 155–156
TeeBeeDee, 281
telephone communication, 147
telephone service
  master phone number service, 43
  three-way calling, 158
  VoIP (voice over Internet protocol), 43, 147
  See also mobile phones
teleporting, 118–120
text messaging, 186–187
  capabilities/functions, 187
  hot spots, finding, 180, 187
  and personal relationship-building, 271
  usefulness of, 15
30 Boxes, 30, 65, 187
37 Signals, 219
Threadless, 217
3G cellular broadband, cellular broadband, 180
three-way calling, 158
Thumbstacks, 56
Thunderbird, 15
Tidy Web, 14
Timbuk2, 176
timeboxing, 69
time management
  availability system, 39–40
  email, discarding, 108–111
  and personal life. *See* personal life-work balance
  tracking time, methods, 242–243
  web surfing, 115, 273

timers
  to stay focused, 69
  for web surfing, 72
TimeSnapper, 243
time zones, working across, tips for, 152–153
T-Mobile, wifi hotspot access subscription, 179,
    181
todocue, 94
to-do lists
  done lists, 69
  in email, 94
  must-do lists, 69
  not-to-do list, 89–90
  text messaging input, 187
  tools for, 30, 64, 66–67
Toodledo, 94
travel
  business cards, 191
  conferences, 192–196
  face-to-face meetings, 188–192
  items to take, 176–177
  laptop bags, 174–176
  mobile phones, 176, 183–187
  web resources for, 189
  workspaces, 178–182
Treos, 45, 66, 184, 185
Trillian, 15, 143–144, 182
TripAdvisor, 189
Tripit, 189
trolls, 12–13
trust factors
  email, 102
  fake versus real identities, 12
  virtual teamwork, 156
Tumblr, 16, 74
Twitter, 14, 16, 40, 74, 147–149, 165
Typepad, 16

Ultra Mobile PC, 45
uncertainty, and burst work, 20–21
Unthirsty, 189
Upcoming, 189
user accounts, OpenID, 10
user names, unique ID, choosing, 14, 206

vanity searches, 131
Verizon, cellular broadband, 47–48, 180
video(s), video sharing, 226
videocams, in headsets, 49–50, 147
video chat, 147, 271
videoconferencing, 147, 227
View Source, 26
virtual assistants, 216
virtualization, 45
virtual private networks (VPNs), 182
virtual teamwork, elements of, 155–156
voice mail, via text message feature, 187
VoIP (voice over Internet protocol), 43, 147
  conference calls, 158
Vox, 14, 15, 74, 261
Vtxt service, 187

Wayback Machine, 207
weak ties, 167, 170
Web
  corporate web, 8
  evolution of, 7–10
  open standards related to, 25
  people web, 9
  social. *See* social web
web applications, 28–32
  office software equivalents, 29–30
  pros/cons of, 29, 31
web content management systems, 216
WebEx, 41, 158
websites
  advertising income from, 214, 245–246
  building, LAMP stack, 28
  design sharing resource, 226
  for online business, 211
web surfing, 113–139
  better surfing, tips for, 135–137
  bookmarks, 121–124
  browsers, fine-tuning for, 121
  information, approaches to, 139
  information sources, 128–129
  memex, building, 125–127
  online mind concept, 131–134
  orienteering versus teleporting, 118–120
  prospective search, 130–131
  RSS feed reader, 116, 127–128
  search engines, 117–118
  serendipity in, 130
  smart phones, 183–184
  social surfing, 115
  time management, 115, 273
  tools for, 116–117
web work
  attention online, rewards of, 21–23
  browsers, 50–54
  burst work, 16–21
  characteristics of, 3–6
  computer equipment for, 43–46
  document creation, 54–55
  future view, 280–284
  headsets, 49–50
  Internet connection, 46–49
  versus knowledge work, 2–6
  and open source, 24–28
  paper-related needs, 58–59
  printers/scanners/fax, 57
  workspaces for, 34–43
Web Worker Daily, 64, 217
webworkerdaily.com, 2
Wesabe, 231, 238
wifi hotspots. *See* hot spots
WiFi Radar, 180

Wikinvest, 238
wikis
  functions of, 150
  platforms for, 127, 150
  for scheduling, 154
WikiSpaces, 127
WiMAX, 48
Windows Mobile, 185
wireless connections. *See* hot spots; Internet
  connection
WordPress.com, 14, 16, 28, 216, 226
word processing. *See* document creation
workaholism, flow/mindfulness as aid, 277
workload, firewall versus social mode approach, 85
workspaces, 34–43
  availability system, 39–40
  coffee houses, 36
  conference space, 41
  connections with colleagues, 40–41
  coworking, 37
  cubicles, 34, 36, 40
  environment of, 38
  ergonomic factors, 42
  home office, 36
  hot spots, 179–182
  human interaction at, 41
  phatic communications in, 142–143
  and productivity, 79
  telephone service, 43
  while traveling, 178–182
workstreaming, 148–149
  benefits of use, 148
  and burst work, 18
  tools for, 149
World Clock Meeting Planner, 153
wrist pain, ergonomic tips, 42

Xing, 15, 149, 165

Yahoo IM, 15
Yahoo! LAUNCHcast, 70
Yahoo! Publisher Network, 214
yield management, 240
Yojimbo, 125
YouTube, 226
  online presence with, 211

Zecco, 232, 238
Zen Habits, 64
Ziegarnik effect, 136
Zoho Office, 29, 55
Zoho Writer, 156
ZoneAlarm, 182
Zotero add-ons, 125